Island on the Edge
Taiwan New Cinema and After

This is the first English-language anthology on the Taiwan New Cinema and its legacy. It is an exciting collection which covers all the major filmmakers from Hou Hsiao Hsien and Edward Yang to Ang Lee and more. Gathering a range of essays that analyze individual films produced since the advent of the Taiwan New Cinema in the early 1980s, it aims to complement Feii Lu's *Taiwan Cinema: Politics, Economics, Aesthetics*, translated by Chris Berry (Duke University Press and Hong Kong University Press, forthcoming).

Taiwan and its internationally renowned cinema are "on the edge" in more ways than one. For all of its history the island has been on the edge of larger geopolitical entities, subjected to invasions, migrations, incursions, and pressures. On the other hand, as one of the "Little Tiger" economies of Asia, it has been on the cutting edge of the Asian economic boom and of technological innovation; in recent years it has pioneered democratization of authoritarian regimes in East Asia.

Chris Berry is the Professor of Film and Television Studies at Goldsmiths College in the University of London. **Feii Lu** is Associate Professor of the Department of Radio/ TV at National Chengchi University in Taiwan.

❖   ❖   ❖   ❖   ❖   ❖

"As the first English-language anthology on Taiwan New Cinema, this is truly a groundbreaking work. The editors have assembled a collection of insightful essays by a group of well-informed and critically astute scholars. The book is essential reading for anyone who wishes to acquire an in-depth understanding of Taiwanese cinema, or more broadly, transnational Chinese-language cinema."
– Sheldon H. Lu, Professor of Comparative Literature and Film Studies, University of California at Davis

"This comprehensive anthology brings out a new perspective on the study of Taiwan cinema. For those who want to go beyond the Taiwan New Cinema movement and explore what happened during the past twenty years, they might begin with this book. It is, without doubt, a major contribution to the long-neglected territory in film history."
– Ru-Shou Robert Chen, Associate Professor and Head of the Graduate School of Applied Media Arts, National Taiwan University of Arts

Island on the Edge

Hong Kong University Press thanks Xu Bing for writing the Press's name in his Square Word Calligraphy for the covers of its books. For further information, see p. iv.

Island on the Edge
Taiwan New Cinema and After

edited by
Chris Berry and Feii Lu

香港大學出版社
HONG KONG UNIVERSITY PRESS

Hong Kong University Press
14/F Hing Wai Centre
7 Tin Wan Praya Road
Aberdeen
Hong Kong

ISBN 962 209 715 4 (Hardback)
ISBN 962 209 716 2 (Paperback)

British Library Cataloguing-in-Publication Data

Secure On-line Ordering
http://www.hkupress.org

Printed and bound by Rainbow Graphic & Printing Co., Ltd. Hong Kong, China.

Hong Kong University Press is honoured that Xu Bing, whose art
explores the complex themes of language across cultures, has written
the Press's name in his Square Word Calligraphy. This signals our
commitment to cross-cultural thinking and the distinctive nature of
our English-language books published in China.

"At first glance, Square Word Calligraphy appears to be nothing more
unusual than Chinese characters, but in fact it is a new way of
rendering English words in the format of a square so they resemble
Chinese characters. Chinese viewers expect to be able to read Square
Word Calligraphy but cannot. Western viewers, however are surprised
to find they can read it. Delight erupts when meaning is unexpectedly
revealed."

— Britta Erickson, *The Art of Xu Bing*

Contents

Contributors

Chris BERRY is Professor of Film and Television Studies at Goldsmiths College, University of London. He has written widely on Chinese cinema, and is the translator of Feii Lu's *Taiwan Cinema: Politics, Economics, Aesthetics*. He is author of *Postsocialist Cinema in Post-Mao China* (Routledge), editor of *Chinese Films in Focus: 25 New Takes* (British Film Institute), co-editor of *Mobile Cultures: New Media and Queer Asia* (Duke University Press), and *The Filmmaker and the Prostitute: Dennis O'Rourke's "The Good Woman of Bangkok"* (Sydney: The Power Institute Press), translator of Ni Zhen's *Memoirs from the Beijing Film Academy: The Origins of China's Fifth Generation Filmmakers* (Duke University Press), and co-translator of Ding Xiaoqi's *Maidenhome*, (San Francisco: Aunt Lute).

Nick BROWNE is Professor, Chair of the Critical Studies Committee, and Vice Chair of the Department of Film, Television and Digital Media at UCLA. He is the author of the book *Contemporary Western Film Theories* (Beijing: China Film Press, 1994) and co-editor of *New Chinese Cinemas, Forms, Identities, Politics* (New York: Cambridge University Press, 1994). A related article, "The Undoing of the Other Woman: *Madame Butterfly* in the Discourse of American Orientalism" was published in *The Birth of Whiteness*, Daniel Bernardi, ed. (New Brunswick: Rutgers University Press, 1996).

Sung-sheng Yvonne CHANG (Ph.D., Stanford) is Professor of Chinese and Comparative Literature at the University of Texas at Austin in the Department of Asian Studies. Her analysis of the relationship between Taiwan New Cinema and contemporary Taiwanese fiction has appeared in such publications as *Wenxuechangyu de bianqian: dangdai Taiwan xiaoshuo lun* (Changes in the literary field: contemporary fiction from Taiwan; Taipei: Lianhe wenxue chubanshe, 2001) and *Literary Culture in Taiwan* (forthcoming, Columbia University Press).

CHEN Kuan-Hsing coordinates the Center for Asia-Pacific Cultural Studies, National Tsing Hua University, Hsinchu, Taiwan, and is a co-executive editor of *Inter-Asia Cultural Studies: Movements.*

Haden GUEST is a Ph.D. candidate in Critical Studies in Film at the University of California, Los Angeles, completing his dissertation project, a study of the post-World War Two American police procedural film. He is currently working on a longer essay on the films of Tsai Mingliang.

Rosemary HADDON (Ph.D., University of British Columbia) is Senior Lecturer in Chinese at Massey University, New Zealand. Her publications include the book *Oxcart: Nativist Stories From Taiwan, 1934–1977* (Dortmund: Projekt Verlag, 1996) and articles on nativism and the fiction of Chinese and Taiwanese women writers. She is currently researching the fiction of Zhu Tianxin for inclusion in an edited volume of Taiwan's *bentu* localist discourse.

Nick KALDIS is Assistant Professor of Chinese in the Department of German, Russian, and East Asian Languages at Binghamton University (SUNY Binghamton). He has written articles on Chinese cinema and is currently completing a manuscript on Lu Xun's *Yecao.*

LIU Yu-hsiu is Professor of Literature and Feminist theories at Taiwan University. She is the author of *The Oedipus Myth: Sophocles, Freud, Pasolini.*

Feii LU is a television and film writer, director, and producer as well as Associate Professor and Chairman of the Department of Radio/TV at National Chengchi University in Taiwan. He is the author of the prizewinning book *Taiwan Cinema: Politics, Economics, Aesthetics, 1949–1994.*

Gina MARCHETTI is an Associate Professor in the Department of Cinema and Photography at Ithaca College. In 1995 her book, *Romance and the "Yellow Peril": Race, Sex and Discursive Strategies in Hollywood Fiction*, won the award for best book in the area of cultural studies from the Association of Asian American Studies. She has contributed essays to several anthologies, including *Classic Hollywood, Classic Whiteness; Keyframes: Popular Cinema and Cultural Studies; At Full Speed: Hong Kong Cinema in a Borderless World; Ladies and Gentlemen, Boys and Girls: Gender in Film at the End of the Twentieth Century; Out of the Shadows: Asians in American Cinema; Countervisions: Asian American Film Criticism; The Cinema of Hong Kong: History, Arts, Identity; Transnational Chinese Cinemas: Identity, Nationhood, Gender; The Birth of Whiteness: Race and the Emergence of United States Cinema; Unspeakable Images: Ethnicity and the American Cinema;* and other collections. She has published articles in *Journal of Film and Video; Genders; Journal of Communication Inquiry; Positions: East Asia Cultures Critique; Postmodern Culture, Post Script;* and others, as well as *Jump Cut* (where she serves on the editorial board). She also is a member of the editorial board of *Popular Communication.* Her current book, *From Tian'anmen to Times Square: China on Global Screens,* will be published by Temple University Press.

Fran MARTIN is author of *Situating Sexualities: Queer Representation in Taiwanese Fiction, Film, and Public Culture* (Hong Kong University Press, 2003); translator and editor of *Angelwings: Contemporary Queer Fiction from Taiwan* (Honolulu: University of Hawaii Press, 2003); co-editor with Chris Berry and Audrey Yue of *Mobile Cultures: New Media and Queer Asia* (Durham and London: Duke University Press, 2003); and editor of *Interpreting Everyday Culture* (Hodder Arnold, forthcoming in 2004). She has published articles on sexualities and contemporary Taiwan media and culture in journals including *Positions, GLQ, Intersections, Critical InQueeries, Communal/Plural* and *Chung-wai Literary Monthly,* and is Lecturer in Cultural Studies at University of Melbourne, Australia.

Ti WEI is Assistant Professor in the Department of Mass Communication at Tamkang University, Taiwan. He received his Ph.D. from the Department of Social Sciences at Loughborough University, England. His Ph.D. thesis, "Global Processes, National Responses: Chinese Film Cultures in Transition," analyzes the dynamic relationship between current globalization trends and Chinese film industries.

Introduction

Chris Berry and Feii Lu

Taiwan and its internationally renowned cinema are "on the edge" in more ways than one. As we outline in this introduction, for all its history the island has been on the edge of larger geopolitical entities, and subjected to invasions, migrations, incursions, and pressures. As one of the "Little Tiger" economies of Asia, however, it has been on the cutting edge of the Asian economic boom and technological innovation, and in recent years it has pioneered democratization of authoritarian regimes in East Asia.

Furthermore, for almost twenty years since the advent of the Taiwan New Cinema in the early 1980s, while they have been at the cinematic cutting edge, filmmakers from Taiwan have also been on the edge of economic disaster, not only locally, but also internationally. Hou Hsiao Hsien's early films *The Boys from Fengkuei, A Summer at Grandpa's, The Time to Live and the Time to Die*, and *Dust in the Wind* won awards at festivals everywhere from Locarno to Turin, Nantes, Rotterdam and Berlin. However, his big international breakthrough came when *City of Sadness* topped the Taiwan box office and won the Best Film award at Venice in 1989, and he has been a fixture on the international festival circuit ever since. His peer Edward Yang picked up a Silver Leopard at Locarno for *The Terrorizer* in 1987, and also became a fixture on the international scene. He reached new highs with *Yi Yi* in 2000, which netted him Best Director at Cannes and numerous other awards. Young directors from Taiwan are also feted. Tsai Mingliang won the Venice Golden Lion for *Vive L'Amour* in 1994, and has picked up at least one major award for every film he has made since. In addition to these and other festival favorites, Taiwan cinema has also produced Ang Lee, whose work combines festival and box-office popularity. With these luminaries and many more, the island can reasonably claim one of the highest per-capita densities of internationally renowned film talent in the world.

Despite the international recognition accorded to Taiwan cinema, there are no readily available books in English on the topic, and only one special issue of a journal (*Modern Chinese Language and Culture* 15, no.1, edited by Yomi Braester and Nicole Huang in 2003.) The translation and publication of Feii Lu's *Taiwan Cinema: Politics, Economics, Aesthetics*, to be jointly published by Duke and Hong Kong university presses, will provide the first history of the Taiwan cinema in English. Lu's work is primarily a social and economic institutional history, grounding discussion of films in analysis of policy initiatives, social change, and economic formations. *Island on the Edge: The Taiwan New Cinema and After* aims to complement Lu's history by gathering a range of work that analyzes individual films produced since the advent of the Taiwan New Cinema in the early 1980s.

Of course, we recognize there is more to Taiwan cinema than the works of the Taiwan New Cinema and its inheritors. Indeed, there are also Taiwan New Cinema directors whose works are not discussed in this anthology, such as Wang Tung, Stan Lai, and Chen Kuo-fu. However, the films considered here are among those that are both best known and most available internationally — although not even all of these are as readily available as they should be. Our hope is that this collection will build on this foundation of familiarity to open the doors for further scholarship and publications on earlier films from Taiwan, on films that are so far less well known internationally, and on films other than feature films. We also hope that it may stimulate distributors to make more Taiwan classic films internationally available.

Island on the Edge

Taiwan's remarkable cinematic achievements in recent years are connected to its complex political, economic, and cultural history. This complex history has not only provided the subject matter for many of its groundbreaking films but also enabled the production and international distribution of these remarkable works.

In 1995 Taiwan's government officially initiated an effort to make the island a regional communications, manufacturing, finance, and media hub. The media part of the project includes reference to the island's illustrious film industry. Dubbed the Asia-Pacific Regional Operations Center Plan, this re-centering move counters Taiwan's long history of marginality.[1]

Until very recently Taiwan's history has been one of marginality, both to the peoples who now constitute its population and to its various governors. Taiwan's earliest inhabitants are widely believed to have had Melanesian roots and to have come to the island from the South Pacific. For them Taiwan was on the edge of their ocean realm. (Some recent theories, in a move that echoes the re-centering of Taiwan, have advanced an opposing theory — that Taiwan is the hub from which the current populations of the South Pacific spread out.) Those indigenous peoples are now called "aboriginal" Taiwanese.

Han Chinese migration began in the fifteenth and sixteenth centuries. As the Chinese took over the coastal plains, the aboriginals moved into the mountains. Most of the migrants came from Fujian Province, across what is now the Taiwan Strait, although there were also some Hakka people. As a result the Minnanese variant of Hokkienese (or Fujianese) is the majority language of the longstanding Chinese population on the island, and is referred to by many as "Taiwanese." For these people Taiwan was an island on the edge of the Chinese mainland.[2]

Finally, in 1949, Taiwan became the offshore retreat of the KMT Nationalist regime and its army upon their defeat at the hands of the Communists. They declared Taipei to be their "temporary capital," again marking in their own minds the marginal status of the island that has been their de facto home ever since. This most recent wave of settlers is referred to as "Mainlanders." However, as Chen Kuan-Hsing points out in his chapter, the local term is *waishengren*, literally "people from outside the province," an ethnic category that makes sense only in terms of Taiwan's particular history. In fact, they came from many different parts of China, spoke many different Chinese languages, and had many different Chinese identities prior to being recoded as "Mainlanders." This ethnic distinction between Mainlanders and Taiwanese, and the complex history of its production, continues to be a dominant tension, supplemented by those dividing these populations from other numerically smaller ethnic groups.[3]

Terms like "people from outside the province" and "temporary capital" also reveal the marginal status of the island in the minds of the KMT regime, even though it constituted the sum total of their territory for forty years and more after their retreat in 1949. In that way, they continue a centuries-old attitude among the island's governors, for most of whom it has been a minor territory on the edge of realms to which they have attached little importance. This was certainly true for the various Chinese dynasties, which paid little attention to Taiwan for centuries. Indeed, Portuguese settled unhindered in the sixteenth century, naming the island Formosa, and the Dutch ruled it from 1624–62. However, for both colonial powers, it was on the edge of their empires and of little importance.[4]

When the Qing dynasty in China was defeated in a war with Japan in 1895, it seems it felt few qualms about surrendering an island on the edge of its imperial realm. The fifty years of colonization that followed Japan's incorporation of Taiwan as the southernmost island in its archipelago underlie the entrenched division between Taiwanese and Mainlanders that developed after 1949. This was because the Japanification pursued by the colonizers on the island widened the cultural gap between the locals and the Mainlanders after the island was returned to Chinese rule at the end of the Pacific War in 1945.[5] As Hou Hsiao Hsien shows in *City of Sadness*, when the Mainlanders arrived they discovered that the local people spoke either Taiwanese or Japanese; very few knew Mandarin, the Mainlanders' national language.

The peripheral status of Taiwan extends not only to the perspective of many of its inhabitants and governors, but also to the rest of the world. "Urban legends" abound in English-speaking countries about Taiwan specialists interviewed for jobs and finding themselves asked questions about Bangkok. More seriously, Taiwan discovered just how far out on the edge of international consciousness it was when the People's Republic took up China's seat at the United Nations in 1972 and Taiwan was forced to withdraw. A vast majority of countries in the world, including the United States, also decided to recognize the Communist government in Beijing instead of the Taipei-based KMT regime as the sole legitimate government of all China.[6]

Many would argue that the shock of this rejection not only propelled Taiwan over the edge into an amorphous space of formal non-existence in the international community, but that it also spelt the beginning of the end for both the KMT's martial law and its hold on government, which has been taken over by the pro-independence Democratic Progressive Party. This shock was also fundamental to the changes in the film industry and in film culture that led to the emergence of the Taiwan New Cinema.

Cinema on the Edge

If the directors of what is now known as the Taiwan New Cinema have something in common, it may be that their concern for filming Taiwan's history has drawn them close to the common experiences of individual people and Taiwan society. This makes their films quite different from the escapist love stories and utopian martial-arts films of the seventies, as well as the traditional Confucian ethics of the "Healthy Realist" cinema promoted by the government. Furthermore, the directors of the Taiwan New Cinema were on not only the thematic but also cinematic cutting edge, both within Taiwan and internationally. They did not pursue the dramatic structures based on conflict that characterized the established mainstream Taiwan cinema, but abandoned the models of stage drama or entertainment to pursue observational realism and modernist expressionism. At a time when the output from the various European and Japanese "new waves," Latin American "new cinema," and Indian "parallel cinema" had begun to drop off, these characteristics also won them a warm welcome at international film festivals and put them on the international cutting edge.

Which film initiated the Taiwan New Cinema is disputed. But in April 1983 the state-owned and largest film studio, the Central Motion Picture Corporation, began shooting *The Sandwich Man*, a portmanteau film featuring short films directed by Hou Hsiao Hsien, Tseng Chuang-hsiang, and Wan Ren. The same year, another major government film studio, the Taiwan Motion Picture Corporation, started shooting another portmanteau work, *The Wheel of Life* (*Da Lunhui*), directed by King Hu, Lee Hsing, and Pai Ching-jui. From the audience's point of view, the former film was directed by unknowns, whereas the latter was directed by the three most famous directors on the island.

However, contrary to expectations, *The Wheel of Life* did not perform well either at the box office or critically. *The Sandwich Man*, on the other hand, was well received critically and a bigger box-office success than had been anticipated. This led one major newspaper to declare, "The release of *The Sandwich Man* heralds the completely new start for the Chinese cinema of Taiwan!"[7]

Although not all the directors of *The Sandwich Man* were born in Taiwan, they all grew up on the island. As members of the first postwar generation in Taiwan, they produced films that represented the collective and individual memories of postwar life on the island. In contrast, the directors of *The Wheel of Life* had all grown up on the Mainland. They made important contributions to postwar Hong Kong and Taiwan cinema, and their films were frequently based on episodes in Chinese history, steeped in Confucian ethical values, pedagogical, and conforming to the government's expectations of cinema and the media.

Other competitors for the title of first Taiwan New Cinema film include the 1982 portmanteau film, *In Our Time*, the directors of which include Edward Yang. Its realist style marked a split from the old school of filmmaking in Taiwan. But from an economic angle, the film that symbolized the potential of Taiwan New Cinema and won attention from both state and private film companies was another 1982 film, *Growing Up* (*Xiao Bi de Gushi*), directed by Chen Kun-hou and scripted by Chu T'ien-wen. Perhaps we should say that *In Our Time* introduced new filmmakers; the new face of Taiwan cinema, *Growing Up*, opened the path for Taiwan New Cinema; and *The Sandwich Man* confirmed its arrival.

In the years that followed there were many works on the cutting edge thematically, because of their focus on local Taiwan history and society, and cinematically because of their pursuit of the observational realism associated with Hou Hsiao Hsien or the modernist expressionism associated with Edward Yang. They included: Hou Hsiao Hsien's *The Boys from Fengkuei* and *A Summer at Grandpa's*; Edward Yang's *That Day on the Beach* and *Taipei Story*; Ko Yi-Cheng's *Reunion* and *Last Train to Tanshui*; Chang Yi's *Jade Love* and *Kuei-mei, a Woman*; Chen Kun-hou's *Woman of Wrath*; Wan Jen's *Ah Fei*; and Wang Tung's *A Flower in the Raining Night*.[8]

The Taiwan New Cinema filmmakers believed in an actively engaged audience rather than a passive one. They abandoned the simplistic black-and-white storytelling methods of the past in favor of a more subtle and complex mode that was closer to real life experience. However, this was something new for an audience accustomed to commercial entertainment. Although some were moved that these films brought them closer to real life, others did not connect with them. As the dramatic plots faded away in the Taiwan New Cinema, so did the audience, and with them the producers and investors, pushing the film movement to the edge of financial non-viability. This crisis was marked by the 1987 publication of the "Taiwan New Cinema Manifesto," which called for "another cinema," discussed in more detail in Feii Lu's chapter on Chang Tsochi's *Darkness and Light*.[9]

Although international critics and audiences continue to speak of new films from Taiwan as part of the "Taiwan New Cinema" or "Taiwan New Wave," critics in Taiwan see 1987 as marking the end of the Taiwan New Cinema after only five years of creative output. (To try to avoid confusion in this volume, we have used only one term throughout: "Taiwan New Cinema.") Of course, this does not mean that the most established Taiwan New Cinema filmmakers ceased production. Indeed, they continued to move in new directions. It was after 1987 that Hou Hsiao Hsien transformed his individual biographical memories into tales of Taiwan's traumatic history, initiating his Taiwan trilogy with *City of Sadness* in 1989. This is unquestionably the greatest achievement since the beginning of the Taiwan New Cinema. Since then, he has also made *The Puppetmaster*, *Good Men, Good Women*; *Goodbye South, Goodbye*; *Flowers of Shanghai*; and *Millennium Mambo*. With *Good Men, Good Women*, he made a radical formal shift, introducing camera movement into his highly refined cinematic repertoire. With his next film he made an equally significant thematic shift, leaving Taiwan's post-war history for the present. *Flowers of Shanghai* was set in the nineteenth century and his most recent film, *Millenium Mambo*, pursues innovation into a future setting. Edward Yang, another leading Taiwan New Cinema director, joined the exploration of Taiwan's recent history when he directed *A Brighter Summer Day* in 1991, and then flirted with improvised acting in *A Confucian Confusion, Mahjong*, and *Yi Yi*.

Waves of new directors have also made their debuts since 1987. They include: Chen Kuo-fu with *Schoolgirl* (1989); Ang Lee with *Pushing Hands* (1991); Tsai Mingliang with *Rebels of the Neon God* (1992); Wu Nien-jen with *A Borrowed Life* (1994); Wang Shaudi with *Sky Calls* (1995); Chen Yu-hsun with *Tropical Fish* (1995); Lin Cheng-sheng with *Footsteps in the Rain* (1995); Chang Tsochi with *Ah-chung* (1996); Yi Zhi-yan with *Lonely Hearts Club* (1996); and more.

Compared with their predecessors, these films are thematically and stylistically more varied. However, they have continued to claim the thematic cutting edge in Taiwan, introducing topics concerning sexuality, alienation, and individual identity. Tsai Mingliang is probably the most evident example of this new trend. At the same time these films have continued to claim the cutting edge at international film festivals everywhere by varying the acclaimed realism of the Taiwan New Cinema with anti-realist elements such as the musical numbers in Tsai Mingliang's *The Hole* or the apparent reincarnations in Chang Tsochi's films. The filmmakers themselves embrace the audience more warmly than their predecessors did, but because of the long-term decline in film audiences and the impact of new media, the economic position of these new directors has been ever more marginal. Except for those few like Tsai Mingliang and Ang Lee who are able to attract foreign funding, most of the new directors rely on government support and operate with extremely low budgets.

Furthermore, as Yvonne Chang elaborates in her chapter in this anthology, whereas the earlier filmmakers operated in largely local terms, the new filmmakers have to work in a hybrid local and global framework. This often manifests itself in their works. As a diasporic Chinese, Tsai Mingliang observes Taipei from a position that is inside and outside simultaneously. Adapting his experience in the theater, he has also carved out a highly individual style. Ang Lee has turned out to be the most successful surfer on the wave of globalization, offering Western audiences a taste of a kind of Confucian ethics mediated through Hollywood technique. Recently, with the blockbuster *Double Vision*, Chen Kuo-fu has tried to follow in his footsteps. Other directors have placed a greater emphasis on the local, such as Wu Nien-jen's investigations of Taiwanese local identity and history, Chen Yu-hsun's interest in new media and their social impact in Taiwan, and Chang Tsochi's innovations on the stylistic foundation of Taiwan New Cinema observational realism, combined with a deep focus on marginalized people in Taiwan society.[10]

Both in terms of economics and culture, 1987 turned out to be a watershed for Taiwan cinema. The new cinema that has emerged in recent years demands its own understanding, but like its predecessors it still pursues the new and stands at the cutting edge locally and internationally. The chapters in this volume delve more deeply into a range of individual films selected from the Taiwan New Cinema and after.

The Chapters

The chapters in this anthology are varied in theme and approach. Most were written especially for the volume and focus on a single film, introducing existing writing on it, and striking out in a new direction. They are published in chronological order of the production dates of the films on which they focus. They cover a wide range of films. However, we did not start out with a list of titles, nor is it our intention to establish a canon. Rather, we were guided in our selection by a search for excellence of scholarship, a determination to cover a representative range of relatively widely available films, and the hope for range and variety.

Some of the chapters undertake institutional analysis and seek to place their films in a larger cultural and economic field. Sung-sheng Yvonne Chang identifies Edward Yang's *The Terrorizer* as a watershed work that traces the shift from government-guided to commercial culture through its satirical representation of literary culture in Taiwan. She also locates the film at the cusp of globalization, noting how the apparent continuity of aesthetic modernism during Taiwan New Cinema and after disguises a shift from determinations of local culture to the demands of the international film festival circuit. Ti Wei also locates Ang Lee's *Eat Drink Man Woman* as a turning point. He notes the shifting thematic interests of Lee's works prior to and after this film, and relates this shift to the arc of Lee's career trajectory

as it moves from primarily Taiwan-derived funding and Taiwan audiences
to globalized funding and audiences.

The international reception of Taiwan cinema is also central to Nick
Kaldis's chapter on Hou Hsiao Hsien's *Flowers of Shanghai* and Fran
Martin's chapter on Ang Lee's *Crouching Tiger, Hidden Dragon*. Kaldis
notes the accusations of self-orientalization that have dominated debates
about Chinese-language cinema's international circulation through the
1990s. In this context, he argues, the dynastic courtesan subject matter of
Flowers of Shanghai promises exotic decadence, but the lack of dramatic
detail, slow pace, and other characteristics of the film frustrate orientalist
spectatorship. Martin is interested in the need for *Crouching Tiger, Hidden
Dragon* to appeal to many different audiences around the world. To
investigate this further, she uses the concept of allo-identification, or
identification with a character different from oneself. Furthermore, she
argues for the valence of Zhang Ziyi's character in the film for a kind of
international pop feminism at the turn of the century, also associated with
such figures as the television character Buffy the Vampire Slayer.

Martin's chapter touches on two other themes picked up by other
writers: the politics of gender and sexuality, and theories of spectatorship
in the cinema. Taking gender and sexuality first, two works make feminist
interventions, and one focuses on sexuality politics. Taiwan cinema is one
of the most male-dominated cinemas in the world, so feminist interventions
are timely. Yet neither essay included here is unappreciative of the films it
analyzes. Indeed, Rosemary Haddon's examination of the female narrating
voice in Hou Hsiao Hsien's *City of Sadness* counters criticisms that women
are passive and that writing is denigrated in Hou's cinema. She argues that
on the contrary, Hou's ability to rewrite Taiwan's history in a way that
inscribes the perspective of those marginalized by and during the traumatic
events of the past is dependent upon his taking up the position of alterity
afforded by a female narrator.

Liu Yu-hsiu's powerful analysis of Edward Yang's *A Brighter Summer
Day* acknowledges the high praise the film has won from local and
international critics for its careful reconstruction of the life experiences of
the often overlooked, less well-off members of the first generation of
Mainlanders to grow up on the island. She goes beyond the apparent
objectivity of the film, however, to trace a structuring and gendered myth
that underlies and drives the film, making possible the patriarchy that its
story constructs on the age-old basis of punishing uncontained female
sexuality. Sexual alterity is also the central concern of Gina Marchetti's
detailed and extensive examination of Tsai Mingliang's *The River*. As she

points out, Ang Lee's *The Wedding Banquet* initiated a cycle of internationally circulated films about male homosexuality in Chinese societies. Two aspects of these films have caught attention; what they have to say about male homosexuality in Chinese societies and cultures in general, and how they relate to the local context. Marchetti pursues both of these angles in her analysis of *The River*.

Concerns about those who are outsiders in Taiwan society because of either gender or sexuality also underlie Chris Berry's examination of Tsai's *Vive L'Amour*. However, his primary interest in how the film's techniques may encourage a certain mode of spectatorship places his work alongside Feii Lu's work on Chang Tsochi's *Darkness and Light*. Berry notes how Tsai reworks the observational realism of the Taiwan New Cinema. Tsai is a poet of loneliness, a condition that it is hard to observe outside the cinema without simultaneously disrupting it. In his films we are brought close to the lonely, but Berry claims Tsai does not place his characters under the microscope, as some have argued, but rather induces empathy for them. Lu also notes how Chang Tsochi reworks the conventions of the Taiwan New Cinema. On the one hand, he deepens the observational realist attention to the lives of ordinary Taiwan people for which the Taiwan New Cinema is famous. But on the other hand, through use of point-of-view shots, he simultaneously and astonishingly draws the audience into the minds of his characters in such a way that it is hard to distinguish between reality and fantasy.

Two chapters interrogate the observational realism for which Hou Hsiao Hsien's cinema is most famous, to give new insights to other inflections in the style. Haden Guest examines *Dust in the Wind* as another turning-point film, one that looks back at his early autobiographical works on the cusp of his shift toward the larger historical themes considered in the films that followed. Noting the apparent realist aesthetic for which Hou is famous, Guest argues for a meta-cinematic and more often overlooked self-reflexive level within this realism. He also notes the anticipation of a growing concern with rhythm in Hou's later films, already emergent in *Dust in the Wind*. Nick Browne's classic work, republished here, examines *The Puppetmaster*. Noticing how the realist depiction of historical events is intercut with scenes of nature, Browne argues against the common idea that Hou is only concerned with the human history of Taiwan. Instead, he suggests, the film embeds these human events in a larger cosmological perspective that transcends them at the same time as they mark Taiwan as the space of home for Hou. Browne also notes the importance of the feminine in Hou's work, a topic taken up by Rosemary Haddon, as noted above.

Finally, one chapter, Chen Kuan-Hsing's, drawn from a work previously published in *Inter-Asia Cultural Studies*, compares two films. This is probably the most intellectually penetrating and moving discussion of the impact of the Cold War on Taiwan and the difficulty of resolving the tensions and contradictions it has produced. Chen takes Wu Nien-jen's *A Borrowed Life*, which is about the travails of the local Taiwanese who endured Japanese colonization, and Wang Tung's *Banana Paradise*, which focuses on the vicissitudes of the Mainland soldiers who came to Taiwan with the KMT, to demonstrate how the mutually incomprehensible structures of feeling produced by their different suffering continue to be incompatible in Taiwan society and culture today.

A Note on Romanization and Acknowledgments

The romanization of Chinese characters remains a fraught and politically loaded issue. During the period of KMT Nationalist government in Taiwan the Wade-Giles system was official on the island — not least because it was different from the *pinyin* system preferred in the People's Republic. Perhaps unsurprisingly, the fall of the KMT has led recently to the fall of the Wade-Giles system in Taiwan. Although there has been an attempt to replace it with a *pinyin* system, the system is slightly different from that preferred on the Mainland.[11] In the face of this history, we have preferred not to take a position by imposing one system of romanization throughout the text. Furthermore, certain places and people are already internationally well known by particular romanizations of their names, and these romanizations may not conform to any of the official systems detailed above.

In these circumstances, and at the risk of some confusion, we have adopted the following policy. Where internationally known romanizations of names already exist, these have been retained. Standard forms of the main filmmakers' names have been adapted throughout the book to avoid confusion. For less well-known names and terms, the internationally best-known system of romanization, i.e. the *pinyin* used in mainland China, has been adopted as a default system unless otherwise noted. Chinese characters are given for key filmmakers' names and film titles in the appendix at the end of the book.

Finally, we would like to thank everyone who has helped to make this anthology possible. First, there are the authors, without whose patience and hard work the anthology would not exist. We would also like to thank our two editors at Hong Kong University Press, Mina Cerny Kumar and Delphine

Ip, for their enthusiasm, efficiency, and professionalism, as well as the press's anonymous readers, whose comments have been invaluable in helping us to improve the book. In Berkeley, Frank Wilderson III helped with the preparation of the final manuscript, and in Taipei, Rendy Hou helped to prepare the filmographies, Yu-lin Chang and Chun-chih Lee helped with film stills, and Ming-huey Jeng and Ning Tai helped to proofread the manuscript.

1

The Terrorizer and the Great Divide in Contemporary Taiwan's Cultural Development

Sung-sheng Yvonne Chang

David Harvey identifies the late 1970s as an epoch-breaking moment when the condition of postmodernity assumed prominence, and a key factor was the extension of production to non-Western locations, including East Asia.[1] Many scholars have since tacitly adopted the same analytical scheme, including its time frame, in their studies of cultural phenomena occurring on the "other side." This seems problematic. Whether or not one chooses to employ the modernity/postmodernity model as a major frame of reference, I would argue it is more justifiable to locate the Great Divide within the historical context of contemporary Taiwan at a point when verifiable cultural reorientations can be discerned, in correspondence with the momentous changes that occurred in the sociopolitical and economic realms.

The lifting of martial law in 1987 opened a "Great Divide" in Taiwan's cultural development, ending four decades of politically dominated cultural production and accelerating the emergence of a new cultural field already increasingly subject to market forces and the effects of globalization. Hovering almost exactly in the space that opened between the old epoch and the new, Edward Yang's critically acclaimed 1986 film *The Terrorizer* is a particularly useful window through which to look back on this decisive moment because of its historical timing and pronounced reflexivity.

During the fifteen or so years *before* the Great Divide — the mid-1970s to the late 1980s — cultural production in Taiwan had already shifted markedly away from political subordination and toward domination by the commercial imperatives of the media and publishing industries. As socioeconomic changes facilitated the growth of middle-class art forms, however, the culture market continued to be shaped by the abiding taste preferences of the "high culture quest" of the earlier Modernist movement (dominant from the late 1950s to early 1970s) and the progressive agenda of the continuing Nativist trend. (Whereas the Modernist movement introduced aesthetic concepts from the West, the Nativist trend, spurred by Taiwan's diplomatic setbacks in the 1970s, was socialistically and nationalistically informed; both were projects pursued by Taiwan's postwar intellectual elites.)[2] In this context, I will argue, *The Terrorizer*'s modernistic critique of middlebrow literature signaled the awakening of Taiwan artists to the evolving genre hierarchy of this transitional period. *The Terrorizer* heralds the arrival of a more specialized, differentiated, and professional cultural order typical of advanced capitalism, and the close of the unique literary culture that formed in martial-law Taiwan.

That the new cultural order in post-martial-law Taiwan is shaped by a commodity market susceptible to the intensifying globalization process is borne out by the trajectory of Taiwan New Cinema in the last decade. If modernism's high-culture impulse informed *The Terrorizer*'s self-reflexivity, the appropriation of modernism in more recent New Cinema films is a very different exercise. Nowadays, Taiwan filmmakers consciously develop strategies to position their works in a re-structured global cultural system.

Before the "Great Divide": *The Terrorizer* 's Critique of Middle-Class Art Forms

Following the inception of Taiwan New Cinema in 1982–83, several unexpected box office hits such as *Growing Up* (*Xiao Bi de Gushi*, 1983) and *Kuei-mei, a Woman* (*Wo Zheyang Guole Yisheng*, 1985) gave it a foothold in the mainstream cultural market, despite the fact that certain elements of the movement harbored an elitist agenda aimed at reforming unsophisticated artistic sensibilities.[3] Building on the elitist cultural trends of the preceding decades, the early works of such talented artists as Hou Hsiao Hsien and Edward Yang clearly departed from the characteristically middle-class outlook of the majority of New Cinema films in the movement's early phase. The tension between this high-culture impulse and the middle-class environment erupted into the "Commerce or Art?" debate of 1985–87, during which many artists began to reflect consciously on survival strategies in a commercialized environment. A parting of ways then took place among New Cinema filmmakers.[4]

A similar reflection on the then-current state of artistic affairs is evident in Yang's *The Terrorizer*. The transformation of the cultural field was having a direct impact on the categories through which art is perceived and appreciated, the classifying schemes applied to artistic products, and the established genre hierarchy. Casting middle-class art forms in an ironic light in *The Terrorizer*, the notably elitist Yang registered the changing climate with a sensibility few other cultural agents displayed at the time.

The Terrorizer features an ostensibly modernistic theme: life imitates art, rather than the other way around. What deserves special attention, however, is the way this is presented, namely through parodic treatment of the film's two would-be artists. They are a middle-class woman whose short stories are published to popular effect in *fukan* (literary supplements to newspapers), and a rich boy whose amateur photography dreams dully of Antonioni's *Blow-Up*. These pseudo-artistic activities are vehicles through which people confined within the anonymously cordoned urban spaces of Taiwan's increasingly affluent modern metropolis pursue their romantic fantasies in a make-believe fashion. The film accentuates the degeneration of both mimetic art forms by repeatedly negating their truth-value: the woman castigates her distressed husband for his inability to distinguish "fiction" from "reality"; the rich boy disbelieves the lover's promises he makes to the giant photo collage he has created of the "White Chick" who fascinates him.

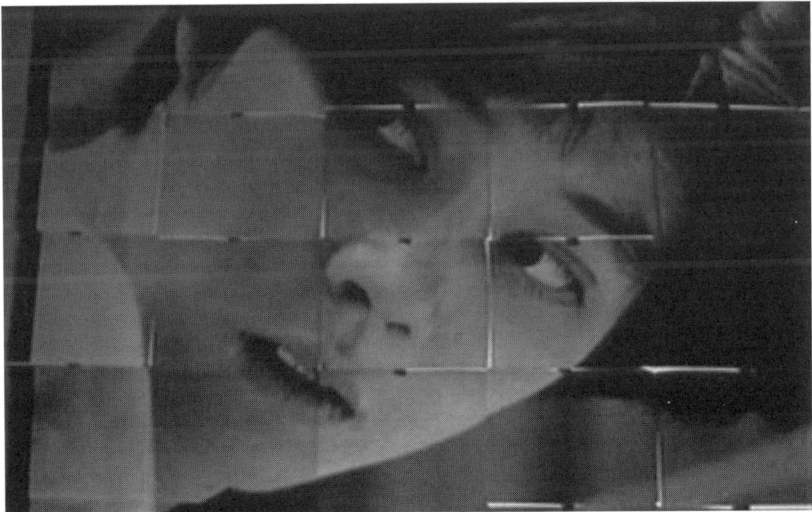

The terrorizer, in *The Terrorizer*.

Two Converging Critical Perspectives

Appearing toward the end of the twentieth century, *The Terrorizer*'s modernistic theme inevitably evoked a sense of *deja vu* among Western critics, well-represented by Fredric Jameson, who applies phrases like "now-archaic modernity," "old-fashioned reflexivity," and "residual modernism" to the film:

> What sets *The Terrorizer* off is not the class status of its characters . . . but the now-archaic modernity of its theme: art versus life, the novel and reality, mimesis and irony . . . . What does stand out . . . is the old-fashioned reflexivity of the themes, the residual modernism of the now-familiar mystery of the imitation of art by life and the correspondence of the novel to the aleatory realities of the real world outside. The very embodiment of the theme around the writing of literature and the pathos of the precarious role of the literary 'creator' strikes a regressive note in a film of this decidedly contemporary stamp . . . 5

Interestingly, local critics interpreted this "residual modernism," whose use of literature as a theme "strikes a regressive note" for Jameson, as a progressive marker. Peggy Hsiung-Ping Chiao lauded *The Terrorizer* as the first Taiwan film to explore the fundamental nature of "film" or "film making."6 Another important critic, Zhan Hongzhi, praised Yang's early skillful use of "international film language."7 The ingenuous remarks suggest that Western-style modernism still served as a privileged high-culture model in late 1980s Taiwan. In short these local critics essentially concurred with Jameson in seeing *The Terrorizer* as a product of "belated" or "derivative" modernism, a view that finds justification in a Eurocentric genealogy of "modernism."8

This, of course, is not the whole story. By the early 1990s a potent interpretive frame that regarded contemporary non-Western cultural products as commentaries on the global "postmodern condition" — in direct contrast to the "belated-modernism" viewpoint — had already become prevalent.9 This is what Jameson seems to have in mind in the last sentence of the quote above, and when he says *The Terrorizer* is a vivid illustration of the idea that "in postmodern times, in the international urban society of late capitalism," characteristically modernistic Gidean moral judgments are "irrelevant or inoperative."10

Here I do not intend to take issue directly with Jameson's interpretation of *The Terrorizer*, or what exactly constitutes the "postmodern condition" in non-Western societies. Rather, my goal is to explore the possibility of building a locally based genealogy in which Yang's use of the modernistic themes is significant for a different set of reasons. The question that Jameson raises about the readership of the middle-class woman's prize-winning short story in *The Terrorizer* is a good point of departure.

The Literary Culture of *Fukan*

As essays in a 1997 conference volume on *fukan* (literary supplements) nicely demonstrate, the *fukan* is a unique modern Chinese journalistic tradition.[11] It is leisure reading and a forum for serious cultural dialogue at the same time. In contemporary Taiwan, major newspaper *fukan* further assume a leading role in literary publications. Between the mid-1970s and late 1980s in particular, *fukan* pages replaced the elitist coterie magazines that had nurtured the Modernist and Nativist trends and emerged as the dominant sponsors and consecrators of new literary production. An overwhelming majority of fiction writers of the baby-boom generation embarked on their literary career by winning awards in *fukan*-sponsored annual contests.[12]

Considerable prominence is given to the *fukan* literary award in *The Terrorizer*: the middle-class wife gives up her regular job to devote herself full-time to writing stories for the *fukan* fiction contest. When she eventually wins the top prize we see eulogistic newspaper headlines followed by a scene in a TV studio, where multiple images of her being interviewed appear on a row of screens. Jameson takes this scene as a commentary on literature's diminished position in the media age, relative to TV and film, remarking: "It is not clear who in the film has actually read this prize-winning production . . ."[13]

But Jameson misreads this. No locally informed contemporary viewer of the film could possibly miss the subtle sarcasm directed at the dominant role played by the *fukan* institution in Taiwan's cultural life in the 1970s and 1980s. Electronically reproduced images of the newly consecrated author sitting for a TV interview were part of the familiar annual ritual of the announcement of the *fukan* literary prize. Through its parodic representation of this public spectacle, the film evokes a unique cultural ambience while inviting the local audience taking part in that culture to contemplate the particular social forces that supported it.

Fukan were the most popular household reading for the educated middle class in post-1949 Taiwan until 1988, when the restrictive press law that banned new newspapers and put a cap on the number of pages newspapers could print was lifted. With regular news heavily censored, newspapers depended on their literary pages to attract subscribers. Before the electronic media were fully liberalized, newspapers were the most modern sector in Taiwan's culture industry. Two of them — *United Daily News* (*Lianhe bao*) and *China Times* (*Zhongguo shibao*) — received special backing from the government and enjoyed exponential growth. Rich in financial and personal resources, *fukan* were windows on the world for residents in the partially closed society. This was exemplified by their exhaustive annual reports on the winner of the Nobel Prize for Literature. *Fukan*-sponsored cultural activities — elegant awards ceremonies, sumptuous parties in luxurious hotel ballrooms, and handsome compensation for contributions to *fukan* pages — created a festive atmosphere and a sense of affluence that mirrored Taiwan's transition in the 1980s from postwar "economy of scarcity" to what Guy Debord calls the "society of the spectacle" in an age of consumption.[14]

Winners of the *fukan*-sponsored annual prizes became instant celebrities, and their works were reprinted by *fukan*-affiliated mainstream publishing houses. *Fukan* literature was widely read by particular sectors of the educated populace, represented well in *The Terrorizer* by the rich boy's girlfriend. The opening scene reveals her bedtime reading to be a book published by Hongfan Bookstore, a publisher immediately recognizable to the film's contemporary viewers. Although the girl appears to be a seasoned fiction reader and is aware of its pulp-entertainment nature, it does not prevent her being influenced by its behavioral models as she demonstrates in her sensational suicide attempt after breaking up with the rich boy.

Despite its unmistakably popular nature, *fukan* literature was highly regarded as legitimate culture in the 1970s and 1980s. The categories through which both consecrating agents (editors, jurors of literary contests, publishers) and writers themselves (mostly of the postwar baby-boom generation) perceived and appreciated literature were deeply influenced by the elitist Modernist and Nativist trends of the previous decades, and *fukan* literature at least pretended to honor these categories. There was, however, a growing conflict between these high-cultural ideals and market demands. Thus, although frustration about her routine life motivated the middle-class wife in *The Terrorizer* to write (in an early scene, staring directly at the audience, she talks about her *ennui* in a language immediately reminiscent of Taiwan's Modernist fiction), her literary pursuit nonetheless follows the typical route by which middlebrow art is consecrated in modern society.

This brings me to my core argument. It is clear that the flourishing of *fukan* literature had a significant impact on the evolving genre hierarchy by which literature is perceived and appreciated by writers and readers in

Taiwan. Unlike the Modernists and the Nativists of the postwar generation, who treated writing as a serious intellectual quest, writers of the 1980s pursued literature as a career, and for them the *fukan* prize was a stepping-stone to professional success. Because of lingering high-culture aspirations from the previous decades, this transition was not fully acknowledged in the literary discourse that prevailed in the 1980s. Critics and writers alike perpetuated the high-culture illusion, resulting in frequent misrecognition and over-legitimization of middlebrow art forms. By maintaining an ironic distance from such middlebrow art forms, *The Terrorizer* achieves a demystifying effect that was only fully appreciated in Taiwan's cultural circles years later.

Fukan-centered Literary Culture and the New Cinema

Some inherent contradictions in the structure of the cultural field in the martial-law period significantly contributed to the gap between the elitist critical discourse and the middlebrow nature of the mainstream cultural output against which *The Terrorizer*'s self-reflexivity represented a meaningful departure. To understand this, we have to look into the political implications of the *fukan* phenomenon before addressing its relationship to Taiwan New Cinema and *The Terrorizer*, which represented the high watermark of that cinema.

The *fukan* institution's cultural hegemony was a product of the cultural control system of Taiwan's soft-authoritarian regime in a society in the process of market transformation.[15] All authoritarian governments closely supervise their mass media, and in the early post-1949 period *fukan* editors were mostly Mainlanders trusted by the KMT government. These and other politically favored cultural agents selectively preserved mainland China's May Fourth tradition in Taiwan, including the role of *fukan* as important publishers of New Literature, a vernacular but earnestly edifying literary form intended by May Fourth intellectuals as their primary means of "enlightening the people." The high-culture status of *fukan* was reinforced in Taiwan even as it was charged with having various political missions.

Sanctioned as the guardian of orthodox "national culture," the *fukan* institution was used by the party-state to teach the official Mandarin dialect to the native Taiwanese population educated by their Japanese colonial rulers before the arrival of the KMT, and for ideological indoctrination. During the Nativist literary movement of the 1970s, *fukan* became a contested site where official and oppositional discourses vied with each other. Through its trusted cultural agents (the *fukan* editors of *United Daily News* were former military personnel) the Nationalist regime was able to monitor and to a certain extent manage the militant Nativist Debate of 1977–78. In the aftermath of the debate, the regime skillfully used *fukan* to restore its cultural hegemony by patching up feuds and reinforcing the dominant cultural ideology.[16]

Fukan editors would face another set of challenges in the 1980s. Society was rapidly outgrowing the KMT's political and social strictures, but the infrastructure of cultural production was still controlled by the state. Resourceful *fukan* editors responded by playing a tactful mediating role between the ruling regime and the social forces demanding change. Successfully translating values of the Nationalist-instituted dominant culture into published work appealing to a highly homogeneous, conservative middle-class reading public, they cultivated a new literary culture that proved to be fertile ground, nurturing the development of a number of important new art forms. These included mainstream theater, *fukan* literature, and Taiwan New Cinema.[17]

A particularly symbiotic relationship developed between Taiwan New Cinema and *fukan* fiction. Both genres tapped into the identity quest of baby-boom-generation artists just then coming of age. Both also drew heavily on cultural resources accumulated during Taiwan's literary renaissance of the 1960s and 70s — a high percentage of early New Cinema works, for instance, were adapted from stories written in the 1960s and 70s. A number of creative talents straddled the two art forms — most notably writer-scriptwriters Chu T'ien-wen and Wu Nien-jen; writer-turned-film-bureaucrat Xiao Ye; and writer-director Zhang Yi — while others, like Zhan Hongzhi, were influential critics in both forms. While New Cinema initially emulated Taiwanese literature's earlier accomplishments, thanks to film's greater translatability and Chinese cinema's sudden rise in the international arena, it soon outperformed literature in both artistic caliber and its ability to address contemporary issues in a meaningful way.

The government cultural bureaucracy, especially the Central Motion Picture Corporation and the Government Information Office, played a positive yet somewhat dubious role in the development of Taiwan New Cinema, simultaneously providing the resources for its inexperienced, non-commercially oriented filmmakers, and imposing restrictions on their artistic expression. Of no less importance were the cultural sections of the mainstream newspapers: *The United Daily News*, *Industry and Business News* (*Gongshang shibao*), and the *China Times*. The mostly baby-boom-generation promoters of New Cinema collaborated with enlightened figures in the cultural establishment, formed pressure groups, and engaged in spirited negotiations with the state, demanding the removal of ideological constraints even as they asked for government assistance in resisting the crude pressures of the market. As demonstrated by articles and historical documents of the time, collected in Peggy Hsiung-ping Chiao's *Taiwan New Cinema* (*Taiwan Xin Dianying*), New Cinema promoters identified "conservative forces" as the worst enemy.[18] These "enemies" included not only those bureaucrats who objected to loosening ideological control, but also many who simply dismissed film as mere "entertainment." The insistence by New Cinema adherents on recognizing film as "culture" or even "high culture" was aimed at establishing an important legal point in their campaign for better access to public resources, because "entertainment" products were subject to heavy taxation.

High-culture aesthetic ideals played a crucial yet ambivalent role in this negotiation. On the one hand, the painstaking aesthetics of New Cinema helped establish film as a legitimate art form deserving public support. The elitist intention of providing cultural edification to the public appealed to the moralist agenda of the government. On the other hand, the high-culture rhetoric concealed the real objective of New Cinema promoters, which was simply to overcome all obstacles standing in the way of the filmmakers producing films, political and commercial alike. The effort was largely successful. Both *fukan* literature and Taiwan New Cinema received enough public funding to regenerate mainstream cultural production, together producing a golden age of sorts in Taiwan's cultural development. The high-culture façade of these mostly middlebrow cultural products explains why the literary and film criticism of the time placed such emphasis on humanitarian ideals, familial relations, and other values promoted in the government-enforced dominant culture.

This mutually beneficial arrangement between the conservative regime and cultural producers also enabled the more genuinely ambitious artistic efforts of Taiwan New Cinema to do reasonably well in the domestic market. This situation, however, did not last. With continuing economic liberalization came increased cultural stratification and segmentation of the market. *The Terrorizer*'s self-reflexive critique suggests consciousness of this changing reality before the Great Divide. If we consider how decisive that divide really was, *The Terrorizer*'s prescience becomes even clearer.

After the Great Divide: the Transnational Cultural Arena

Forces unleashed by political and economic liberalization after the lifting of
martial law moved the evolving cultural field even more decisively in the
directions alluded to above. The Nationalist regime gave up its efforts to
enforce a conservative dominant culture through state-sponsored cultural
institutions, shifting cultural production firmly into the hands of the
consumer market. Economic liberalization, meanwhile, ushered in the global
marketplace, with its huge array of cultural products for local
consumption.[19] The impact on local cultural producers was thoroughly
disorienting. This was evident in the late 1980s and early 1990s in
pronouncements declaring the death of this or that art form, including *chun
wenxue* ("pure literature," exemplified by *fukan* fiction), Taiwan New
Cinema, and Little Theater (an avant-garde or postmodern theater
movement in the late 1980s).[20]

Local cultural production survived, however, but only by adapting to
deep structural changes in the cultural field. Certain aspects of the
development of Taiwan New Cinema after its alleged "death" may help to
illuminate the nature of this change. As the vanguard of Taiwanese cultural
products entering the global system, the New Cinema at once carries the
legacy of local cultural developments in the previous era and exhibits
features that are clearly the result of its interaction with rules governing the
field of transnational film production.[21] The continued and increasingly
sophisticated employment of the legacy of modernistic themes and
aesthetics by such auteur directors as Hou Hsiao Hsien, Edward Yang, and
Tsai Mingliang has definitively shaped their individual styles. However, this
unexpected minor renaissance of modernism in the hands of Taiwan
filmmakers long after its heyday in the West is simultaneously a constitutive
element of the uniquely inclusive process of cultural globalization, a process
that obliterates temporal and spatial boundaries.

There is little doubt that the "belated" appearance in Taiwan of an
alienating and dehumanizing capitalist urban culture constitutes a purely
domestic reason for many salient modernistic features in Tsai Mingliang's
Vive L'Amour (1994), *The River* (1996), and *The Hole* (1998), which treat the
monstrosity of the city as an emblem of modern civilization. Tsai's seemingly
anachronistic cultural critique speaks powerfully to the phenomenon of
"compressed modernity" in regions formerly designated as "third world."
Comparing depictions of Taipei in *Vive L'Amour* and *Dust in the Wind* (1985),
a Hou Hsiao Hsien film made a decade earlier, gives a good idea of the
compressed timetable of the country's capitalist urban development.[22]

Both films feature "marginal" inhabitants of Taipei, with much of the city's wealth and glamour beyond their reach. The contrast, however, is sharp. Traces of poverty, the overriding theme in many New Cinema films of the 1980s that is also responsible for the painful separation of the young lovers in *Dust in the Wind*, all but vanish in Tsai's more contemporary urban parable. And so do meaningful human relationships, something that at once overburden and console Hou's youngsters who, like many others in the 1960s and 70s, find menial jobs in the capital city while sending cash back to their families in the impoverished countryside. If *Dust in the Wind*'s solemn humanitarianism is reminiscent of postwar European "new realism" — the motorcycle incident readily evokes *The Bicycle Thief* — *Vive L'Amour* cool-headedly portrays the vacuity of modern existence through self-conscious adoption of artistic devices of the existentialist theater and the European art film of the "classic" period.

The mirror effect achieved — between the materially affluent end-of-the-century Taipei and European cities of the 1960s that have featured in the French New Wave — is, of course, not coincidental. It superficially points to a linear conception of modernity: societal modernization in the capitalist mode progresses in a linear mode, and so does the cultural modernism that it generates. This explanation, however, is at best only partially valid. Also to be taken into consideration are the institutional factors conditioning Tsai's adoption of those highly consecrated modernistic devices.

The Nationalist government's political maneuvers in post-Cold War diplomatic power struggles significantly aided the Taiwan New Cinema's debut on the global stage. Since the late 1980s, encouraged by the initial recognition Taiwan New Cinema received at international film festivals, the Government Information Office has tactfully enlisted film in Taiwan's diplomatic struggle for "international living space" against mounting pressure from the People's Republic of China. Government-sponsored annual trips to the festivals introduced Taiwan New Cinema to a particular sub-field of transnational cinema — the international film festival circuit. This subjected the filmmakers to the creative standards, rules, and conventions governing what is generally understood as the international art film, and they found a niche there. In the same way that national epics — with the Cultural Revolution as their centerpiece — helped Zhang Yimou and Chen Kaige to insert their work into the global market for mainstream art films, modernistic thematic and aesthetic devices helped to position Taiwan New Cinema in the early to mid-1990s.

The idea that artistic modernism is used as cultural currency by Taiwanese auteur directors does not necessarily invalidate other interpretive frames, such as that of "compressed modernity." However, viewing transnational film production as a "field" in the Bourdieuian sense allows us to conduct a more complete contextual analysis. Because cultural agents always employ specific tactics to achieve specific effects, studies of Taiwan New Cinema since the early 1990s must take into account how the operational rules of the art-film world and the expectations of art-house moviegoers affect Taiwanese filmmakers' position-taking strategies.

Consider Edward Yang's latest film, *Yi Yi* (2000), as a metaphor of this global rather than purely domestic set of determinations. Characteristically modernistic themes — the privileging of artistic/technological innovation, "showing people what they cannot see," as something redemptive, capable of redressing the rampant materialism and lack of spirituality — are cast in a decidedly postmodern milieu in Yang's latest masterpiece. The US, Taiwan, and Japan are not seen as representing different stages of capitalist modernization, but rather as occupying different slots on the same computer-software production chain, a distinctive feature of today's information-technology-based global capitalism.

However, as the metaphor of *Yi Yi* indicates, this globalized scenario is also regional. At the same time as Taiwan New Cinema directors have found a festival circuit niche by emulating classic artistic modernism, their exchanges of financial and cultural capital in Asia have increased remarkably in both type and volume in the last decade. For instance, whereas Hou Hsiao Hsien's venture into the realm of pure aestheticism continues contemporary Taiwanese artists' quest for high culture modeled on the West, his "long take" technique has traveled mostly within the broader Asian civilizational framework, attracting followers in the People's Republic of China, Japan, and South Korea.[23]

Also particularly noteworthy is the exponential growth of network formation and business cooperation among filmmakers within the "Greater China" cultural-linguistic sphere, consisting of the People's Republic, Taiwan, Hong Kong, and the Chinese diaspora. New labels such as "Chinese-language film" or "Pan-Chinese cinema" have been invented to give an identity to this burgeoning "transnational" phenomenon.

The commonalities linking the components in this new transnational cinema are multiple, but one example would be the "aesthetics of the commonplace" that has its roots in the 1940s Shanghai associated with author Zhang Ailing (Eileen Chang). Zhang's sophisticated urban romance has fascinated Chinese readers for more than half a century, making her a legendary cultural icon in Hong Kong and Taiwan,[24] and since the 1980s her appeal has rebounded with full vigor in post-socialist China. "Greater Chinese" films and literature inspired by Zhang's work and aesthetic style include Yim Ho's *Red Dust* (*Gungun Hongchen*, 1990), Stanley Kwan's *Red Rose, White Rose* (*Hong Meigui, Bai Meigui*, 1994), Peter Chan's *Comrades, Almost a Love Story* (*Tian Mimi*, 1996), Ann Hui's *Eighteen Springs* (*Bansheng Yuan*, 1997), Hou Hsiao Hsien's *Flowers of Shanghai* (*Haishang Hua*, 1998), and Wong Kar-wai's *In the Mood for Love* (*Huayang Nianhua*, 2001).[25]

Conclusion

The first part of this chapter argues that the modernistic themes of *The Terrorizer* may be considered "residues" of Taiwan's own Modernist movement of the 1960s and 1970s — Edward Yang's formative years. With its professed goal of emulating Western high culture, underpinned by American liberal ideology, Taiwan's Modernist literary movement may be seen in turn as a potent "alternative cultural formation" (to borrow Raymond Williams's term) in Taiwan's early martial-law period.[26] As I have noted, lingering high-culture aspirations were prominent in the Taiwan New Cinema movement of the early 1980s. That decade, however, also included rapid movement of the cultural field toward market-driven standards of artistic value, so that by the time we get to *The Terrorizer* the context has changed to the extent that its "alternative" nature is defined against the rise of this more commercial culture rather than against politically imposed culture. The modernistic device of self-reflexivity in *The Terrorizer* enables the film to maintain a critical distance from the objects it represents, namely the various middlebrow art forms that thrived in this cultural milieu.

After the Great Divide, while Taiwan New Cinema directors have continued to employ modernistic themes and aesthetic devices, the globalized cultural environment has come into play. Their appropriation of classic features of European modernism now reflects strategic self-positioning, dictated by the trade-specific operational rules governing the art-film circuit, the primary venue where Taiwan filmmakers have participated in the transnational cinema. Configurations of classic modernism in Taiwan New Cinema films from this period, therefore, ought to be considered in conjunction with specific aspects of transnational cinema, including network formation, the circulation of aesthetic trends and technical innovations within or across regional and cultural-linguistic spheres, cultural producers' position-taking strategies, and the interaction between the field's internal operational rules and such external factors as civilizational affinities, stages of modernization, and geopolitical concerns.

2

Reflections on the Screen: Hou Hsiao Hsien's *Dust In the Wind* and the Rhythms of the Taiwan New Cinema

Haden Guest

Hou Hsiao Hsien's seventh feature film, *Dust in the Wind* (1986, Central Motion Picture Corporation), marks a crucial yet rarely acknowledged turning point in his career as one of the most influential and internationally acclaimed filmmakers to emerge from the Taiwan New Cinema of the 1980s. Although recent years have witnessed a surge in Western scholarship on Hou's films, *Dust in the Wind* remains one of his least discussed works, mentioned briefly within only the broader surveys and thematic analyses of Hou's oeuvre.[1] Indeed, outside Asia, writing on Hou has been notably selective, principally focused on the director's best-known and most widely distributed works, especially his magnum opus, the so-called Taiwan trilogy composed of *A City of Sadness* (1989, Era International), *The Puppetmaster* (1993, Era International) and *Good Men, Good Women* (1995, 3H Films Ltd.). To date the most engaged work in English on Hou's films, by scholars such as Chris Berry, Bérénice Reynaud, and June Yip, has dealt primarily with the trilogy and its challenging treatment of historical narrative and issues related to Taiwanese cultural identity.[2]

With the hope of contributing to a more comprehensive assessment of Hou's oeuvre, this chapter returns to *Dust in the Wind* and re-examines it as a complex and important transitional film that sheds new light on key developments in his work. Situated roughly half-way through Hou's directorial work thus far, the film does, in fact, suggest a clear division between his early autobiographical films — all based on episodes from either Hou's or his collaborators' adolescence and made under the aegis of the

Kuomintang-controlled Central Motion Picture Corporation (CMPC) — and his subsequent "mature" work, including his celebrated trilogy.[3] As Hou's final work for the CMPC, and his last in a series of autobiographical coming-of-age stories, *Dust in the Wind* arguably represents the end of the Taiwan New Cinema's most formative period and a turn away from the particular realist style and subjects favored by the movement.

More than simply a chronological milestone, *Dust in the Wind* is also partially cast as a retrospective gaze. It looks back at the "new wave," which was encouraged and sponsored by the CMPC and already drawing to a close by the end of the decade. Indeed, I will argue that the film's elegiac coming-of-age story is also a meditation on the precarious situation faced by the Taiwan cinema in general during the late 1980s, brought on by, among other factors, the surging popularity of foreign, and especially Hong Kong, films despite the international renown Hou and his fellow new-wave directors achieved.[4] Resonant throughout *Dust in the Wind* is the failure of Hou's first mature films to capture the steady domestic audience hoped for by the institutional and creative "founders" of the Taiwan New Cinema, who had brought about an unprecedented level of creative freedom and government support.[5] In this way the film offers a response to the criticism of many in the film community who openly questioned the very project of the new wave in the face of its apparent inability to revive the island's faltering motion-picture industry.[6]

As will be shown, a closer examination of *Dust in the Wind* reveals an important meta-cinematic dimension of Hou's early work that has rarely been discussed by critics or scholars. A deliberate self-consciousness remains an absolutely essential component of the particular "realism" explored in *Dust in the Wind* and across Hou's early films in general. This quality is especially significant as well in his breakthrough film *The Boys from Fengkuei* (1983, CMPC). These two films in particular can be seen to question subtly the very goals and means of the Taiwan New Cinema that they so effectively represent, with both, moreover, attempting to understand the specific presence and role of the cinema in the everyday lives of their subjects and audience.

In addition to its meta-cinematic aspects the importance of *Dust in the Wind* for this chapter also lies in its partial break with the pattern set by Hou's earlier CMPC films and, simultaneously, its anticipation of certain major ideas explored more fully by his most recent work. Chief among these is a heightened concern for *rhythm*, both as a structuring device and a larger thematic concept. This idea becomes absolutely central to Hou's later films, *Goodbye South, Goodbye* (1996, Shochiku) and *Millennium Mambo* (2001,

3H Productions) and in both gives way to a renewed attention to music and musical motifs. *Dust in the Wind* introduces a new formal complexity to Hou's films. It raises the stakes of the "art cinema" explored by his movies and the Taiwan New Cinema in general, reorienting their shared realist agenda to point toward the ambitious attempt of Hou's later work to redefine the very parameters of narrative cinema.

The opening minutes of *Dust in the Wind* contain the first in a series of poetically charged allusions to the cinema that are carefully woven throughout the film. Returning home to their mountain village from school, the film's protagonists, the young couple Wan (Wang Jingwen) and Huen (Xin Shufen), pause at an open plaza to watch an enormous cloth movie screen being stretched into place for a public showing later that night. Caught in an early evening breeze the cloth screen billows like a giant sail, its blank surface sprung to life in rhythm with the windswept landscape surrounding the village.

This sudden animation of the movie screen in place of an absent, expected film offers a powerfully emblematic gesture for the type of formally innovative art cinema defined by the Taiwan New Cinema and carefully refined within *Dust in the Wind*. As a type of literal blank canvas, the "empty", isolated screen further suggests the mode of active and engaged spectatorship demanded by Hou's work, and this film in particular. Indeed, *Dust in the Wind* is marked by a heightened stylization that both summarizes

The outdoor movie screen in *Dust in the Wind.*

and dramatically expands on aesthetic and narrative strategies honed in his earlier work, taking to a new level, for example, the restrained spatial and temporal ambiguity featured in *The Boys from Fengkuei* and *The Time to Live and the Time to Die* (1985, CMPC).

Although the film's basic story of alienated youth in post-"economic miracle" Taiwan addresses Taiwan New Cinema's favorite subjects, it does so with a decidedly sober tone — an austerity that is somewhat unusual for Hou. Contributing to this general tone is the resolutely minimal characterization that defines the young protagonists, accentuated by the understated presence of non-professional actors standard to Hou's early work. In addition, while Hou's earlier films are marked by abrupt temporal ellipses and a notable exploitation of off-screen space, *Dust in the Wind* goes further, shaping both mise-en-scène and narrative through a deliberate fracturing of space and time.

Typical is the scene of Huen's first arrival in Taipei, which flaunts a careful temporal disorientation. The scene opens with an image of a railway-station clock giving the exact hour yet without any clear indication as to how much time has passed since the last scene, or what has transpired between them. Without explanation the scene continues into an extended long shot showing Huen walking away from the camera with an unidentified older man, their backs turned and their conversation entirely unheard. The sudden arrival of Wan adds further confusion as the youth and the unidentified man break into a sudden, violent confrontation while the camera maintains its fixed, distanced position, cutting to a medium shot only after the action has reached a climax. This scene also exemplifies the exacting mise-en-scène refined throughout the film — what David Bordwell calls Hou's "precision staging" — with a pillar purposely obscuring the faces of the fighting men.[7]

The same movie screen glimpsed at the start of *Dust in the Wind* appears again in a later scene, this time with a large crowd, including the young couple visiting from Taipei, gathered in the village plaza to watch a film. Significantly, the movie, revealed in a series of telling clips, is *Beautiful Duckling* (*Yangya renjia*, 1964, Lee Hsing, CMPC), a well-known classic of Taiwan's "Healthy Realism" movement, a "local style" of filmmaking that emerged in the early 1960s as a response to mainland China's Socialist Realist cinema.[8] Taking Italian neo-realism as its avowed model, Healthy Realism centered on an image and ideal of Taiwan that favored rural settings and small-town communities, and gravitated toward themes of "cultural harmony, agricultural progress and development."[9] Such a design is clearly visible in the bucolic country scenes on the movie screen that conspicuously feature plentiful harvests and happy farmers.

With this pointed reference to an earlier but now clearly outdated model of genre production, *Dust in the Wind*, itself sponsored by the CMPC, implicitly measures its treatment of present-day Taiwan against that of its official government predecessors. Indeed, Hou's film offers an immediate response to the Taiwan of Lee's Healthy Realism, swiftly undercutting its bucolic fantasy by showing it to be both an outmoded and now totally inappropriate representation of the island nation. In this way an implicit on- and off-screen contrast is established, between the sunny utopia of the film-within-a-film and the reality of the impoverished mountain village in which it is screened. Unlike the peasants in *Beautiful Duckling*, the adults of the village undertake dangerous and unstable work in a nearby mine. The bitter plight of the local miners is best expressed by the serious mining injury incurred by Wan's father. Because of the accident, whose traumatic effect on the boy and his family echoes through the film, the father is a largely absent, ethereal figure. Locked into a seemingly perpetual strike to protest against unfair labor conditions, the miners are further deprived of wages and the means to support their families. As if to underscore the total disparity between reality and cinematic representation, the village is not even able to provide the electricity needed to project the film in its entirety, with a power failure unexpectedly derailing the show and plunging the village into darkness. This literal "short-circuiting" of the film underscores its ultimate irrelevance to the mining town.

The rejection of the pastoral nostalgia seen onscreen and typically associated with the cinema of Healthy Realism is also, however, a comment on a specific development in Hou's career that marks the distance between *Dust in the Wind* and his earlier work. The first accepted script of Hou, who began as a low-level CMPC employee, was, in fact, assigned to Lee, the director of *Beautiful Duckling*.[10] Rather than simply an object of critique the inclusion of Lee's beloved classic is, then, equally homage, or an autobiographical aside. Lee's influence is, moreover, clearly apparent in Hou's first three feature films, light musical comedies that all feature idealized depictions of rural Taiwan.

The spirit of Healthy Realism is also visible in Hou's later mature work, such as *A Summer at Grandpa's* (1984, CMPC), which follows a young brother and sister sent for a school vacation from Taipei to their grandfather's home in a small rural town. Although an indirect encounter with a pair of thugs temporarily disrupts the children's stay, the setting of the film nevertheless offers a vision of harmonious co-existence with nature in verdant and picturesque landscapes not unlike those so central to the Healthy Realist movement. Although this idea of the rural is openly embraced by the frolicking children in *A Summer at Grandpa's*, it is rejected by the distracted adolescents in *Dust in the Wind* who stand before its spectacle at the outdoor theater, exchanging stories about their difficult lives in Taipei.

Dust in the Wind instead offers a markedly different vision of the Taiwanese landscape from the postcard images shown at the village cinema. This distinctive approach to the representation of the lush hillsides and seascapes is seen throughout Hou's film. Following a similar logic to that of the railway station scene discussed previously, landscapes in *Dust in the Wind* — most shot from an extreme and fixed distance — are presented as rigorously abstract compositions that obscure specific characters and objects within them. Take, for example, the early scene in which Wan's father returns from the hospital after his crippling accident in the mine. The reunited family members are barely visible, tiny figures moving along a bridge, sublimated within a distanced and extended long shot of the landscape as they walk home from the station. The absence of dialogue, which is again unheard and unintelligible, is pronounced because of the family's much-anticipated reunion.

The explicit reference in *Dust in the Wind* to an earlier idea of cinematic realism significantly recalls an important scene in Hou's first major feature film, *The Boys from Fengkuei*, in which the youths sneak into a local movie theater only to find Lucino Visconti's epic of Italian neo-realism, *Rocco and His Brothers* (*Rocco e suoi fratelli*, 1960, Titanus) playing as an improbable matinee. Like the citation in *Dust in the Wind*, the insertion of Visconti's film, at the moment of the Sicilian family's arrival at their Milan apartment, makes clear the historical and cultural distance from Hou's realist film to its precedents and implicit models. Yet, while *The Boys from Fengkuei* is undoubtedly antithetical in form and spirit to the Italian film's operatic melodrama, there is suggested nevertheless a deeper commonality between the two films. Indeed, the boys' subsequent voyage from their small town to find work on the main island recalls the path of the Sicilian family shown on screen. And a later scene of the boys' first hours in the city closely echoes an equivalent moment in *Rocco and His Brothers*, with the Taiwan youths and the Sicilian family both eagerly staring through bus windows and absorbing the bustle and electric wonders of the modern city so different from their former homes. As if to underscore further the neo-realist model claimed by the Taiwan New Cinema, a scene in *Dust in the Wind* also reads like a "quotation" from the Italian neo-realism classic *The Bicycle Thieves* (*Ladri di bicicletti*, 1946, de Sica, Produzioni De Sica). Here Wan, like the hero of Vittorio de Sica's film, is simultaneously and overwhelmingly faced with the sudden theft of his motor scooter, the danger of losing his vehicle-dependent job and the moral indignation of his girlfriend when he threatens to steal a replacement.

The Boys from Fengkuei provides another unusual and revealing cinematic statement to which *Dust in the Wind* seems to offer an implicit response. The boys, now in the city, are tricked by a local con man into buying tickets for "European films" they believe to be in color, Cinemascope and pornographic. Told the illicit theater is on the eleventh floor of a seemingly deserted building, the gullible youths instead find themselves inside a gutted concrete shell commanding a panoramic view of the city. The empty window frames are, as a boy sarcastically comments, widescreen in dimension, and the vista over the city is an unwelcome substitute for what they had hoped to see.

As in their earlier encounter with the Visconti film, the boys — unable to find a spectacle to sate their juvenile desires — are again disappointed by the promise of the cinema. This time, however, the object of scrutiny is the cinematic apparatus itself, described as a type of false cinema whose transparent "screen" opens up unexpectedly to the outside world. Considered as such this comic episode becomes an ironic and almost self-deprecatory comment on the avowed and ultimately quixotic project of the Taiwan New Cinema to reach out to the "new" youth audience with films, occasionally color and widescreen, that claim to depict their specific culture and everyday experiences.

A similar description of the cinema as only hesitantly interwoven into the everyday lives of Taiwan youth is also found in *Dust in the Wind*, in which a Taipei movie theater offers a second explicit figure of the cinema. A frequent meeting place for the young couple, the theater is also the unusual home of a friend of Wan who works as a painter of oversized movie billboards in a studio that shares a wall with the movie screen itself. Situated on the other side of the screen, the dark and cavernous billboard studio, which is nestled somewhere at the back of the movie theater, reads as a sort of negative of the theater itself; it is a space of work rather than recreation, and its inhabitants, as the employees of the theater, are denied time to attend the cinema regularly.

Similar to the village cinema, this movie theater is also the vehicle for an extended contrast of *Dust in the Wind*, and implicitly the Taiwan New Cinema that it exemplifies, with another alternative mode of cinema — the popular martial-arts films that seem to be the theater's exclusive offering. This incongruous pairing of Hou Hsiao Hsien and kung fu is first established as an audio effect within the billboard studio, where the blaring martial-arts soundtrack echoes as background noise throughout the space. As an ironic counterpoint to the general austerity that characterizes the film's soundtrack, the muted gatherings of the young couple and their friends in the studio are accompanied by the totally inappropriate audio hyperbole of clashing swords and fistfights. The punctuation of the scene's minimal dialogue by the loud sound effects and dramatic, rushing music from the theater parallels two entirely antithetical ideas of cinematic "action" — the violent fights and acrobatics heard off-screen set against *Dust in the Wind*'s controlled understatement of performance and dialogue.

This encounter with kung fu cinema is expanded into another scene in the theater, in which Wan and Huen sit impassively and nearly expressionless before a martial-arts film.[11] The clips seen quickly reveal the visual equivalent of the sounds heard previously in the studio: hyperactive fight scenes punctuated by sudden zooms and rapid-fire editing. Placed within *Dust in the Wind*'s somber evocation of alienated youth, this fragment torn from a cinema of action and spectacle is made strange, its aggressive stylization vividly underscored. A complete contrast with the aesthetic and narrative restraint refined in *Dust in the Wind*, the martial-arts film — and the cool, indifferent reception given it by the young couple — seems to measure the distance between the Taiwan New Cinema and its commercial nemesis, the overwhelmingly popular contemporary Hong Kong cinema that effectively dominated the box office throughout the late 1980s. Beyond this ironic meeting between the martial-arts film's kinetic camera and performance and *Dust in the Wind*'s sparse and reluctant camera, the movie theater is also, however, part of the film's broader meditation on the cinematic apparatus.

Like the village cinema, with its temporary cloth screen and power outages, the Taipei theater is presented in a state of casual disarray, a disorder embodied by the scruffy backrooms cluttered with the disassembled fragments of the garish hand-painted movie billboards. These fractured and partially painted images break down popular cinema into the smaller constitutive units of advertising's call to the audience. In similar fashion to the many traffic signals, which are "neutralized" and stripped of their functional meaning in the abstract cityscapes that recur throughout *Dust in the Wind*, these billboard images are fully integrated into the film's controlled aesthetic. The movie theater, like the village cinema before it, embodies a vision of the cinema as an almost organic entity spilling out into its larger environment, its soundtrack and disordered images floating up haphazardly and incongruously into the everyday. In this regard the architecture of the theater itself recalls the false cinema in *The Boys from*

Fengkuei, with both suggesting the barrier between the cinematic spectacle and the world that surrounds it to be as thin, if not transparent, as the screen itself. This point is emphasized by Hen-Chu's studio, where a small hole punctured in an adjoining wall allows a shaft of light from the movie screen to pass through — a reverse projection from the theater out into the "real world."

Variously described in *Dust in the Wind* as a faulty and hesitant apparatus, these different figures of the cinema are, in fact, included among a range of machines that exert a major presence throughout the film and act together as a motif and structuring metaphor. This design is immediately apparent in the opening hypnotic "traveling shot" from the front of a train passing through tunnels on its way to the mining village. Rhythmically alternating between the darkness of the tunnels and the bright and verdant hillscape, the sequence describes a patterned movement between darkness and light that extends through the first introduction of Wan and Huen as they stand inside the train's cabin. This immediate association of the young couple with the mechanical rhythm of the train is essential for the rest of the film. For just as the train pulls them in and out of the daylight, its passage also depicts the same restless path that will carry them throughout the film, unmoored and overwhelmed, repeatedly back and forth between their village and Taipei, suspended between the two locales and at home in neither.

This rhythmic oscillation between light and darkness also operates at a deeper level in *Dust in the Wind* as a function of the film's purposely oblique narrative, a structure of calculated gaps and absences that frequently withholds crucial information and renders the passage of time nearly impossible to gauge with precision. This narrative strategy is made clear in a telling scene in which Wan writes to his younger sister late at night, accompanied by one of the film's rare instances of first-person voice-over narration. Directly echoing the violent halt of the village projector earlier, this brief and dimly lit scene is suddenly interrupted by total darkness, abruptly cut short by a power outage that suddenly turns off Wan's makeshift lamp. An expression of Wan's ultimately unstable position, this sudden and almost comic interruption poignantly describes the film's narrative as a type of potentially faulty machinery that deflects the characters within it.

This same idea is given literal form in the menial jobs taken by both Wan and Huen in a printing press and dress factory respectively — mindless labor that locks them to the droning repetition of machines and forces them into a near-automaton state of half-attention. As with the train, the restless and futile motion of the primitive machines symbolizes little hope for change or improvement. Against the halting rhythm of machines at sudden rest and in motion, the characters in *Dust in the Wind* are notably impassive, at times swept away completely, like the family from mainland China carried to shore in a broken fishing vessel later in the film. The futility if not impossibility of motion is, in fact, a dominant condition of characters throughout Hou's early films, a state embodied by the almost expressionless and immobile poses frequently commanded by Hou's preferred non-professional actors. In these films characters also seem to be inevitably struck down by sudden and violent mishaps or serious infirmity: the diseases that gradually restrict the speech and motion of the mother and father before taking their lives in *The Time to Live and the Time to Die*, for example, or the freak accidents that swiftly cripple the fathers in both *The Boys from Fengkuei* and *Dust in the Wind*.

In these last two films the traumatic maiming of the two fathers is explicitly linked to the cinematic apparatus, in both cases revisited by their sons while watching a film, with their memories figured as an interruption and distortion of the films. Thus in *The Boys from Fengkuei* the son has a sudden flashback to his father's accident during the screening of *Rocco and His Brothers*, the soundtrack of the Italian film extended and layered over the images of the memory sequence. In *Dust in the Wind*, meanwhile, Wan is abruptly pulled into the memory of his father's injury by a sudden fever that overwhelms him as he watches a mining documentary on television. Adding symmetry to the film's opening is a hypnotic television shot that rides along the tracks into a coal mine. The motion of another train is now the "vehicle" for the delirious visions that assault Wan as he passes out. A different type of motion characterizes the entirely subjective sequence that follows, seen from Wan's feverish point of view. Crafted in a style distinct from the film that contains it, it imitates the feverish rush of Wan's mind with a quick montage of seemingly disconnected and barely recognizable images — his father being pulled from the mine after his accident, a priest chanting directly at the camera, and Wan's grandfather discussing the naming of his newborn grandson.

Like the other figures of the cinema that appear in the film and *The Boys from Fengkuei* before it, this sequence rests on a tension between the cinematic and the extra-cinematic, an ambiguity figured as a near-transparency of the screen. In this way the sequence begins with a rare camera movement, closing in to "enter" the television by passing through the screen into Wan's visions on the other side. The attempt of *Dust in the Wind* to describe and understand the logic of its characters' lives — the specific rhythms that shape their restless passage between country and city — takes another form. Here the film seems to turn away from the physical rhythms of the machines that define the characters' immediate environment and inward toward a new subjective realm matched by a heightened fluidity of time, space, intimate memory, and desire that condenses and transforms the aesthetic and narrative logic of the film.

The overall attempt of *Dust in the Wind* to describe and understand the rhythms that define the lives of its characters and their environment offers an important key to Hou's more recent work, and specifically *Goodbye South, Goodbye* and *Millennium Mambo*. Indeed, both films extend the earlier work's concern for rhythm to another level. While dealing with a vastly different subject — the contemporary Taiwan of nightclubs and petty criminals — these films' characters are again caught in restless and futile cycles, given to a constant rushing around without any singular purpose, although now often openly bored and under the influence of drugs or alcohol. In both recent films the specific motivations for individual actions are almost totally obscured, rendering indecipherable the seemingly endless "business" transactions in *Goodbye South, Goodbye*, and the almost interchangeable fights between Vicky (Shu Qi) and her lover in *Millennium Mambo*. Indeed, the many extended driving scenes in *Goodbye South, Goodbye* and the dances in *Millennium Mambo* give way to an almost meditative quality paradoxically equivalent to the long silences in Hou's earlier works.

Both *Goodbye South, Goodbye* and *Millennium Mambo* are instead more concerned with the larger, abstract design of their characters' lives, motivated by a sort of cryptic sociology, a total immersion within the specific subcultures depicted within them: the world of gangsters on the one hand and the nightclubs/rave "scene" on the other. This gives way to a virtual catalogue of the colors, patterns, textures, and shapes that define these worlds — the gangsters' garish Hawaiian shirts and cluttered backrooms, the nightclubs' hallucinatory colored lights. The almost perpetual "techno" soundtracks that bind both films' open, meandering narratives give literal form to the films' attempt to understand the larger rhythm or design of these worlds while enhancing their deliberate narrative abstraction. Impatient and easily bored, the main characters of both *Goodbye South, Goodbye* and *Millennium Mambo* ultimately remain cryptic figures, adrift and absorbed in a distracted world of rhythmic motion and mesmerizing surfaces, in tune with the music that surrounds them.

3

A Borrowed Life in Banana Paradise: De-Cold War/Decolonization, or Modernity and Its Tears

Chen Kuan-Hsing

De-Cold War/Decolonization

When this chapter was in its initial stages I was in Seoul, where I could not help being confronted by exceedingly emotional scenes of North-South family reunions.[1] Flooded by scenes of tears between 15 and 18 August 2000, all Seoul was turned into a space of "mourning Korean modernity," in the words of Kim Seongnae, describing the 1948 Cheju Incident.[2] The all-too-familiar, overwhelming sentiment resurfaced to echo our situation in the late 1980s and early 90s, when visits from Taiwan to mainland China were officially permitted. Loaded with gifts and longing for home, groups of *waishengren,* eager to reunite with their relatives, passed through the old Hong Kong airport.[3] My father was one of those travelers. Escorted by my elder brother, he made the visit after my mother died in the early 1990s. He came home to Taipei in silence, not even mentioning the living conditions of his children in the Mainland, and never went back again before he died in 1995. Although my mother's only sister and her family, who had moved from the Shandong Province to Beijing, are still living there, she refused to go back to see them as long as the communists were still in power or even to have contact with them. She said they might be used as a "political weapon" for communist propaganda. In both instances — North and South Korea, and in Taiwan and China — "national" and "personal" histories clearly intersect. For those involved, the emotional plane of affective desire seems to overshadow any other aspects of these "reunions."

Can we say then, at least in these two instances, that this is finally the end of the Cold War in Northeast Asia? Contrary to this mainstream tone, my main argument is that *this is not yet the Post-Cold War era.* Moreover, Cold War effects have become embedded in local histories and will not be dissolved even if the Cold War really is announced to have finished. Empirically, the Cold War structure in the East Asian region is not finished, although the general sentiment is that it is on its way out. The US air force and army still operate in Japan, Okinawa and South Korea. On a cultural-political level, the excitement generated by the escalating televisual effects of the two Kims' summit, the downfall of the Kuomintang in Taiwan, and the rise of former oppositional forces — South Korea's Kim Dae-Jung, and Chen Shui-bian in Taiwan — are signs the Cold War structure is still in place.

More than ever, with the Cold War structure loosening up, the conjuncture has arrived for undertaking critical work to "de-Cold War." To de-Cold War, at this point in history, does not just mean to get rid of Cold War consciousness or to forget that episode of history and to look towards the future, as all the state leaders and politicians have called for. It means to mark out a space to begin to reopen unspoken histories and stories, in order to recognize and map out the historically constituted cultural-political effects of the Cold War. The task is parallel to and connected with the historical project of *decolonization* on various levels of abstraction in the Third World. These two historical lines are convolutedly intersected. Decolonization movements on all fronts since the end of the Second World War have been "invaded," intercepted, and interrupted by the structure of the Cold War. Divided into capitalist and socialist blocs, led by the US and the USSR, capitalist East Asia had to avoid conflict within the anti-communist camp. Therefore, historical issues of Japanese colonialism in Taiwan or Korea could not be tackled, because the Japanese, South Korean, and Taiwanese states had been locked into the pro-American bloc. To revisit such issues would lead to confronting "internal contradiction" within the capitalist clique.

To pursue the issue further, although the motor forces were predicated on the expansion of capital, the era of territorial colonialism and its subsequent anti-colonialist moment were mainly organized and conducted along racial-national dividing lines. International socialism, as a class-based decolonization movement initiated within Western Europe, had to negotiate with a nationalist anti-colonial struggle in the colonies of the Third World. In retrospect, without proper class politics in place largely because these places had not entered the industrial mode of production needed for class politics to emerge, Third World nationalism based on the logic of inside/ outside and organized along the "color" line was the engine to end territorial colonialism.

Historical-structural conditions have a bearing on living subjects and groups, collective or otherwise. Kim Seongnae's intervention in "Mourning Korean Modernity" analyzes how South Korean state violence worked under the rhetoric of anti-communism in the 3 April 1948 Cheju Incident, which is strikingly similar to the 28 February 1947 Incident and the White Terror of the 1950s in Taiwan.[4] More importantly, her ethnographic work documents the painful experiences of the survivors and the victims' families up to today. Taking a lead from her analysis, but without the capacity for ethnographic research, I want to center on two Taiwan films to bring out critical issues involved in living histories, and to demonstrate how these structural effects have been able not only to shape specific national space but also to work on the bodies, consciousnesses, and desires of "innocent" people, constituting "ethnic" conflicts among different populations. Much like the Korean family reunion scenes cited above, tensions during emotional encounters will be the focus of analysis. These two films, *Banana Paradise* (1989) and *A Borrowed Life* (1994), are the strategic sites chosen to reveal how the entanglements of colonialism and Cold War in contemporary Taiwan have produced different "emotional structures of feeling,"[5] which have become the "emotional-material basis" of ethnic conflicts.

The two films cover roughly the same period of post-war Taiwan from the late 1940s to the early 1990s, centering on two subject positions. In *A Borrowed Life*, Duosang is a *benshengren* ("local province person," or Taiwanese) working-class man of Minnanese background, shaped by colonial history. In *Banana Paradise*, Menshuan and Desheng are lower-class *waishengren*, mainly molded by the Cold War. I wish to show that, because living subjects inhabit different structures, the two axes of colonialism and Cold War have produced different historical experiences, affectively constituting identities and subjectivities in different ways. This split might explain the impossibility of constructing a shared "imagined community" and "great reconciliation" between *benshengren* and *waishengren*, and between mainland China and Taiwan. In other words, we need to bring the divergence of the emotional structures of feeling into our analysis, so that decolonization and de-Cold War projects may converge and begin their transformative work.

First, we have to clarify that, unlike gender/sexuality, class, race, and "ethnicity," *benshengren* and *waishengren* are not analytical but living concepts and political constructions emerging in the concrete historical processes of everyday life. The dividing line is 1945–49: those who came to Taiwan before then are called *benshengren* (people living in Taiwan province), and those who came after are *waishengren* (people from outside Taiwan province). Among *benshengren*, Minnanese (who speak the language of southern Fujian province) are the majority. However, this simple division cannot account for the entire range of identities of those who have lived in Taiwan. For instance, the *waishengren* population has no common language or customs, and the term *waishengren* is only meaningful in relation to *benshengren*. Similarly, there is no unity of *benshengren*. Some came to Taiwan earlier than others; they include different ethnic groups, and there is no single language.

A Borrowed Life — The Logic of Hierarchy: Japan > Taiwan > Mainland China

Released in 1994 and directed by well-known Minnanese screenwriter and novelist Wu Nien-jen, *A Borrowed Life* was the first film to take on the issue of colonial effects in post-Second World War Taiwan. "Duosang" is a local version of the Japanese term for father, and is used by the protagonist's son and narrator of the film, Wenjian. Lian Qingke is Duosang's Chinese name, but friends and neighbors of his own generation call him by his Japanese name, Seiga. He was born in 1929, thirty-six years after Taiwan became a Japanese colony in 1895, and so he received a Japanese education. The film begins in the late 1940s, right after the end of the war. Working in a declining gold mine, Duosang maintains his family on a minimal salary. When the mine closes, the mother has to do construction work while Duosang plays mahjong to kill time. Five years later, Wenjian goes to the city to work and study, and Duosang becomes a coal miner. Duosang becomes the village head. According to the narrator, this is because most of the villagers have moved out to look for work. At 53 years old in 1984, like his friends who work in the mine, his symptoms begin to emerge. He retires two years later with a small payout, which he gives his younger son to start a small business. At 58, he has to be hospitalized and must live out his days on oxygen support. When he is put into the emergency room to wait to die, one year later in 1990, he defenestrates himself on a stormy night. Despite the simple plot, *A Borrowed Life* is a complex film. The linear narrative parallels historical changes in postwar Taiwan: the KMT took over the political regime and rural community life was interrupted by economic development and urbanization. Deserted by capital, rural working-class populations were losing control over their own lives. Beyond the dominant father-son relationship, intergenerational conflicts manifest lines of tension. Duosang's children's patriotism, shaped by the KMT state nationalist education, stands against his cultivated "Japaneseness" and his defense of his masculine dignity as head of the family.

Languages adopted by different characters, crystallized in the same family space, mark their times. Duosang operates in Minnanese and Japanese. Late in his life, he picks up a little Mandarin. Eldest son Wenjian speaks Minnanese but narrates in Mandarin. His sister argues with Duosang in Minnanese and Mandarin. Wenjian's son (and Duosang's grandson) is educated solely in Mandarin and can neither speak nor understand Minnanese. Over three generations, the daily mixing of Japanese and Minnanese gives way to the mixing of Minnanese and Mandarin, and then to the official language of Mandarin. By the 1980s, after thirty years of official Mandarin education, some younger urban Minnanese like the grandson could no longer speak the "mother tongue." Brought up in the colonial era, Duosang has to rely on Japanese, just as his children were forced to adopt Mandarin. In the era of Mandarin dominance, Duosang's generation has become a silent generation "without language" or power.

References to Japan run throughout the film. Duosang listens to the radio in Japanese, frequents a Japanese-style *jiu-jia* (bar) with his mine "brothers" to sing Japanese songs, watches Japanese movies, prefers Japanese female bodies (to those displayed in *Playboy*), curses in Japanese, and has a never fulfilled desire to visit the Imperial Palace and Mount Fuji in Japan. In various episodes, the tension explodes. For example, while Wenjian is out buying noodles, his sister asks Duosang to help with the homework by drawing the national flag. When Wenjian comes home, he witnesses the ensuing fight:

> *Daughter (complaining to Wenjian):* Look at this awful national flag Duosang has drawn! How can I hand this in? *(She shows him the drawing: the sun on the flag, which should be white, is red.)*
> *Duosang:* I helped you out, how can you complain? How could the sun be any color except red? Only the devil would see the sun in white.
> *Daughter:* Lu Haodong painted it white.
> *Duosang (getting angry):* He is illiterate! You're as stupid as he is! Really stupid! What color is the sun on the Japanese flag? White? Nonsense!
> *Daughter (yelling in Mandarin):* Everything's Japanese with you! Who are you? Wang Jingwei? [6]
> *Duosang (unable to understand Mandarin, getting angrier):* Don't think I don't understand Bagin Huei. *[Mandarin]*
> *Daughter (in higher pitched Mandarin as she realizes Duosang cannot*

understand her): You are a traitor, a running dog! You are Wang
Jingwei!
Duosang (appealing to Wenjian): What is she saying now? Baka yarou!
["Fuck" in Japanese]
Wenjian (trying to cool things down): Nothing.
Duosang (before he walks off): Baka yarou!

For the daughter, molded by nationalist education, red is simply not the
right color. For Duosang, it is "common sense" for the sun to be red, based
on his knowledge of the Japanese flag. She draws into the argument the
original designer of the flag, Lu Haodong, but Duosang tries to maintain his
masculine authority by trashing Lu as illiterate. What really upsets the
daughter is Duosang's invocation of the Japanese flag as an assumed
reference point, contrary to the anti-Japanese education she received from
the state. Without any feeling for Duosang's historical experiences, she uses
"Everything is Japanese with you!" as a personal as well as nationalist attack.
In this context, it is no accident that she switches to Mandarin and accuses
him of being a Han traitor by citing the stereotypical sign, Wang Jingwei,
whom she learnt about from school history books. She has to attack in
Mandarin because this is a resource she can draw upon and hide behind, and
also probably because she is either too emotional to translate into Minnanese
or does not really want to hurt her father. Switching to the "outsider"
language, Mandarin, further upsets Duosang. Wenjian tries to mediate.
Knowing that if he translates there will be a true explosion, he tells Duosang
she is saying "nothing."

It would be simplistic to reduce this intergenerational encounter to
nation-state identifications: the hybrid use of languages already marks a
more complex situation. For Duosang, the red sun on the Japanese flag is
the obvious reference point: he may not even know the color of the KMT
national flag, and he reads the KMT sun with twelve rays as equivalent to
the sun on the Japanese flag. This desire to map one onto the other expresses
a will to continuity. If that reference point constitutes part of his subjective
knowledge and hence subjectivity, it is only "natural" for him to mobilize that
system of knowledge to defend his identity. The same applies to the
daughter. She cannot understand the huge difference in their experienced
reference systems, and therefore does not concede. This is an irresolvable
situation: it is impossible to seal the gap or to mutually recognize generation
difference, shaped by the changing totality of the social. It can only end with
curses from the powerless patriarch.

However, it is important to recognize that only through such emotional
confrontations can Duosang's pain and his "Japanese" structure of feeling

be felt, shared by, and hence handed down to, the next generation. The eldest son, Wenjian, is more able to understand and sympathize with Duosang's passion. In the end, he becomes the "inheritor" of Duosang's structure of feeling, and takes the picture of his deceased father with him when paying a visit to the Imperial Palace and Mount Fuji to fulfill Duosang's final wish. The film ends with sad music as a moved Wenjian reads words that appear in white on a black screen:

> 1991, January 11
> Duosang finally sees the Imperial Palace and Mount Fuji
> It is the first snow of winter in Tokyo
> Duosang is speechless

The mood mixes final fulfillment with a chilly sadness. This is the fulfillment of a longed for dream, but without any sense of achievement. The Imperial Palace and Mount Fuji stand in the cold winter, covered by the first snow of the season, no longer able to symbolize the sublime power of the Empire. Finally arriving in Tokyo, "Duosang is speechless" is a culminating point of sadness. What can he say? The "speechless generation" had to jump out of the window and commit suicide to maintain its minimal dignity. Can the fulfillment of a wish after death cancel out an entire life of agony? Throughout the film, Wenjian — the son, the inheritor, and the emphatic narrator — never makes any "negative" judgment about Duosang's endorsement of Japaneseness. His sympathy for his father's suffering is made clear in several attempts to help him at his workplace and to offer him money, although Duosang's dignity makes it impossible for him to accept. Wenjian's sympathetic identification with Duosang is recognition of his father's "borrowed life," of a desperate drive to move out of it, and of a sense of hopelessness about leaving the course of this "borrowed life."

Banana Paradise — Anti-Japan > Anti-Communism > Going Home

Banana Paradise was directed by Wang Tung and written by Wang Shaudi. Released in 1989, not too long after contact across the Taiwan Strait was made possible, it was shot from the perspective of "old soldiers" (*laobing*) from mainland China.[7] The first scene is set in Northeast China during the cold winter of 1948. Menshuan is a naive teenage boy from a peasant family in rural Shandong Province. His father sells his family property to send him to join a slightly older "brother" from the same village, Desheng, who is a cook for the Kuomintang army. Defeated by the People's Liberation Army, their unit has to move to Taiwan. Neither "brother" has any idea where Taiwan is. They think it must be nearby, and are told that it is known for growing the best bananas. Having moved to Taiwan, they immediately run into the era of the anti-communist purge. Both of them get into trouble because they naively picked up the wrong names on the Mainland. Because other soldiers laughed at his nickname, He Jiumei (Ninth Sister), Menshuan changes it to Zuo Fugui. This literally means Left Prosperity, which is seen by the authorities as pro-communist. Desheng conveniently selects a name from the list of existing unit members — Liu Jinyuan. Because Liu did not come to Taiwan, Desheng can simply assume his identity. However, it turns out Liu is suspected of being a communist spy years back on the Mainland. This was the era of fear, locally remembered and marked by the slogan, "Watch out, communist spies are right around you." Tortured by security forces, Desheng escapes to another army unit, adopts the new name Liu Zhuanxiao, and is put in charge of the kitchen and food supply. He befriends a local peasant family, headed by Ah-Xiang and his wife, whom Desheng calls Banana Sister because they grow bananas. Ah-Xiang's family treats Desheng as a family member, and they become his only shelter so far away from home. Having contracted the anti-communist phobia, Desheng launches a paranoid attack on his own commanding officer, accusing him of being a communist. He then goes mad when beaten by security personnel and is taken care of by the warm peasant family. Menshuan runs away when he comes under suspicion. He happens to meet a dying man, Li Chilin, his wife Yuexiang, and their newborn son, Yaohua (literally, "Glorify China"). After Li dies, Menshuan takes over his identity, using Li's university degree in English to take an air force job arranged for Li before he died, so that he can support Yuexiang and Yaohua. Of course, the illiterate Menshuan cannot really do the work, especially in English, so the "family" has to leave the air force and seek out "older brother" Desheng's help. With sympathetic support from Ah-Xiang's family, Menshuan studies and finally passes the civil servant examination to become a lifelong petty bureaucrat, taking care of "his" family and his mad brother, Desheng. Years later, contact with the Mainland is permitted in the late 1980s. Not knowing his real "family history," Yaohua uses the excuse of a business trip to go to Hong Kong and reunite with his Mainland grandfather. Anxious about the reunion phone call from Hong Kong, Yuexiang has to tell Menshuan the surprising news that she is not Yaohua's real mother. Much as Menshuan has taken over Li Chilin's identity, she was not Li's real wife but promised Li to take care of his son. Never having had sex and only having pretended to be spouses,

Menshuan and Yuexiang embrace for the first time, in tears. When the son finally calls home, Menshuan has to talk to Yaohua's grandfather on the phone. Bursting into tears, he calls him "Dad," as if he were speaking to his real father.

Cast in the mode of poignant black humor, and very different from *A Borrowed Life*'s unsentimental technique, *Banana Paradise* was the first Taiwan film critical of the Kuomintang regime. (Interestingly, it was produced by the Central Motion Picture Corporation, a KMT organ.) The sympathetic representation of these innocent "nobodies" — Menshuan, Desheng, Yuexiang, and the local peasant family — stands in sharp contrast to the cruelty of the security officers. Representing the violence of the state, they are the only negative figures in the film. *Banana Paradise* was released only two years after the lifting of martial law in 1987, when politics was still under the shadow of the police state. Under this shadow, the film's critical stance towards the state is mediated by the strategy of black humor throughout. Suspected of being communist spies, the little "nobodies" prove to be apolitical innocent ones, and the representation of the sneaky and brutal security guys correlates to the stereotype of communist spies. The "banana paradise" is rather an anti-communist "white terror" hell. Like many others in that era, Desheng, Menshuan, and Yuexiang are all forced to assume serial identities. This causes them to be mistakenly identified as communist spies or to assume other identities for the rest of their "borrowed lives." But sooner or later these well-intentioned necessary "lies" are exposed and it becomes clear nobody is whom they are assumed to be. As the audience, we do not know the real name of Desheng, who became Liu Jinyuan, then Liu Zhuanxiao. Menshuan is simply a nickname, and he became He Jiumei, Zuo Fugui, and finally Li Chilin. He is not Yaohua's father or Yuexiang's husband. And Yuexiang is not the dead man's wife, and therefore not Yaohua's mother. In the end we are not even sure whether if the name Yuexiang is that of Li's wife or her own. Not to have one real identity, or not to be able to have one, or not to be able finally to reclaim one's real identity constitutes the central problematic of the film.

In *A Borrowed Life*, the *waishengren* population does not enter Duosang's everyday world directly. In contrast, encounters between *benshengren* and *waishengren* are emphasized in *Banana Paradise*. After Desheng escapes from being tortured as a communist suspect, he adopts the new name of Li Zhuanxiao and works in another military unit. By then he has begun to act "abnormally," with a victim complex, imagining strangers to be real communists who want to kidnap him. When Menshuan and Yuexiang finally find him in Ah-Xiang's family, Desheng suspects that

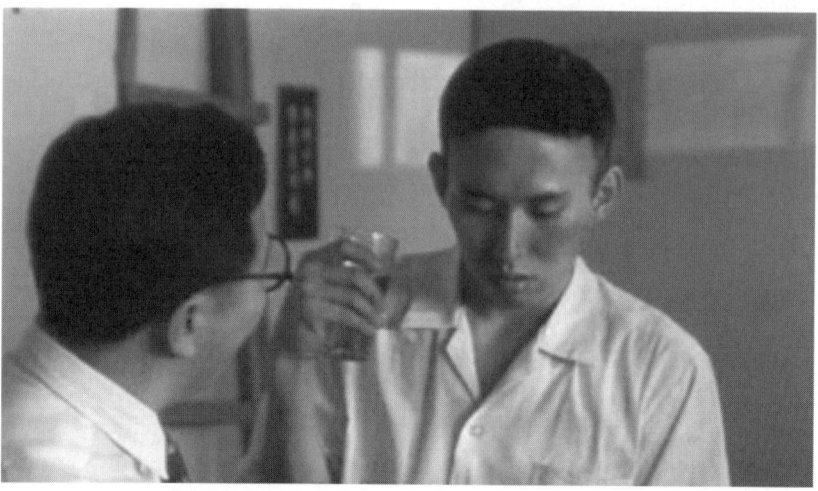

"How did you get to be called Menshuan?" — *Banana Paradise*

Yuexiang is really an agent sent by the security forces to spy on him and is just using her relationship with Menshuan as a cover. Taking Desheng in, the peasant family treats these *waishengren* away from home warmly. Living with the family, Desheng gradually develops a sexual interest towards Banana Sister's teenage daughter, Ah-Jane. In one scene, Desheng loses control, holding her and wanting her to marry him. Scared, she cries out for her father, Ah-Xiang, who angrily chases Desheng away with a stick. Desheng flees and at first cannot be found. There is a gunshot. Desheng has been tracked down by a team of soldiers in the fields. At this moment of life and death crisis, Desheng desperately seeks refuge in his adopted home. Ah-Xiang and Banana Sister intervene to save his life.

Despite a romantic representation of the open-mindedness of ordinary folk (the *laobaixing*), the film has not covered up real conflict. This manifests itself in Desheng's uncontrollable desire for Ah-Jane, resulting in unforgivable sexual harassment. His desire mixes passion, lust, and loneliness. Feeling betrayed by his conduct, the family does not even ask Desheng and his friends to leave. However ashamed he is, Desheng still has to "come home" for help when he is about to be persecuted by the soldiers. Banana Sister, Ah-Xiang, and Ah-Jane generously forgive and rescue him again. Desperate and powerless, Desheng projects his longing for home onto Banana Sister, treating her as his mother, his shelter. In tears, he hysterically shouts, "Ma! Ma! I miss you so much! Ma, I want to go home! Ma, I miss you!" This is a highly loaded and compressed moment, condensing unrepresentable feelings of love and loss. But what could the tears and hysteria in this scene entail? Patriotic, anti-communist, resenting harsh treatment, and with no home and no mother to re/turn to, Desheng has gone hysterically mad. In this moment of emotional condensation, is he adopting Banana Sister as his "new" mother in this "new" home? Yes, but not quite. (A similar vicarious projection will happen to Menshuan.) At this critical juncture, the suffering Menshuan, afraid of being deserted, quickly moves into the scene and reminds Desheng of his responsibility to take him home: "You cannot go mad . . . . I have had enough bananas here. I don't want to eat any more. Damn it, you brought me here, and now you have to take me home." Is Menshuan the barrier against Desheng's adoption of "Taiwan" as his new home?

This is the heart of our concern: why can Desheng's generation of *waishengren* not readjust and adopt Taiwan as their new home, or their only home? The figure of "home" evokes an entire set of structured feelings: "Ma," "missing you," "going home," and "a life of suffering." "Going home" has been a persistent desire and hope for lower class *waishengren* like Menshuan and Desheng, who have no resources or capital and have suffered in the "forced" migration process. Nothing can disrupt their real imagination of final homecoming. They never thought they would stay "here," never mind establish a new home here. Even when a new home is established, it is only transient and temporary: "We'll return eventually." Parallel to the KMT state's determination to recover the Mainland, the returning-home mindset was gradually forced to readjust from the 1970s onward, but has never really diminished. For this generation of *waishengren*, to adopt Taiwan as *the* home or to say "I am also a Taiwanese," a *benshengren*, is difficult if not impossible. It is difficult for them to imagine and impossible to believe the harsh reality that Taiwan has been and is their only home. This unacceptably harsh reality can only be grasped later after they do indeed return home to the Mainland after the 1980s. But in the 1960s and 70s, if Desheng gave up his identity as a Shandong person to become "Taiwanese," it would also be unacceptable to Banana Sister. How would she position herself in relation to Desheng? Very few of Desheng's generation stayed on the Mainland after going home in the late 1980s, in part because mainland Chinese consider these *waishengren*, and especially the second generation, "Taiwanese." For the second generation like Yaohua, born or growing up in Taiwan, it is much easier to utter, "I am a Taiwanese, and my home is in Taiwan" (although he would not deny that he is "at the same time" a Chinese).

Within this mindset of assumed entitlement to be in Taiwan, often expressed carelessly, later proved to be the psychic foundation and core of political, cultural, and "provincial" conflicts. For *benshengren*, Taiwan is home, in the past, the present, and the future. There is no other home to go back to: we are the host, you are the guests, and therefore Taiwan is ours and not yours. This mindset is expressed very clearly in Banana Sister and Ah-Xiang's interactions with Desheng and Menshuan. At the lunch table, after rounds of liquor, Desheng shows his sincere gratitude; "Banana Sister, you've been so nice to me. When I go home, I will hire palanquins to take each of you to Shandong and we'll drink out of a large bowl." Banana Sister replies, "I'll be sure to bring a big basket of bananas, so that you will have plenty to eat." Ah-Xiang seems a bit embarrassed and interrupts, "Bananas are too cheap [to bring as a gift]." Banana Sister insists, "They're famous [local products]." In the course of this exchange, the relation between host and guest is obvious, and friendly. But later, Menshuan frankly expresses his anger and fear to Desheng by saying, "I have had enough bananas here. I don't want to eat any more." Sympathizers like Banana Sister and Ah-Xiang could perhaps understand their desperation and their suffering, as well as the desire to go home. But, if such an overt expression occurred at the height of the *waishengren/benshengren* conflict in the 1990s, would this not hurt *benshengren* feelings? How would Taiwan independence movement enthusiasts, equipped with strong "Taiwanese consciousness," respond to Menshuan's statement? Would they not think that *waishengren* like Menshuan and Desheng could come and go at will, without any commitment to Taiwan?

With no opportunity to go home or contact relatives in the "communist bandit territory" for forty or fifty years, *waishengren* have had to find ways to live on psychically, although their drive to go home has never died out. When the opportunity finally arrived in the 1980s, a huge "returning home" (*fanxiang*) movement followed.[8] How might people like Menshuan, who have multiple and adopted identities, confront these new challenges? In what names and with what identities could they possibly go home? Could they go at all?

After making repeated efforts to find his father's relatives on the Mainland, Yaohua finally succeeds and prepares to go to Hong Kong and meet his grandfather and aunt. To surprise his father, he does not tell his parents about the reunion, and they think he is simply on a business trip. At the airport, he asks his wife to make sure her parents-in-law are home when he calls with the grandfather that evening. To prevent Menshuan and Yuexiang from going out, she has to reveal the secret. Menshuan and Yuexiang retreat in shock to the bedroom to strategize. Menshuan asks Yuexiang to tell him more about Li's family, so that he will know how to react properly and the secret will not be exposed. After a long silence, Yuexiang reveals the truth: "Menshuan, I'm not Li Chilin's wife." Forced to confront deep wounds she would not otherwise want to reopen, she continues:

> Fleeing war, I lost touch with other family members. My prayers went unanswered, and I was forced to flee back to my old home. On the way, I discovered it had already been burnt down. I had no place to go. Turning round, I ran desperately. However, I bumped into local gangsters. They captured me and secured me with metal hooks. They separated my hands and pulled my legs apart. I lay on the ground. They tore my clothes. The wounds were very painful, very painful!

Weeping, she tears the buttons on her cheongsam, as if returning to the original site and restaging the trauma. Menshuan kneels in tears, holding her tightly, wanting to protect her, and sharing her pain. Yuexiang continues:

> Luckily, Mr Li and his classmates were passing through, and they saved me. I feel so. . . . I did not know it could last until now. Later, on the road, his wife died from disease. A big man, holding a baby, and crying so pitifully! At that moment, I swore to raise this good-hearted man's child as my own, and to love and protect him. I did it.

When the awkward phone call finally comes, Menshuan and Yuexiang walk hesitantly out of their bedroom. The daughter-in-law picks up the phone. Menshuan is forced to take on the role of the son, Chilin. In the process, he becomes completely absorbed into a real emotional state, as if he were talking to his real father and crying at the news of his mother's death. In this intense moment of "reunion," tears overwrite and conflate the gap between the "real" and the "imaginary." When Menshuan repeats, "Your son is not filial," he is not simply releasing his own guilt at not being able to take care of his parents, but also releasing his long-suppressed grief. Overwhelmed by sorrow, Yuexiang, Yaohua, and Yaohua's wife are also in tears. One can imagine that Yuexiang's tears do not just express her sympathy for Menshuan and the Li family, but also for her own sad past: the loss of her own family during the war, the rape, and the tough process of supporting these two men, Yaohua and Menshuan, throughout her life. Like Wenjian in *A Borrowed Life*, the tears of the younger generation, Yaohua and his wife, are recognition of the lives of suffering of the earlier generation. Participating in mourning family history, they also inherit their parents' structure of feeling. Perhaps it is during such moments that postwar generations of both *waishengren* and *benshengren* more or less partake of the emotional structure of earlier generations, which has become the emotional foundation for the two populations.

The film ends with yet another piece of black humor. Menshuan's petition to extend his retirement age is turned down by the personnel office. He claims that the official record of his age was a mistake, that he is much younger, which might well be true. But because Li Chilin was about ten years older than he is, once Menshuan assumes his identity and his degree his real age no longer counts. The officer tells him that if the age he is claiming is correct, he must have got his university degree by the age of eleven, to which he cannot respond. This becomes a big joke in the office. Younger people working in the same office have always thought he was an old fool and had no respect for him. Approaching the end of his career, he is insulted again. He has to live as "Li Chilin," like it or not. He has to go on until the end of his life with Li Chilin's identity superimposed on the body of Menshuan. Isn't this also "a borrowed life"?

Colonialism and the Cold War: The Entanglements of Double Structures

"A borrowed life" connects Duosang and Menshuan, though they live their lives very differently. The analyses of the conditions brought out in the films prepare us to account for the divergent formations of the structures of feeling produced by the complexity of history.

If *A Borrowed Life* is about post/colonial effects of the representation[9] of Japanese colonialism, and *Banana Paradise* is about the effects of the Cold War, juxtaposing them, one cannot help but identify "tears of suffering" as the affective trope common to the historical experiences of the two different living populations. But, as structural effects, the specificities of these "tears of suffering" have very different historical trajectories. The intersection of colonialism and Cold War is crystallized in the scenes of tension analyzed above. In *A Borrowed Life*, Duosang, who has been formed by Japanese colonialism, is in conflict with his own children, who are shaped by Cold War KMT apparatuses such as nationalist education, the forced use of Mandarin as the official language, and attempts to evacuate Japanese influence.[10] On the other hand, in *Banana Paradise*, overshadowed by the Cold War structure, colonialism is neither in the foreground nor in the background. In my view, this is the key to understanding the difference: "colonialism" does not seem to exist in the structure of historical memory for *waishengren*, just as "Cold War" does not occupy a central place in that of *benshengren.* If historical reality is that these two populations have to go on living together, "reconciliation" would only be possible by establishing mutual recognition of the historical trajectories of each other's histories of "suffering." However, this cannot be done with the politicians' very superficial call for a temporary suspension of the unification versus independence controversy. On the contrary, to be able to look forward is to look backward, courageously confronting the past, and moving towards the future.

4

Hou Hsiao Hsien's
City of Sadness:
History and the Dialogic
Female Voice

Rosemary Haddon

Forgetting, I would even go so far as to say historical error, is a crucial factor
in the creation of a nation, which is why progress in historical studies often
constitutes a danger for [the principle of] nationality. Indeed, historical
enquiry brings to light deeds of violence which took place at the origins of
all political formations, even of those whose consequences have been
altogether beneficial.[1]

A violent episode in the nation's historical past, referred to as *Ererba*, or the
2–2–8 Incident, is the sequence in *City of Sadness* (1989) that viewers tend
to remember the most. For reasons discussed in more detail later, *Ererba*
is a taboo incident in Taiwan's past, and its treatment in Hou Hsiao Hsien's
film broke new ground in the reconstruction of history. The presence of this
incident in *City* was a factor in the film's acquisition of the Golden Lion
award in 1989.[2]

In the film, the representation of *Ererba* is mediated through the violent
business relations of the Lims (Lins), a family that functions as a microcosm
of the state and re-enacts the bad ethics associated with the incident. At first
glance, the mediated nature of the representation appears to obscure the
meaning of *Ererba*, which was a tragedy generated by race, and calls into
question Hou's ethnic loyalties with respect to the originary moments of the
incident. Indeed, in the aftermath of *City*'s release, film critics and political
historians debated the representation of *Ererba* in relation to Taiwan's
politics, history, and identity.[3] In this chapter, I argue that Hou's intention
is not obscured in the film and that, on the contrary, the representation

provided the filmmaker with a framework within which to condemn the incident and the Nationalists (KMT) who perpetrated the tragedy for the purpose of establishing statehood. Hou's condemnation is articulated through the diaristic voice-over of a dialogic female voice, that of Hiromi (Kuanmei), whose alterities position her outside the "official" discourse of the KMT. Hiromi's gendered difference enables Hou to express his empathy without compromising his integrity or his identity as an émigré from the Mainland at a time when Taiwan's *bentu* (localist, also known as "nativist") movement was nearing a peak.[4]

City is known as Hou's "post-Martial Law film"[5] and is the first in a trilogy about Taiwan's recent historical past. Apart from this film, the trilogy includes *The Puppetmaster* (1993) and *Good Men, Good Women* (1995), both of which investigate Taiwan's historical periods that were previously off limits. Set in the transitional period of 1945–1949, *City* documents the events that took place during the intervening years between the end of Japanese colonialism (1895–1945) and the establishment of Nationalist rule. Their rule was set in place after the Nationalists suffered defeat, then withdrew to the island after the Chinese civil war and set up a government-in-exile that remained in place for fifty years.

As is depicted at the outset of the film, the end of Japanese colonialism was accompanied by euphoria and a hope for enlightened Chinese rule. The hope was short-lived, however, due to the repression that erupted on 28 February 1947 and resulted in an estimated 18,000 to 28,000 casualties. Immediately after the incident, the repression was whitewashed, and both *Ererba* and the *Baikong* (White Terror) purges that followed it were banned from public discourse during the era of Martial Law (1947–1987). The lifting of the Law brought to an end the forty-year-long amnesia and resulted in the restoration of *Ererba* to public memory and to the annals of local history. *City*'s contribution to the process of restoration locates the film within the discursive global trend of the reconstruction of the past.

Ererba appears as a series of intermittent episodes in the second half of *City* and brings to a denouement the film's themes of violence, tragedy, and loss. The episodes are based on Lan Bozhou's *Huang mache zhi ge* (*The Song of the Covered Wagon*, 1988), a piece of reportage (*baogao wenxue*) that documents the lives of Taiwan's socialist underground during the colonial period. Lan's work was compiled from documents, photographs, and excerpts from the diary of Zhong Liho, a well-known Taiwanese fiction writer who traveled to China during the 1930s and 1940s. More importantly, *The Song of the Covered Wagon* contains the recorded interviews of individuals who were associated with Zhong Haodong, Zhong Liho's older brother who is the model for Lin Laoshi (Teacher Lin), the leftist leader in the film.[6] The interviews recount the travels of Zhong Haodong and Su Yunyu (née Jiang Biyu) to China during the War of Resistance against Japan, and their subsequent ideological shift to Marxism.[7] Finally, *The Song of the Covered Wagon* records Zhong's purge during 1950–1953, an event that provided the model for the arrest and execution of the leftist activists in the film.[8] *City*'s reworking of these events reflects Hou's imperative in bringing to light the troubled events of the past and in evaluating the wrongs that shaped subsequent history.

City's cinematography comprises a "dialogic web of multiple, heterogeneous and fragmentary stories" and "wisps of narratives" that are arranged with little attention to plot.[9] According to Li Tuo, the film does not "write" the historical events of the past so much as it uses the "device of cinematic narration to explore 'the writing of history'."[10] Inserted into this web, Hiromi's voice-over oversees the exploration as it articulates segments, stories, and broken bits of narrative. The segments include a separation; the arrest, torture and derangement of a brother-in-law; the killings that took place in Taipei; and the casualties of *Ererba*, who are brought into the hospital where Hiromi works as a nurse. More important, Hiromi narrates the story about Teacher Lin, the activities of his group, and their quest for a utopian socialist ideal in the years before *Ererba*. Hiromi's narration forges a path through the complex network of truths and untruths and the false and authentic histories that have hitherto surrounded the incident. In doing so it dispels the mystique that has shrouded *Ererba* since its whitewashing fifty years ago.

Ethic of National Construction

When the will is sincere, the mind is rectified; when the mind is rectified, the personal life is cultivated; when the personal life is cultivated, the family will be regulated; when the family is regulated, the state will be in order; and when the state is in order, there will be peace throughout the world.[11]

Billed as "The saga of a family — The saga of a nation," *City* consists of a story within a story, which mirror each other in theme, ethos, and spirit. In the saga about the family, the Lims' ethical malaise mirrors the spiritual void in the nation, which is the subject of the second level of narration. Embedded within both is an etiological inquiry into Taiwan's social and political life.

The link between the family and the state recalls the "nation-family," or the "roots and branches," in traditional Chinese thought. The *Daxue* (Great Learning), which contains the ethical blueprint for family and social life, elaborates that there is never a case when "the root is in disorder and yet the branches are in order."[12] Conversely, there is never a case when the practice of *ren* (humanity) and *yi* (righteousness) is absent in the branches and yet the roots remain secure. The replication of this construct in *City* points to a Confucian ethic in the political unconscious of the film and signifies the presence of a traditionalist ideal to critique the nation-state. *City*'s discursiveness, which is edifying rather than entertaining, differentiates the film from Hollywood movies with their ethos of pleasurable viewing. The discursiveness similarly differentiates it from its escapist Taiwanese forebears and the transnational, globalized films of the Fifth Generation of Chinese Filmmakers that came into being in response to the international cultural market.

In the film the narrative commences with a transitional event in the life of a Taiwanese family — the birth of a son. The event is synchronized with a voice-over, that of the Showa emperor, announcing Japan's wartime defeat at the end of colonial rule. The narrative then moves on to the family's daily life and concludes with the eventual extinction of the Lim family line: at the end of the film, all that is left is an old man, a mental cripple, women and their progeny. The rest of the Lim males are "all either dead, missing, or in Guomindang prisons."[13] Metaphorically, the family is a microcosm of the state, and its decline because of malaise suggests that the nation is similarly fated to end.

The Lims include the widowed gangster, Ah-luk-sai (A Lushi), whose four adult sons figure as characters in the film. (In this chapter, I present the names of the sons in Hokkien orthography out of respect for the film's primary language of Hoklo.) The oldest, Bun-heung (Wenxiong), is a hood and operates the family nightclub, which goes by the name of Little Shanghai. The nightclub is a cover for a gambling establishment and is patronized by prostitutes, gangsters, and black marketeers. The presence of these figures disturbs the Lim ethics and is a sign of the didactic subtext in the structure of the film.

Bun-heung divides his time between running the nightclub and shipping illegal goods between Keelong (Jilung) and Shanghai. The dealing leads to skirmishes and, eventually, to Bun-heung's death at the hands of black marketeers. Although Bun-heung is a black marketeer, he is the family member most attuned to Taiwan's social and political realities, that is, its colonial and neo-colonial heritage.[14] Bun-heung despairs, "We *benshengren*

[Taiwanese] are so pitiable. First, the Japanese come, then the Chinese. Everyone eats the Taiwanese, everyone takes advantage of them and nobody loves them." His comment sums up the island's historical dispossession and its problematic sovereignty that was set in place at the end of the war.

The second son, Bun-hsim (Wensen), is a doctor who was conscripted by the Japanese during the war. Bun-hsim was sent to the Philippines and disappeared, although his wife continues to hope that he will one day reappear. Bun-leong (Wenliang), the third son, was similarly sent overseas during the war and returns from Shanghai with post-traumatic stress disorder. This son becomes caught up in the family's gangster activities, is arrested by the KMT authorities on charges of being a spy, and is tortured in jail. At the end of the film, he is reduced to a pitiful state of irredeemable derangement.

The fourth son, Bun-chhing (Wenqing), is a deaf-mute, a photographer-intellectual, and a collateral member of the political underground. In the story, Bun-chhing falls in love with Hiromi, and they marry and have a son. Bun-chhing's alterities, which are based on his disabilities, position him outside the praxis of familial and national life. Excluded through difference, he is aligned alongside Hiroe (Kuanrong), Hiromi's brother, and Hiroe's

Hiromi writes to communicate with Bun-chhing.

leftist intellectual friends. The Japanese names that are given Hiroe and his sister reflect the hybrid nature of Taiwan's historical past. The siblings are given Japanese names in recognition of the language policy of the colonial government during the period of militarization. This policy compelled the local population, such as the brother and sister, to adopt Japanese names throughout the remainder of colonial rule.

Hiroe's intellectual friends are headed by Teacher Lin, a shadowy figure who emerges and re-emerges in the film, then finally disappears. From the sidelines, Lin and the members of the group ponder their fate as they discuss the new regime. Allegorically, they play the role of the conscience in the emerging nation, but are relegated to the part of the other in the ideology of the state. One by one, in the violence associated with *Ererba*, the intellectuals are purged, imprisoned, or shot, their fate mirroring that of Zhong Haodong in "The Song of the Covered Wagon." As though prescient of his fate, Bun-chhing takes a final photograph in the lead-up to his arrest. The photograph includes himself, his wife, and his baby son, and is a reminder of the power of dignity in counteracting tyranny.

The story about the Lims and Hiroe and his friends is linked through diagetic agency to the saga about the state. Through the means of letters, intertitles, random chitchat, and the diary written by Hiromi, the story intercepts the narrative about the birth of the KMT state. The narrative is *Rashōmon*-like in construction and contains conflicting interpretations of the 1947 events.

The *Ererba* cover-up is the cornerstone in the "official" history, or master narrative, about the birth of the state. Shortly after the incident, a play of mirrors danced over the truth about *Ererba*. The masquerade enabled the KMT's neo-colonial agenda to move forward unchecked. Buttressing the Nationalist strategy was the claim that China was in a state of rebellion and that once the "Communist bandits" (*gongfei*) were defeated, the Mainland could be recovered (*fangong dalu*) and the Chinese people could be reunited (*minzu tongyi*) under the Republic of China flag. The rhetoric, which amounted to a type of KMT-ese, or KMT-speak, echoes Mao-speak during the Maoist period in China and supported the KMT in its claim as the legitimate Chinese government.

Chen Yi, the Nationalist governor from 1945–1947, is the foremost articulator of the whitewashing and, through voice-over, apprises his listeners of a disturbance and the rationale for Martial Law. Chen Yi rationalizes that the Law has been set in place in order to deal with "rebel insurgents" (*luandang pantu*) who, he maintains, are responsible for the disturbance, despite the fact that, at the time in question, Taiwan's

Communists comprised only seventy adherents and had no power to instigate such an uprising.[15] The subterfuge that Taiwan's communists instigated the disturbance is a sign of the untruth at the heart of the "official" history.

The "unofficial" history presents an alternative viewpoint about the creation of the state. As the history unfolds, the narrative reveals the facts, which include government incompetence, the smuggling of rice and cigarettes, unemployment, corruption, *daluan* (chaos), and the disappearances, arrests, and deaths associated with *Ererba*. The history, which points to a genocide, was elided by the officially sanctioned creed. The "unofficial" story is managed dialogically by Hiromi, who is empowered with the will to resist tyranny and to subvert the master narrative.

Feminization of Narration and Voice

> The act of writing thus gave these women a measure of control in a situation where what had seemed immutable ideals and beliefs were in a state of total collapse. . . . The intellectual resistance of the dehumanizing terror both shaped and reflected an inner struggle to maintain spiritual and ethical values in a human world devoid of humaneness.[16]

Gendered resistance is a strategic, subversive tactic in counteracting tyranny. Like her counterparts elsewhere, Hiromi resists tyranny through the act of writing, which is the creative activity that women have historically resorted to during times of literary repression. Hiromi's counterparts include Anne Frank, Edith Stein, Simone Weil, and Etty Hillesum, all of whom kept personal records of their experiences during the Holocaust.[17] As Hiromi writes in her diary and reads aloud from it, like her counterparts, she mirrors her humanity and her will not to surrender to despair. At times the diary appears trivial; nonetheless, Hiromi's empowerment is self-evident and signifies her social and moral consciousness about the impending political events. This view about the empowered aspects of Hiromi's writing differs from that of Lu Tonglin, who claims that writing plays a negative role in Hou Hsiao Hsien's films.[18] Lu maintains that women play passive and subordinate roles in Hou's films as "either instruments or voices of their male counterparts."[19]

As a testimony of resistance, the diary records Hiromi's gendered subjectivity, her awareness of the political situation, and her moral and personal outlook as the terror reaches a peak. The diary alternates between emotion and objectivity owing to Hiromi's observation of and participation in the private and public spheres of everyday life. In the diary there is a link between her emotive experience in one sphere and her understanding of the political events in the other. The existence of both spheres in the diary evokes the full quota of meanings about the life of a woman survivor.

As a survivor, Hiromi's writing reflects her initiative in recording the horror of the political events as they impinged on her world. This initiative is proactive and suggests neither the subordination nor the passivity associated with a woman who is used by men. The "personal" discourse of diaries and letters has, as a genre, been historically denigrated. Hou's use of it is innovative and renders *City* a "cinema of correspondence" that examines the links between emotion and intellect in the lives of women.[20] As is the case with Anne Frank and Edith Stein, Hiromi's diary is more than a tool that records a woman's observations of the world; it is a valuable resource that conveys a vital perspective about the course of history. Through its subversion of the "official," or master, narrative, the diaristic voice transforms *City* into a sympathetic drama about the victims of a "holocaust."[21]

Hiromi evokes the maternal attributes that are traditionally associated with the empathic feminine ideal. Engendered by empathy, her subjectivity derives from her interactions and her interpersonal connectedness shaping the subjective female self.[22] Such a self informs the familiar social patterns of female ethical life.[23] Hiromi's concerns, which extend to the fate of Hiroe, Bun-chhing, their baby, and the casualties of *Ererba,* recall Edith Stein, the Jewish German autobiographer who was gassed at Auschwitz in 1942. Stein's World War I wartime experience as a nurse's aide inspired her view that woman's "empathic understanding" of her immediate others extends outward to include the pains and travails of humanity at large.[24] These words apply to Hiromi, whose humanity and spiritual resourcefulness enable her to feel empathy for others despite the growing threat to the lives of her brother, her husband and herself. Hiromi's image in the film is that of a stereotypically petite and compliant Hokkiennese; this image, nonetheless, belies her ability in resisting and/or negotiating not only terror but also tyrannical social structures such as those in the realistically conceived agnatic Lim family.

Near the outset, Hiromi arrives by sedan chair at a hospital where she is employed to work as a nurse. The hospital is in the mining town of Kim-kuei-chiu and is a setting for the action of the film. In the dramatization of this character, Hiromi provides services that are reminiscent of a caregiver: she cares for the patients in the hospital, who include the casualties of *Ererba.* Her empathy does not stop with the wounded, however; it extends beyond the environment of the hospital to encompass the wider social world, including the numerous events that transpired with *Ererba*. Through voice-over, Hiromi recounts an "incident" (*shijian*), the mutual slaughter of Taiwanese and Mainlanders and the formal declaration and implementation of Martial Law. In the wake of the incident, Bun-chhing and Hiroe travel to Taipei, which Hiromi notes has "become transformed into an extremely dangerous place." An intertitle reinforces the news about Taipei and advises that the city has become the scene of the "deaths of large numbers of people." Despite the mounting tensions, Hiromi continues to write, her determination reflecting her desire to retain her spiritual values and her ethical concerns in a world devoid of humanity.

Hiromi's alterities, which are ideological and gendered, are othered in the same way that those of Hiroe, Bun-chhing, their friends and the Taiwanese in general are othered through the ideological determination of the state. With their occupation, the Nationalists formulated an identity that was based on the exclusion of genealogies and ideologies that were non-Nationalist in orientation. These things included communism, colonialism, Taiwan's hybridity, and its diverse linguistic alterities,[25] all of which were denied or labeled inferior in the KMT bid for supremacy. The Nationalists' political reality included their tendency to idealize the pre-1949 past and their claim that Communism was a temporary aberration that would be overthrown by the Chinese people and that would disappear with the future reunification of China under the KMT. As for the Taiwanese, their ethnicity was compromised, in this view, because of their enslavement (*nuhua*) under the occupying Japanese. Throughout the forty-year period of history that followed *Ererba*, the island was commandeered into the mythmaking through the claim that, culturally and politically, it was an integral part of China. The suppression of local history included the erasure of the colonial heritage, Taiwan's hybridity and its diverse linguistic alterities that, in real terms, mark the island's cultural differences from China. As June Yip points out, the Guomindang skillfully deployed the "rhetoric of nation to integrate Taiwan into a larger 'Chinese' cultural identity and to weave a seamless narrative of Chinese nationhood" that denied these alterities.[26] The inclusion of these alterities in *City* reflects Hou's sensibilities with respect to Taiwan's geo-historic space.

Hiromi's voice-over engenders a counter-discursiveness that disrupts the monolithic, myth-making aspect of the KMT's master narrative. With this voice, space is opened up for the "unofficial" history that is reconstructed from fact. The "unofficial" history narrates the events that, one by one, took place with *Ererba*. The events include the disappearance of Teacher Lin, the exile of Hiroe to a mountain retreat, and Bun-chhing's first arrest owing to his leftist political connections — the latter conveyed through a letter to Hiromi from her sister-in-law. Through the recitation of these events, an alternative truth emerges about both *Ererba* and the underground, one that stands in opposition to the claim of insurgency formulated by Chen Yi. In the cinematic unfolding of the "unofficial" history, the reconstructed facts are foregrounded in a series of long takes of the type that characterize the camera work of Hou's films.[27] One such take focuses on Bun-chhing as he sits on the ground in his cell, unaware of the guards as they march down the hall and come to a halt immediately outside the cell. The guards summon not Bun-chhing but instead a cellmate, who stands up and proceeds to his execution. Before he departs the cellmate writes two lines that memorialize the socialist dream about the Chinese ancestral land —"In life I am separated from the ancestor-land, in death I return to the ancestor-land. Both life and death are fated; I leave with no regrets" (*Sheng li zuguo, si gui zuguo. Sisheng tianming, wu xiang wu nian.*) The cellmate breaks into the opening lyrics of "The Song of the Covered Wagon," re-staging in dramatic form the execution of Zhong Haodong, a victim of *Ererba* who sang this song as he went to his execution.[28]

The scene leads shortly thereafter to the routing of Hiroe by the police and the arrest of Bun-chhing for a second and final time. With this act, Bun-chhing is erased like his friends, purged through a nexus of violence and a malaise that derives from lack. The remaining Lims, who are enframed in a final shot, drive home *City*'s themes of tragedy and loss. *City* concludes with an intertitle that, inscribed with irony, displays the announcement that in 1949 the KMT withdrew to Taiwan and set up its capital in Taipei.

Implicit in the dialogic unmasking is the cinematic authorial voice — the moral and ethical sensibilities of Hou Hsiao Hsien. Hou's presence remains in the background of the film, but moves to the foreground in the dialogic unfolding of the "unofficial" story of the text. His presence is articulated through Hiromi, who communicates the feminine values of empathy and recites the arrests, disappearances, and purges that took place during *Ererba*. In the film, Hiromi's voice-over is cinematically synchronized with scenes of familial private life, but when her voice-over describes public events, the audio track shifts to an omniscient or quasi-omniscient third-person narration that is that of Hou Hsiao Hsien himself.[29] This technique allows Hou to comment on the tragedy in a way that conveys his ethical views, his perspective on cultural life, and his political vision about contemporary national life.

Peggy Hsiung-Ping Chiao comments that *City* represents a "search for the origin of history" that, the critic implies, is innately Taiwanese.[30] Taiwan's history is composed of numerous strands and a hybridity, which is the result of the legacies of colonialism, neo-colonialism, traditionalism, modernity, and linguistic and ethnic alterities. Many of these elements have been recently resurrected for the purpose of re-writing history. In the process the categories of class, generation, and ethnicity come into play in the creation of hegemonies that presume selective interpretations.[31] Through its discourse of gender, Hou's examination merges into the present moments from these strands that have been forgotten, suppressed, denigrated, or elided, opening up space thereby for a range of interpretations. Hiromi's diary, which is the means for foregrounding these moments, simultaneously highlights the value of women's discourse in the writing of history.

5

A Myth(ology) Mythologizing Its Own Closure: Edward Yang's *A Brighter Summer Day*

Liu Yu-hsiu

The international acclaim for Edward Yang's latest movie, *Yi Yi* (or *A One and a Two*, 2000), has aroused a new wave of enthusiastic attention to his earlier films. Among them *A Brighter Summer Day* stands out because the two films share important similarities and form meaningful contrasts.[1] Yang's visual style, which is characterized by long shots, fixed framing, and profound silences, and "which reached an apotheosis in 1991's *A Brighter Summer Day*," is seen as essential to the later film's power.[2] This continuity on the technical level is matched on the thematic level: both films aim at presenting a panoramic view of Taiwan society with poignant historical depths. In *Yi Yi*, Yang finally manages to create a new era and "his new Taipei," but in the earlier film he endeavored to cast a nostalgic glance at 1960s Taipei. This glance has become a sort of official portrait of the city: "We [critics in Taiwan] are accustomed to seeing *A Brighter Summer Day* as the historical approach Edward Yang assumes to penetrate the surface of the sad city."[3]

Jonathan Rosenbaum also sees *A Brighter Summer Day* as preoccupied with history. He echoes Stephen Teo in emphasizing that the characters, as a result of their diaspora from mainland China, are enmeshed in a sense of perpetual exile and at the same time try desperately to adapt.[4] Similarly Yeh Yueh-Yu focuses on the juxtaposition between the poverty and constriction of the "soldiers' villages" (where the low-ranking soldiers from mainland China take up residence with their families) and the American rock 'n' roll the second generation are enamored of, this contrast itself being a clue to the complexity of the political and economic background.[5] Another critic, Saul Austerlitz, says of *A Brighter Summer Day*, "In Edward Yang's subtle mise en scène, his Taiwan is a country dominated by the detritus of other cultures."[6] This historical aspect of the film will be the focus of my investigation.

The film tells how the first and second generations of the so-called Mainlanders — those who came from mainland China with the Kuomintang in 1949 — engage in power and sexual games, and how they try to adapt to the new social environment in Taiwan. The protagonist, Si'r, is a senior high-school student. He participates in gang activities because his elders are burdened by responsibilities, inconsiderate, and often unjust, and because his girl betrays him. Ming, Si'r's girlfriend, lost her father in the civil war. She and her mother, who suffers badly from asthma, depend on unwilling relatives, who are themselves destitute exiles from mainland China. Ming's mother is hired as a housemaid for the parents of Si'r's best friend, Ma. Lured financially and sexually, Ming falls for Ma and thus upsets the boys' friendship. Ming was originally the girlfriend of Honey, the noble leader of the Park Gang who entrusted her to Si'r before his murder by the treacherous leader of the Soldiers' Village Gang. Si'r takes a samurai sword left behind by the Japanese colonists and sets out to avenge himself on Ma. But instead, he runs into Ming, falls out with her, and kills her, stabbing her repeatedly while shouting: "You're disappointing! You're disappointing!" Si'r disappears behind bars, with the others lamenting the fall of someone so young and promising.

Strangely, the femme-fatale theme, or blame-the-woman theme, has been submerged into the impression that in the self-enclosed world of the film "all the characters are conditioned by the social environment, with little space for individual choice,"[7] and that "everybody can be the murderer when there are no innocent victims."[8] The following analysis will attempt to argue that this is basically an effect of the superb structure, or structurality, of the film.

The Bricolage of the Film Set

Many viewers, mostly male, give vent to the strong emotions aroused by *A Brighter Summer Day*. One of them says, in a way typical of such viewers, "We can feel the mysterious force that is pushing Si'r toward the act of killing Ming. . . . The overwhelming power of *A Brighter Summer Day* comes from a subjective reality that is built up on the basis of a solid objective reality."[9]

This impression is closely connected with another widely shared view that the film is preoccupied with history. Shen Jiao Du, a personal website devoted to cultural criticism, spells out the connection: "Edward Yang does his utmost to build up the film set in order to reconstruct the somber age [of the 1960s]."[10] The objectiveness or historicity of the film is a result of reconstruction. We can then ask to what extent is the reconstructed history aesthetic or ideological instead of factual?

According to Yang Shunqing, who participated in the script writing, set designing, and acting, director Yang remarked: "The older audience members are witnesses; here lies the difficulty in making a film about events of thirty years ago. Every single household item, as well as every piece of clothing, requires tremendous effort to *find*."[11] Edward Yang and his crew did not create — they found. Thus they were forced to become literally what Lévi-Strauss calls the "bricoleur-mythmaker." Just like the bricoleur-mythmaker they were constricted in using only "the remains and debris" of the past, the "fossilized evidence of an individual or a society."[12] They laboriously searched for and collected a huge quantity of "fossilized evidence" for potential use on the sets, while the director "made good use of whatever was available, rearranging and reconstituting, like a magician pulling off wonderful tricks."[13]

Here we need to ask whether what has been assembled by the bricoleur-director results in the reappearance of a cross-section of history. Let us examine another passage from the notes of Yang Shunqing:

> Director Yang specifically asked the entire crew to assist in set designing. Unless everything was in place, it was meaningless to try to shoot. In the end it was as if time had turned back. Many curios had been utilized: the coal-burning cooking stove, the hot water flask, the old handbag, the old wristwatch, the old eyeglasses, the desk calendar of thirty years ago, comic books and elementary and high school textbooks, the parents' wedding photo, the photo of the Japanese girl, paper money, lottery tickets, calendars, and posters.[14]

What we notice here first is director Yang's insistence on everything being "in place." His obsessive meticulousness cannot be explained purely by his desire to represent the past faithfully, but is also partly motivated by his idea of the internal structure and coherence of everything on the screen. Take the photo of the Japanese girl. Thematically, the Japanese girl exemplifies the fantasized ideal of female purity, in contrast with heroine Ming's infidelity.[15] The small samurai sword used by the girl to commit suicide and preserve her chastity, the male characters imagine, is the same one used by Si'r to kill Ming at the end of the film. We learn from the shooting script (hereafter referred to as the script) that the sword is a crucial prop because it will be the murder instrument at the climax of the film. However, the script does not mention "the photo of the Japanese girl"; its inclusion in the film results from the internal expediency of the film as a self-enclosed system. There is a certain inevitability in the plot whereby Si'r, taking the sword to confront his friend Ma, who has been dating Ming, ends up killing Ming instead. The wonderful subtlety of this coincidence comes from the fact that the sword imagined as belonging to a faithful girl who has used it to commit suicide out of loyalty to her beloved — a sword thus endowed with a specific historical significance — is absolutely appropriate for the killing of an unfaithful femme fatale. There is no real evidence the Japanese girl did kill herself with the sword. Plausibility is derived not so much from our impression of Japanese culture as from the meaning and function assigned to it by the structure of the film. In other words the film makes use of the image of the Japanese girl in conjunction with the sword in order to constitute the dichotomy and contrast of the good woman killing herself for love and the bad woman being punished with murder.

There are many similar examples. Yang Shunqing mentions that during production, the crew "discovered one suitable location after another: the abandoned factory (the original site for shooting the nighttime dates) was replaced by the tennis court, and mysteriousness and silence replaced chaos and secrecy; the rifle range was moved from the mountainous area in Guandu to Wanjin Army Base in Neipu, Pingdong County, and consequently the infinite wide-open plain took the place of the mountains."[16] Here it is worth investigating why the locations were changed. Setting the dates in an abandoned factory as indicated in the script would have reflected more faithfully the socioeconomic conditions of Taiwan in the 1960s. Why change it? It is precisely because whenever sticking to the historical landscape is detrimental to the film's structure, director Yang lets structure take precedence over historicity. Abandoning the connotation of chaos, secrecy, and inaccessibility and opting for mystery, wide-openness, and infinity, the film strives to avoid the sense of claustrophobia and searches for something transcendental instead. Provided with the illusion of something ultimate to transcend to, the film's self-enclosure is accomplished.

Similar endeavor can be seen in two important examples concerning characterization. The first is the portrayal of Si'r's father. In the script he is distant from his children, who are frequently reminded of his authority by both himself and his wife. In his relation with her, he adopts the traditional male attitude; sometimes he even shouts at her so much that Si'r laments in his diary, "If they were a little kinder, I would love them more."[17] In the film all the scenes concerning the father's authoritarian behavior (except the scene near the end when he chastises his second son) are eliminated, turning him into a loving father who treats his children more as equals.

The second example is the portrayal of Si'r's mother. In the film she is the most flawless character. In the home she is self-sacrificing, while outside the home she is a responsible teacher and has a realistic understanding of and open-minded attitude towards the conflict between Taiwanese and Mainlanders in Taiwan. Thus, she is seen as an entirely kind and wise person in the film. In the script, however, she is more worldly. Her character thinks everyone in the bureaucracy conspires to profiteer and suggests her husband take part rather than risk being treated as a pariah by his colleagues. Her disregard for social justice infuriates her upright husband and incurs his contempt. This delineation of Si'r's mother shows her as a potential threat to men and society, hence to some extent not unlike Ming. Because of the shortcomings in her personality men cannot trust or respect her, which is why she fails to maintain a harmonious relationship with her husband. The film version omits all the negative personality traits, making Si'r's mother a perfect wife, mother, and citizen.

Comparing the script with the film, we have discovered that the film transforms Si'r's parents into role models as husband and wife, father and mother. Not only have individual characters or elements been made more exemplary, but the relations between these elements also seem more rational and coherent in the film. For instance, in the script there is a scene where Si'r's father sees blocks of ice being transported in the corridor of the Garrison Command Headquarters. Such a scene clearly communicates authorial criticism of the brutality of a patriarchal institution. Although included in the principal cinematography it was edited out of the finished film. Why? One of the main reasons must be the consideration that the Garrison Command's interrogation and imprisonment of innocent citizens is analogous to Si'r's father's beating his second son and wrongly accusing him of stealing in a later sequence. To avoid an association of Si'r's father with the Garrison Command that would taint the father's image, the film chooses to conceal the brutality of the authoritarian institution. In fact, the father's method of disciplining his son is influenced by his experience in the headquarters, and the beating is partly the father's way of venting frustration with the bureaucracy. Precisely because of this dialectical relation the violence and cruelty in the Garrison Command Headquarters have to be diminished. Consequently the character of Si'r's father stands out more clearly as a reforming force against patriarchal power and for a new ethics of equality and mutual trust.

The same can be said about the character of Si'r's mother. After the elimination of her "femme fatale" traits she becomes the antithesis of Ming. The latter is destructive to others and to herself, while the former is infallibly virtuous and wise.

After the properties and positions of the two fundamental units (the father and the mother) are defined, all the other components needed to build the structure become evident. So do their "natural" positions — naturalness being an effect of any well-organized structure — and the relation(ship)s between them. Hence, the male characters — the father, Si'r, the noble leader Honey, Honey's treacherous and cruel counterpart Shandong, the other gang members, and the bureaucrats — become mutually antithetical yet complementary elements. When put together these form a coherent system. Concomitantly, the female roles all fall into place and constitute an interlocking order, with the mother at the apex and Green at the nadir. Under normal conditions there is no place for the heroine Ming within this female system. Green is unequivocally a vagrant female element with a clearly mapped-out trajectory. By contrast Ming's character traits are ambiguous. On the one hand, she is some Big Brother's woman. On the other hand, complex intrinsic and extrinsic factors make her an object of desire for all the young male characters, and hence a destabilizing force. To restore harmony and equilibrium within the system her death is imperative. This interpretation derived from structural analysis is in accordance with film critic Liu Daren's perception that the death of Ming is the film's attempt to "establish a new world and a new moral order."[18]

The script repeatedly makes it clear that Ming likes to flirt with different male characters, but the film greatly downplays her promiscuity to set her apart from Green. Ming's ambiguity and the impossibility of classifying her must be emphasized to drive the film to its logical conclusion that she be killed.

The completed film, in which Chang Dachun detects "a national implication,"[19] and which Huang Jianye calls "a national fable,"[20] is exactly what Lévi-Strauss calls a "bricolage", in which the signified of the old structure becomes the signifier in the new.[21] In this case the reconstruction is done by the director and his crew. According to one of the screenwriters, Yan Hongya, Edward Yang studied the script meticulously. "If any details were inappropriate or inconsistent, he would not think twice about changing the wonderful established plot so that sections that were not integral parts of the structure were steadily eliminated."[22] The segment about the torture of suspects in the Garrison Command Headquarters is perhaps an instance of "wonderful established plot" that is "not integral" and has therefore been done away with.

The use of vehicles in the film is an interesting example of the mythopoeic activity the film crew is engaged in. Yan Hongya specifically points out that "the vehicle which crushed Honey to death was a bus [in the script], but became an army truck in the film."[23] The change is subtle and significant. The use of an army vehicle as a murder weapon implies criticism both of Shandong — the leader of the Soldiers' Village Gang and a patriarchal figure — and of the army — a brutish patriarchal institution — and kills two birds with one stone. Yang Shunqing also records that because the production department found an abundant source of old-fashioned vehicles, they "even put two antique fire trucks in the big Japanese-style wooden house where [the Wanhua Gang] run their gambling den."[24] These two fire trucks seem gratuitous, but in fact serve an intricate function. They create the association of something gigantic, solid, and courageous with the Taiwanese Wanhua Gang, who will initiate the two incidents of meeting Honey — the exiled upright leader of the Mainlanders' Park Gang — and of setting out to avenge his death. Thus the fire engines and the army truck, Honey and Shandong, the Wanhua/Park gangs and the Soldiers' Village Gang form antithetical pairs.

The dichotomy between the army truck and the fire trucks cannot be grasped through reason, but can be intuited. The same goes for the last few scenes of the film. The detention officer throws into the garbage can the music tape given as a present to Si'r by his buddy "Elvis Presley the Junior." Si'r's second sister bursts into tears in the middle of singing in the church choir. The malfunctioning radio at Si'r's home suddenly gives out names of students who have passed the college entrance examination, for which Si'r was supposed to have worked hard. Scenes like these are not easy to comprehend but can move the viewer emotionally and trigger a series of inexplicit mental activities. Through such mental activities the viewer may realize that Si'r's crime or suffering is the function of a comprehensive, if not entirely perfect, system. Thus the film successfully "makes the audience sense, not just through rational thinking" that Si'r's killing of Ming is "a sort of self-sacrificing religious act to save the world."[25]

The human mind is capable of thinking without recourse to reason; it can operate intuitively via the use of metaphor. Metaphorical language conveys, as Lévi-Strauss sees it, the primitive apprehension of "a global structure of signification,"[26] which issues from "a need to impose a grammatical order on a mass of random elements."[27] We can say concerning

A Brighter Summer Day that the screenwriters, the director, the entire production crew, and the audience have all engaged in the construction of such a "grammatical order."

It would be more precise to say that this "grammatical order" is generated by the intrinsic demand of the system, which works in a devious way. Those who took part in the making of the film reiterate the director's emphasis on structure. Yan Hongya, for instance, records Edward Yang's opinion in his notebook: "Structure is the most essential and solid foundation. A perfect structural principle enables an artist to proceed with confidence and a sense of security."[28]

Following the director the crew also immersed themselves in the beauty of structure, as attested to by the recollections of Yan Hongya, Yang Shunqing, and others. But despite the director's claim of total control over his work, his crew's accounts seem to imply that a universal and independent structural mechanism was in operation autonomously, leading the film crew to select appropriate elements for proper disposition. Yan Hongya testifies:

> After the shoot began . . . I often dreamed of going to the theater to see what the finished film looked like. In one of the close-ups, the only thing left was a portrait frame within which flowed the colors of the rainbow. In the dream I thought it was refreshing and powerful and I wasn't surprised at all. Waking up, I knew it was unreal, but understood perfectly the psychology behind my reaction in the dream — the bridge of *A Brighter Summer Day* has been built; on such a secure framework, all magical transformations are feasible.[29]

This "secure framework" is unmistakably an instance of what Lévi-Strauss calls "the global structure of signification." It is as if the moment the bricoleur-mythmaker successfully connects with the global structure, free association enables him — as well as the reader/viewer — to plug into that global circuit board and draw its current of signification, so that "all the magical transformations become feasible."

Under such conditions an everlasting and far-reaching myth or "national fable" has been born. The entire creative process took place in the realm of collective human understanding, beyond any individual subject. It is exactly this kind of mythopoeic activity that leads Lévi-Strauss to see "not how men think in myths, but how myth operates in men's minds without them being aware of the fact."[30] This appears to be exactly what transpired on the set: a myth operated through the hands and minds of Edward Yang and his crew, thinking for itself and dictating its own completion.

A Myth(ology) Mythologizing Its Own Closure

In the preceding section I have tried to illustrate how both filmmaker and audience — myself included — have engaged in a structural (or structuralist) game. As a result of constant self-critiquing in the process of bricolage film production, this game has to a certain degree advanced from the realm of the intuitive and achieved the status of sophisticated knowledge. We may claim that the various versions of *A Brighter Summer Day* — the script, the four-hour long test run, the three-and-a-half hour theater version, and the three-hour video — as well as the production notes and all the examinations of each version for structural coherence, are all mythical thoughts and simultaneously the dissection and elucidation of mythical thoughts. In short *A Brighter Summer Day* is both a myth and a study of myth — in other words a mythology.

Apparently, the mythology can be liberating. As the various versions of the film and its production records show, the constituting elements can be arranged differently and the meaning they produce has no absolute stability. In this myth(ology), meaning has no transcendental existence but rather hinges entirely on the interrelations and correspondences of the elements within the system. Thus, "the truth of the myth does not lie in any special content, it consists in logical relations . . ."[31] In his critique of Lévi-Strauss's mythological project, Jacques Derrida expresses his fascination with the latter's "stated abandonment of all reference to a center, to a subject, to a privileged reference, to an origin, or to an absolute archia."[32] It is fascinating to see that on the mythological level *A Brighter Summer Day* reflects similar abandonment of all reference to an absolute truth. In this film Taiwan culture began to think what Derrida calls "the structurality of structure."[33] It has taken a big historical step; an event of great significance, a rupture, has happened.

In the history of Taiwan feature films *A Brighter Summer Day* indeed represents a big step, and one in the Western, progressive direction. Zhan Hongzhi, who was in charge of the film's marketing, explained that this film managed to attract plenty of foreign capital. As a result, its choice of subject matter and methodological experiments were free from regular box office constraints.[34] The film's methodology also relied on a kind of foreign "capital": the methodological concepts adopted were inspired by the director's experience abroad and his long-term immersion in Western art and culture.

However, where has the film's meditation on "the structurality of structure" led us? To what extent has it liberated us? It is notable that in all the reports and interviews in which Edward Yang or his crew express views about *A Brighter Summer Day*, the film's structure and techniques are repeatedly discussed but the subject matter is hardly touched on. It is only too obvious that they are trying, probably unconsciously, to distract their own as well as the audience's attention from the content by focusing on the form. Does this mean that the content is not important?

Of course not. On the contrary, Edward Yang's three previous features are linked by central themes of the femme-fatale phenomenon and patrilineal power transference. *That Day at the Beach* (1983) seems to sing the praises of two women, but deep down is a lament on the failure of power transference from father to son. In *Taipei Story* (1985) the protagonist Ah Long, an embodiment of the legacy of Taiwan's history, dies nihilistically for a woman for no good reason. The film implies that women are responsible for the tragedy. *The Terrorizer* (1986) is a long dialectical meditation on the theme of the femme fatale.

In *A Brighter Summer Day* the themes of the femme fatale and power transference converge and become fully developed. This is worth exploring because it hints at the direction in which the postmodern culture of Taiwan is going: the reconsolidation of patriarchal power and the sexual structure by way of an endless meditation on its own structurality. The film ingeniously conceals the brutality and violence of patriarchal institutions in order to preserve the good image of the father. It erases the normal woman's

Edward Yang's femme fatale: Ming in *A Brighter Summer Day*.

potential threat to man to set up a dichotomy between the virtuous woman and the femme fatale, justifying the imprisonment of the former and the destruction of the latter. With the elimination or concealment of these problematic components, the father seems to become the brother while remaining the father, and the brothers and the brotherly father form an alliance to ensure the survival of the same power structure by delimiting women as Other.

As for the film's self-critique and self-scrutiny, they are motivated by the necessity of rationalizing the omissions and concealments indicated above to prove the inevitability of the system as a whole. Here we see Edward Yang, the master structuralist-director, has employed the same strategy used by Lévi-Strauss. Lévi-Strauss, the author of *The Structures of Kinship* and the theorist of patriarchal relations, repeatedly belittles the Oedipal myth. Since Freud has theorized this as the founding myth of today's patriarchal culture, the human mind has become inconveniently and embarrassingly conscious of the Oedipal structure. Unwilling to give it up, Lévi-Strauss strives to avert attention from its content by focusing on its structurality. Structural games are, Lévi-Strauss contends, "intellectually satisfying in proportion to the complexity of the operation and to the ingenuity required in manipulating them."[35] In this way a mythical system "produces the illusion that the underlying equations are solvable"; this solution that is not a real solution "is a way of relieving intellectual uneasiness and even existential anxiety."[36] Like so many others, Lévi-Strauss and Edward Yang share a common source of anxiety: the awkward situation after the Freudian exposure of Oedipal desires.

In his paper on Lévi-Strauss, Derrida suggests that once representation — of father, God, center, truth — has begun it has no end. We can only conceive of its closure as "its playing space," within which the representation of the tragic fate of representation — "its gratuitous and baseless necessity" — continues.[37] This appears to be exactly what men — Lévi-Strauss, Derrida, and Edward Yang — are doing, and just because all this is conceived, or constructed, to have a "gratuitous and baseless necessity."

Postscript

The above analysis is a revision of an article I published in Chinese in 1993. Interestingly, many critics, mostly male, have voiced indignation against the feminist stance I took. This view leads to the corollary that, "it is beside the point to argue whether Ming is faithful, or whether Edward Yang attempts to build the Otherness of women with the murder of the unfaithful woman."[38]

Such instances of self-defense on the part of men attest to the working of exactly what my article exposes. This is patriarchy with its self-perpetuating structure, which Lévi-Strauss — wishfully — found "always unfolded in the same way, engendering here and there identical configurations."[39] In this way men have been trying hard to cling to the same citadel, however decrepit and inconvenient it has become.

Among these critics one, and only one, finds himself cornered and therefore turns round to confront the feminist stance. He says my article on *A Brighter Summer Day* "forestalls the possibility of any refutation. . . . But I doubt whether such refined analysis is not another attempt to achieve self-enclosure. Lévi-Strauss meticulously collects all the anthropological remnants. Edward Yang, with the same meticulousness, collects all the traces of a 'national fable.' And so does Liu Yu-hsiu with the legacies of the patriarchal myth(ology). Between them where is the difference?" Then he plunges himself into a kind of soul-searching: "Why can't I endure hearing any contemptuous words about *A Brighter Summer Day*? Am I still enclosed in that same myth?"[40]

Such self-reflection is very touching indeed, just like Edward Yang's development after *A Brighter Summer Day*. Now, asked by an interviewer about the perpetual theme of the conflict between man and woman in his movies, he explains that it reflects "the spear-and-shield relationship of the two sexes," and that he wishes to present in this way "some elements of Taiwan society, as well as some essential elements of human nature."[41] Partly at least for this reason, *Yi Yi* is generally regarded as presenting Edward Yang's new Taipei, a city seen from a male perspective that is to a great degree freed from patriarchal constraints.

6

Hou Hsiao Hsien's
The Puppetmaster:
The Poetics of Landscape

Nick Browne

The recent reception of Hou Hsiao Hsien's *City of Sadness* as a political film has displaced critical attention from an investigation of the dominant aesthetic tendencies evident in the accumulating body of work by Taiwan's premier director. This has complicated the problem of situating the distinctive features of his aesthetic project by seeming to bring the work closer, and in some cases even to subordinate it, to the theoretical discussions of "Third Cinema" and contemporary critiques of colonialism. These discussions are valuable in instituting the question of where Hou stands on the map of the contemporary world cinema and in regard to the critical agenda of Western cultural theory. This tendency to subordinate Hou's work to doctrine of this kind, however, seems to me a misapprehension of the general significance of his achievement.

Hou's work is informed by three major general modes: autobiography, history, and cultural critique identified, respectively, with *The Time to Live and the Time to Die*, *City of Sadness*, and arguably, *Daughter of the Nile*. I would like to inquire into the autobiographical scenes in Hou's work by focusing on their major instances — in *The Time to Live and the Time to Die* and most centrally, in his recent *The Puppetmaster*.[1] Through the examination of the narrative structure of autobiographical form and its historical embeddedness, we might take as an object of study the relation of the autobiographer to the larger culture. That is, we might consider the assertion that the natural, not the political, history of Taiwan is the significant cultural subtext of this oeuvre.

The Poetics of Space

The Puppetmaster is sustained by a complex formal structure that goes well beyond the narrative design of Hou's putative autobiography in *Time to Live*. Though derived from factual materials as to narrative and setting (the film was shot in Hou's childhood home), the earlier film presents itself stylistically as fictional drama. Dramatically, it is almost wholly circumscribed in its order and meaning by the representation of the familial and of the protagonist within that structure. It is an example of a cinema of mise-en-scène and architecture that together trace changes of the family against a backdrop of familiar and repeated daily or annual occurrences and places: preparing food, eating, bathing, boys playing in the central square, the changing of seasons, and the sun and rain. Against this backdrop of pattern and routine are events of short duration: the grandmother's wandering and return, the fights, the visit to the brothel, the courtship of the sister, and so on. The big events, that is, the long ones, are the declining health of father, mother, and grandmother that leads eventually to their deaths, the survivor's mourning and his time to live, his growing up. This action is centered on a physical place, chiefly the family's house and the surrounding neighborhood. The decoupage effects a systematic interpenetration and continuity between the two spaces, whether looking into the house, or inversely, from within the house looking out. The perspective, in other words, is transitive. The house is in the Japanese style — with movable screens and partitions — and the framing and composition of shots realize at the same time a definition of filmic space that is graphic in its frontal plane (its sense of arrangement of form and color), and three dimensional, creating a space for action that is normally articulated in multiple planes of recession. The approach to mise-en-scène favors the lateral, thus determining the actor's profile and movement. Thus the internal screens that articulate the space sometimes eclipse the action, but only for a moment, when the action is quickly recentered in a legible space. There is much in the deployment of this style to suggest that the creation and maintenance of this formal pattern should be taken as the instanciation of a mode of human order — I would say a Confucian one. Thus constructed, "place" is the space of transparency of familial relations, of mutually implicating obligations and privileges. That is, the internal screens are more of a compositional device than a dramatic one. The publicness and serenity of this order are striking, disturbed only by the perturbation of the events we have indicated.

"Outside" is the space of the neighborhood beyond the house and family.

There is a world of conflict and change beyond this habitus, but it is only indirectly presented. One night, for example, while the family sleeps, there is a rumbling in the dark and, the following morning, simply the imprint of tracks on the road. On other occasions there are public announcements over the radio and articles in the newspapers; at one point a flag is shown flying at half-mast. But these are of the nature of allusion, part of the setting, non-events as far as the life in the house is concerned. The order of the house — and this is the deeper implication of both Hou's narrative and his style — is disturbed only by events from within.

The Puppetmaster presents the autobiography of Li Tien-lu, from the time of his birth shortly after the Japanese instituted their administration of the island to their departure at the end of World War II. It assumes the form of autobiography but only in a secondary way: it is an autobiography in the third person — for Hou is the filmmaker but not the subject. The complexity of the film's design consists of three integrated principles of composition: the alternation of the on-screen presence of the puppetmaster recounting events from his life (six times by my count) in a presentational mode with dramatizations by actors of events from his life in a representational mode; the insertion into the dramatized diegesis of scenes of a number of puppet shows, and operas (eight, I believe), and the constitution of the question of their meaning within the culture of their time; and the systematic alternation of spaces inside houses and the lives they imply with the space of the outdoors, and, in this, the constitution of a complex dialectic around the theme of "place," or, if you like, of "location," of the figure of the puppetmaster within Taiwan's aesthetic and political culture. All this is explicitly held in place by an autobiographical and historical narrative frame subtended by the precise period of Japanese administration. Later, I want to introduce a fourth consideration, but first, let me take these three points in reverse order.

I will concentrate first on the dialectic of space, or more exactly, the question of the "location" of the action. The operas are all staged indoors and all the puppet shows outdoors. But the place to begin is with the houses, that is, with the practical matter of shelter. In part, the film's recounting of Li Tien-lu's life-long vicissitudes of family and employment assume the form of questions of residence, not as an external circumstance or merely as a sign, but as an instanciation of his autobiographical situation. That is, by both birth and marriage, the puppetmaster is located in the woman's family house. He is born and lives in the house of his mother's father and is given the name, despite the objections of his father, of his maternal grandmother — Li rather than Shu. After marrying, he moves into the house of his wife's family. The function of women, however — mother, step-mother, and wife — in both the educational and the sentimental spheres, is either pictured as negative or inconsequential. His family life, including his wedding, is hardly mentioned and not shown. Rather, there is an extended dramatization of life with his girlfriend — Li Chu, whose nickname is Lu — situating the respective realms of sexuality and domesticity in structures of feeling that inform his story.

The narrative recounts three kinds of events — relations with relatives, the vicissitudes of employment, and relations with the government — presented, when all is said and done, under a common aspect: the unfolding of fortune, that is, of predestination. Under this ontology of narrative design, events in his world are less chosen than pre-decided — notably by social structure and, even more emphatically, by physiology. Relations with relatives are formulated through sickness, health, and survival. Of the nine deaths of family members recounted in the film, that of the grandmother indicates best the skein of fatality in the clan. One day, the puppetmaster reports, the maternal grandmother falls sick and the puppetmaster's mother prays to give some years of her own life in exchange for her recovery. Shortly afterward, his mother contracts TB and dies in July, an inauspicious month, the puppetmaster remarks, in the lunar calendar. Then, because of a conflict with her son's new wife, the grandmother is obliged to move out of the family house and live with another grandson. Shortly after her arrival the grandson dies. The grandmother then moves to the residence of her daughter-in-law, but she soon dies too. When the grandmother returns home, the new wife falls sick. In desperation, the puppetmaster's father makes his son an unusual offer — in return for caring for the grandmother the boy can keep all his earnings as an apprentice. The young puppetmaster agrees. One day, some time later, the grandmother asks for some candy, but the young puppetmaster refuses to get her any. The grandmother then falls down and refuses to get up. For ten days she lies in a kind of catatonic state, but neither a Western nor a traditional doctor can find anything wrong. The puppetmaster is advised, however, that if he were to leave the place where she is lying, she will die. Soon after he is called away to another place by the Japanese to do a job and, as predicted, his grandmother dies. Eventually he returns home to bury her.

These events make up a belief system of personal substitution, contamination, fatality, and survival, which indicates and foregrounds the special status, and, in a sense, the strength of the person of the storyteller. The logic of narrative events institutes a system of magical causality through physical co-presence of persons and defines an order whose meaning is evident only through inferences across gaps closed by superstitious belief and presumptively ordered by a scheme of fate — bizarre coincidence defeats plausibility and serves as testimony of an order beyond the visible. In this sense, strict linearity of events is an emphatic affirmation of magical causality and hence, of the validity of superstition. This narrative and its logic condenses the link between destiny and the body.

The Politics of Puppetry

The recounting of the changing organization of the aesthetic world of opera and puppetry, my second topic, serves to reflect changing political circumstances. At the onset the Japanese administration tolerates a range of aesthetic media: Peking opera, native Taiwanese opera (each with distinctive content and style), and northern, that is to say, courtly styles of hand-controlled puppetry. The Taiwanese cultural materials consist of three elements: the selection and teaching of classical poetry in the schools, the subject matter for the depicted scenes of the vernacular — that is, Taiwanese opera — and the topics of the puppet theater proper. Among the three, there is a common iconographic and thematic link, one important to the meaning of the film: the depiction of the travels of a group of men and women on a boat across the water. "The Legend of White Snake," performed as a puppet show in the film, is the most detailed and extended exemplification of this situation. Its complicated narrative points to the unstable harmony with the forces of a nature-god, and the legend is ultimately embedded in a widely celebrated Taiwanese ritual intended both to commemorate the injustice done to the white snake and to pacify her. The theme of maritime uncertainty resonates through these cultural texts.

With the onset of the Sino-Japanese War the puppetmaster reports that both Taiwanese opera and outdoor puppet performances are banned, reducing his opportunity for employment to approved stage operas. The extended episode with the prostitute Li Chu is recounted in this context. The sequence opens with a new operatic scene of maritime uncertainty very much like the scene from "The Legend of White Snake" depicted in the puppet show, in this case indicating the possibility of robbery by roving pirates of two women and a man occupying a small boat on a lake. Their story is developed through an on-stage/off-stage dialectic of real life and artifice. Eventually the puppetmaster's intrigue and intimacy with this lady-prostitute deepens — she offers to lend him money to become a proprietor of his own brothel (he refuses) and eventually follows him to another city.

There are two defining moments in the film's presentation of her: her game to test this fidelity by sending him another seductress, and the occasion of her being photographed in the studio and the discussion between them of which picture to keep. Both pose questions of appearance, matters that the film treats as distinctively feminine — moments, in other words, of theatricalized self-presentation. In these instances her "person" undergoes a change, or a kind of metamorphosis. For him, acting on the stage is a temporary matter, a departure from his more consistent role of puppetmaster. Through the contrast between the actress and the narrator, the film stages and engenders spectacle, putting the woman on the side of the shape-shifter.

Li Tien-lu eventually formally affiliates with a pro-Japanese theatrical troupe playing anti-American agitprop and takes up residence in a kind of dormitory for local militia. He begins speaking a mixture of Taiwanese and Japanese. His relationship with the Japanese is respectful and even cordial. Japanese administration, while bureaucratic, is shown to be orderly, fair, and even faintly humorous. After the Japanese evacuation he joins a new troupe and returns to Taipei. The film ends with the scene of warplanes being salvaged in order to pay the puppetmaster to stage a show thanking the gods for their protection.

Taiwanese farmers taking Japanese warplanes apart in *The Puppetmaster*.

The Poetics of Landscape

The dialectic that the film sets in motion between the space of the house and the space of nature is more than simply a formal system. The house is presented as a space of enclosure, and of familial conflict, and as a retreat for the sickly. The spaces are dark, musty, and without windows, the only lighting coming from above. These spaces make a striking contrast with the scenes of sky, water, golden fields, and enormous towering green trees. Compositionally, these images of nature are represented using panoramic shots of both vertical and horizontal expanse with minimal or slow movement, sometimes of persons, other times of gently rising smoke. These are essentially non-narrative descriptions. They are frequently the prelude to a scene of the puppet shows, which are invariably staged in the open air and announced by firecrackers. The dramatic force of the interpolation of these "quiet" shots into the flow of the story constitutes the sense of a distinct break or escape from familial trouble, spatial enclosure, and formally from narrative. These images of nature, some of the most beautiful in cinema, form and concentrate a dialectic with the house, whose meaning is paradoxically related to the progressive construction of a sense of nature as the puppetmaster's shelter and home. After leaving the family house he, in fact, becomes a vagabond. He has no fixed residence and often takes shelter where he works, according to the vicissitudes of employment. At one point he is obliged to take up residence in the shop of a coffin maker. "Homelessness," in other words, is presented here as the condition of narrative contingency — of working out what the film designates as his fate.

This, it seems to me, is the context for situating the scene of the puppetmaster's first on-screen appearance — the only one to take place outdoors in nature — in which he tells the story of the grandmother's illness. Behind him, workers are putting a roof with new timbers on an addition to an old house. This is the background to his account of the wandering fateful itinerary, of his grandmother's coming and going seventy years before. It is a complex scenic image of permanence and change in which the puppetmaster has arrived home, as it were, in his natural setting and in clear possession of his own history. Throughout the film "homelessness" is thematized through the conceit of the contingent journey, that is, through the recounting of a story.

In this way, we can return from a different direction, through the narrative structure of the film, to the third compositional dialectic, that between the spaces inside houses and those outdoors. It is probably plain by now that I have come to see the puppetmaster as a paradoxical figure belonging to this second order — that of the natural world. This is, moreover, the defining location of his work — in the small theaters set up under trees in the open fields. The paradox consists of the fact the puppet theaters are also a cultural emblem of symbolic shelter. Hou's frontal, up-close display of these architectural constructions constitutes privileged moments in the film. It is here that the world is enacted under the control of the puppetmaster's hands and voice, and it is here that the English translation of the title of the film betrays its subject. Perhaps another translation, like "My Life as A Dream on the Stage," would point more clearly to the real themes of this autobiography and to the film's display of the dialectic of art and life. The import of the Japanese as agitprop in the film's later scenes — its schematic opposition of treachery and heroism in a kind of military melodrama — is not taken seriously by the film. Rather, the dominant and common theme of the most prominent stagings turns on the constellation of images and situations related to "The Legend of the White Snake." Without entering into the psychoanalytic registers that could be called on to account for the form and outcome of this story, we might reflect simply on three elements: the metamorphosis of the snake under the force of sexual desire into the form of the woman, that is, the modulations and substitution between the feminine form and that of the creatures of another nature; the role of the male figures in the story, whether the poet, priest, or boatman, as fixed emblems of the laws of social or religious control and eventually as the woman's betrayers; and the centuries-long imprisonment of women under the weight of masculine religious authority that is indirectly associated with a sense of precariousness and even of danger, which consistently threatens the security of the boat's journey. The legend, in other words, though it is not reported completely in the film, is a cogent dramatization in miniature of the role of the woman in the patriarchal unconscious. The woman in this story is the transfigured term whose movement between natural and domestic forms and back constitutes the threat to a stable system of human mimesis in a traditional aesthetic dialectic that relates the natural landscape to the itinerary of human life. It is on this point that Hou's filmic incorporation of traditional theater exceeds it, constituting the work's fourth dialectic of composition, that of the relation between theater and film.

The historical period recounted by the puppetmaster's autobiography is the one just before the filmmaker's birth. We should be clear, though we keep speaking about "autobiography," that Hou is producing a biography based on the subject's autobiographical text. The accounts of growing up by Hou Hsiao Hsien and Li Tien-lu are, in fact, very different. The strongest contrasts are between the sense of home and "homelessness" in the way I have developed it, and stylistically between the transparency of dramatic and spatial relations between home and neighborhood in *The Time to Live and the Time to Die*, and the complex dislocations among home, residence, and place traced by "My Life as a Dream on the Stage." In so far as the puppet stage is the instanciation of a mode of human order, this film about Li Tien-lu stages the puppetmaster at the crossover point of traditional aesthetics — the dialectic between the patterns of human life and the natural world, and between the real and the staged (that is, the imaginary). In this sense, the contrast between the depiction of the vernacular Taiwanese aesthetics of the puppet show and its other, the opera, presents a system of traditional order and control that includes as well the pragmatic intentions of the performance of these displays in ritual. Ritual, in other words, seeks to close the circle of the aesthetic, the pragmatic, and the transcendental.

In Hou's aesthetic ontology the natural order is to be apprehended as the beautiful, even as the sublime by means of description, that is, through non-narrative images of the stillness of landscape. They are moments of the narratively unrepresentable and stand as points of stasis in the narrative system of Hou's film. The status of the visible *per se*, that is, of the phenomenology of appearance of the natural order is different from the meaning of narrative disclosure in human events. At one level in this film the aesthetics of the visible are those of metamorphosis and so are linked to the representation, we might say the "staging" of femininity in "The Legend of the White Snake." Through the film's incorporation of traditional puppet shows we can see that the metaphysics implied in Hou's biographical mode with its task of constituting the dialectic of action and landscape is different from the hyper-narrative, autobiographical stories of contingency and fate that Li relates. Hou incorporates, in other words, the recounted action into another aesthetic system, his own, with two signal dimensions: the assertion and acknowledgment of an imagined or claimed aesthetic paternity that links his role as contemporary filmmaker with the vernacular Taiwanese tradition, and the composition of a meditation on Taiwanese landscape as the natural mise-en-scène of his life. Hou, in other words, claims the physical place of Taiwan as his home.

In sum, the category of "history" in *The Puppetmaster* is more genealogical than political. In *The Time to Live and the Time to Die* the only significant time was family time. In *The Puppetmaster*, politics has real effects and consequences, but they are viewed as incidental and temporary against the landscape and the larger pattern of life. The events of this biography are those of work, fatality, and the charm and loss of his lover. Women, however, serve only as temporary and interrupted shelter in Li

Tien-lu's story, figured as disappearance, image, and memory. In this light, the value of any post-colonial critique must confront and come to terms with the aesthetic ontology of Hou's work and the equivocal place it accords to political administration.

The depiction of the withdrawal of the Japanese at the end of the war in the film's concluding sequences gives rise to one of the most incongruous and beautiful images of world cinema — the dismantling of the military aircraft abandoned on the open plain of tall grasses, cupped and protected by a ring of soft blue mountains in the distance. Like the complex male/female image of the "Legend of the White Snake," it is a condensed and paradoxical image, which leads me to conclude, though I will not seek to argue it further here, on the importance of femininity in the aesthetics of landscape and on the filmic representation of Taiwan as a small boat on the open sea.

7

Where Is the Love? Hyperbolic Realism and Indulgence in *Vive L'Amour*

Chris Berry

Four Paradoxes

Despite its title, Taiwan filmmaker Tsai Mingliang's *Vive L'Amour*, winner of the Golden Lion Award at the 1994 Venice International Film Festival, displays a marked absence of love.[1] There are three isolated characters and an empty apartment in contemporary Taipei that they each use and where they sometimes meet. Most of the time they are alone, doing little. Even when they are not, one is struck by their alienation from the people around them. This absence of love in *Vive L'Amour* is the first paradox. It may account for the dominant international response to Tsai's films so far, which, as Fran Martin points out in her recent essay on *Vive L'Amour*, has been to place them in a lineage of films about the urban alienation characteristic of modernity.[2] Martin's essay joins an alternative stream of writing, much of it in Chinese but also represented in this volume by Gina Marchetti's chapter on *The River*, which places Tsai's films more firmly in local culture and the emergence of local lesbian/gay/queer or *tongzhi* culture in the 1990s.[3]

The other three paradoxes are all associated with the mode of filmmaking adopted in many of Tsai's films, and especially *Vive L'Amour*. I call this mode hyperbolic realism because it performs its realism so excessively as to draw attention to itself, making it a limit-case realism. Ordinary realist acting involves only one paradox. Acting implies an audience, but to produce the desired illusionistic effect, realist acting requires actors to disavow the presence of the audience, most obviously by never looking directly at the camera. Hence the saying that good acting is not acting at all.[4] This is the second paradox.

Yet in *Vive L'Amour* the realist mode is pushed to a limit where it threatens to draw attention to itself. Acting may imply an audience, but loneliness implies the absence of others, and what is performed most in the film is loneliness. As we watch characters engage in various private distractions we become more and more aware of our presence and pretended absence. This is the third paradox. But because this is a realist film, the presence of the audience for the performance of loneliness is still disavowed, so although there is an audience the characters are still alone. This is the fourth paradox.

In focusing on this hyperbolic realist mode, my aim is not to return to an investigation of style divorced from the Taiwan context, but rather to suggest that this mode brings together questions of style and context. I argue that the complex paradoxes of the hyperbolic realist mode are necessary not only to put the spectator in touch with the experience of loneliness that is at the heart of the film, but also to produce a consoling effect of what I call indulgence in the audience's relationship to these lonely Taiwan people, all of whom are not only literally but also metaphorically homeless and outside the kinship systems of the local culture. This indulgence is where the love is in *Vive L'Amour*.

Acting So Real It Shows

In a discussion of the performance of gender and drag, Judith Butler observes that "it may be that performance, understood as 'acting out,' is significantly related to the problem of unacknowledged loss."[5] Just as the performed quality of gender is usually made invisible so that it appears natural, and the loss of other options involved in taking up one gender or the other is hidden, so mainstream cinema engages realism as a style that hides and naturalizes its own performed quality, making it appear present and full or "real" to the spectator rather than a text.[6] In this sense it could be said that the loss that realist style acts out and tries so hard to disavow is the loss of the real (or even the Lacanian Real) entailed by the entry into discourse.

The illusionist realism associated with mainstream Hollywood cinema has also been argued to install the spectator in a variety of desiring positions in relation to the world of the film. These range from Mulvey's argument for either a male-identified sadistic or fetishistic scopophilic attitude toward women on the screen to Studlar's idea of a masochistic relation where, sitting still in the dark before the giant screen and giant images of female stars, the spectator is still male-identified, but like the dependent infant being ministered to by its mother.[7]

Butler also points to certain forms of performance that subvert the usual effort to (re)produce seamless repetition. She analyses drag as a hyperbolic form that draws attention to the loss entailed in taking up and performing one gender or the other. As such it does not so much destroy or undermine gender as teeter back and forth at a limit point of ambivalence and paradox, exposing loss, persisting in performing roles that require it, and simultaneously perverting them to produce new roles.[8]

Vive L'Amour is a hyperbolic realist text that performs realism so rigorously and thoroughly that it teeters back and forth at its limits. Just as drag does not simply negate gender but takes on an ambivalent stance toward it, so *Vive L'Amour* engages in the same realist style that it exposes. Director Tsai Mingliang has spoken of a desire to make the film "like life," a concern that most realist texts fail in this regard, and that hence there is a need to rewrite those codes to make them more plausible again.[9]

Although the characters are alone for much of the film, there is also a constant play of seeing and being seen that threatens to remind the audience that this is a film. In the opening shot, for example, the camera is trained in close-up on a key dangling from an apartment door in the corridor of a building. A young man sneaks up from the out-of-focus background and snatches it. Before he takes the key he looks around to make sure no one is watching. Of course, a whole camera crew and the audience is watching and his action may remind us of that, but the actor sticks with realist conventions and, pretending to be unaware, takes the key anyway.

In the next scene he buys a bottle of water in a 7-Eleven store. Here, the camera is fixed on a security mirror, watching the man in it as the audience is watching him. We already know he is a thief of sorts, and the focus on the security mirror suggests to us that he may steal again. However, this narrative expectation is thwarted. Furthermore, the young man catches sight of himself in the mirror. He holds the look. This look runs counter to the usual conventions of realist cinema, for it is also a look straight at the camera and audience. But at the same time it is justified in terms of the codes of realism by the presence of the mirror. By holding his look for a while he rouses a certain suspense about whether or not the usual conventions of realism are about to be broken, and whether or not we as the audience are about to be caught looking. But after a moment he just brushes his hair from his forehead and moves on.

The erotic potential of the play of looks is more emphasized in the next sequence. A slightly older man who may be in his twenties is drinking coffee at a table in a bar. A fashionably dressed woman of about thirty sits at a table next to his. Pretending to be unaware of each other, they sneak the occasional glance. She then goes to the bathroom and checks her make-up in the mirror, comes back, and heads out to the street. What follows is a game of cat and mouse in which they cruise each other through the evening streets of Taipei, all the while pretending to be unaware of each other's presence as she leads him back to the same empty apartment whose key the other young man has stolen.

As Mei-Mei and Ah Jung enter the apartment for a one-night stand the voyeuristic play is stepped up a notch. This is not only because the audience is watching them make love, but also because we know the other young man, Hsiao Kang, is also in the apartment. He has taken a bath and settled in a different room from the one they use. There he has tried to commit suicide by slashing his wrist with a Swiss Army knife. In a sense, they all threaten to catch each other in the act, but in the end, although Hsiao Kang is aware of their presence, no one disturbs anyone and the film moves on, repeatedly rousing suspense in this manner but delivering little pay-off.

At times, such as the scene just described, the film teeters on the brink of farce. The second sex scene between Mei-Mei and Ah Jung, which takes place toward the end of the film, is an even more obvious instance, at the same time invoking the potential voyeurism of the audience even more powerfully. When Mei-Mei and Ah Jung enter the apartment, Hsiao Kang is already there again. He quickly hides under the bed. With the audience concentrating on whether he will be discovered, narrative expectations are diverted again and we are caught by surprise when he begins masturbating, pulling a handkerchief from his trouser pocket and pushing it down into his crotch without missing a beat. Again, this is an activity that is usually solitary, so the voyeuristic effect is further heightened, yet hardly in a manner that gratifies. We watch him and listen to them as he also listens to their lovemaking on the bed above.

Face to Face Alone

The description I have just given could lead one to think that *Vive L'Amour* is a playful sort of art-house film, self-referential and amusing, drawing attention to the codes of realism and how unrealistic they are, but at the same time re-installing them at a higher level.

However, despite all the invocations of voyeurism and narrative drive, *Vive L'Amour* disables the production of either Mulvey's desiring subject or Studlar's masochistic subject.

I have already argued there is little pay-off whenever voyeuristic responses or investment in narrative is aroused. Even when Mei-Mei and Ah Jung have sex, they are not glamorized or romanticized through soft lighting and whispered dialogue. Instead we are more likely to notice the almost driven, desperate way they go about their business. Indeed, they do not even bother to find out each other's names. Their performance remains blank to an audience, lacking in any meaning deeper than the temporary relief of loneliness.

Indeed, it is the confrontation with loneliness that the audience is impelled into that is central to the frustration of Mulvey's desiring subject. The construction of the desiring subject requires an object; it requires a self-and-other relationship, or at least the illusion of such a relationship, to be put in place and sustained for its existence. However, as critic Edmond K.Y. Wong (Huang Chien-Yeh) writes, in Tsai Mingliang's films and television series "ordinary people live like insects under examination in a laboratory; unconscious actions, walking, sitting and sleeping gradually emerge as the manifestations of loneliness."[10] Instead of meaningful narrative and exchanges between characters allowing for the sustained engagement of the spectators, most of the time we are witness to events that turn out to be meaningless and empty beyond their status as signifiers of despair, loneliness, alienation, isolation, banality and boredom. The hyperbolic realism of the film only enhances these qualities. This includes a refusal of extra-diegetic music. Given the lack of interaction between characters, this results in a soundtrack consisting largely of silence and diegetically motivated sounds, focusing the attention of the audience on the aloneness of the characters even more. In this sense we are as aurally deprived as the characters themselves.

If we are encouraged by this to identify with the loneliness of the characters and to merge ourselves with them, this would seem to suggest the masochistic aesthetic outlined by Studlar. And indeed, just as the film invokes voyeurism and narrative drive, it also invokes the merging and stasis of the masochistic aesthetic. Perhaps the best evidence for this type of engagement is at the end of the film. After being teased and tickled through long, silent loneliness in the kind of waiting game of deferred gratification and sensory deprivation that so often characterizes masochistic practice itself, catharsis is finally delivered. The morning after the second one-night stand with Ah Jung, the camera follows Mei-Mei as she walks on and on through a half-finished mudscape of a park.¹¹ Coming to a great amphitheater of benches where there is only one other person, an old man, she sits down. What follows is an extremely long-take close-up of her face. She starts to cry, neither silently and elegantly nor in a distraught and melodramatic manner, but whining and sniffling. She stops, lights a cigarette, and then cries some more.

Each time I watch all that misery in *Vive L'Amour* I find myself suffused with a strange joy. I do not believe this is just *schadenfreude* on my part. Rather, it is a sense of plenitude, similar to that produced by the standard realist film and yet different. How can we understand this difference?

A lonely walk in the park in *Vive L'Amour*.

They Are Alone, We Are With Them

Vive L'Amour is not the only film in which the performance of negative feelings and emotions by the main actors enables or demands the kind of spectatorial relationship I am having trouble describing. Maybe I can give a better sense of the something more that is going on by discussing them, too. During the same period that I was watching *Vive L'Amour*, I was also looking at a number of documentary films from around Asia, among them Byun Young-Joo's *The Murmuring*. Byun is a Korean documentarian and feminist activist. In 1995 she made *The Murmuring* (*Nazn Moksori*, South Korea), about former Korean "comfort women" forced into service by the Japanese Imperial Army during the Second World War. The focus is the continuing struggle of some of these women today. The film dwells on their complaints and their impassioned and often lengthy expression of their grievances. Just as *Vive L'Amour* impels the spectator to attend to the loneliness of its characters in scenes that offer little apparent narrative progression or other amusement, so *The Murmuring* seems to demand we attend to the lengthy lamentations of the former "comfort women" beyond the time needed simply to comprehend their complaints.

A number of other documentaries deal with women, rape and war, or more specifically with the "comfort women." Examples include Helke Sanders' *Liberators Take Liberties* (*Befreier und Befreite*, Germany, 1992), which focuses on the rape of German women by Soviet soldiers at the end of World War II,[12] and *Fifty Years of Silence* (Ned Landers, Australia, 1994), which documents the case of Jan Ruff-Ahern, a Dutch Indonesian former "comfort woman" now living in Australia.[13] The sufferings of most of these women have not been acknowledged until recently, not least because social attitudes in most patriarchal societies mark raped women as defiled.[14] However, now they have come forward, their public performance of their testimony is highly varied. In both *Liberators Take Liberties* and *Fifty Years of Silence*, the Western women are calm and self-controlled in their accounts of their suffering. This forms a contrast to the emotional complaints of the Korean women in *The Murmuring*.[15]

Writing about the 1992 International Public Hearing on Post-War Compensation by Japan held in Tokyo, George Hicks notes a similar phenomenon. Where Ruff-Ahern is controlled, he notes that the Korean and Chinese women are far more emotional, in some cases screaming out their hatred of the Japanese and requiring medical attention.[16] Hicks is clearly more comfortable with Ruff-Ahern, and his account suggests he may think the Chinese and Korean women's performance is manipulative and exaggerated.

Byun Young-Joo's *The Murmuring* also includes long passages in which the women become very emotional. Because Byun has chosen to include this material, I assume she does not find this performance distasteful or believe it will alienate spectators.[17] If so, what sort of spectatorial relationship is this performance of grievance and suffering intended to enable? And why do I find it resonates with my relation to *Vive L'Amour*?

I have found a possible answer in another documentary. *Tolerance for the Dead* (*Mot Coi Tam Linh*, Vietnam/UK, 1994) is by the remarkable

Vietnamese essay filmmaker Tran Van Thuy. In it he details the great care Vietnamese culture demands for the dead, and the revival of such rituals and ceremonies in socialist Vietnam today. The living cannot be at ease unless they are performing their duties of care for their dead kin correctly, and neither can the dead.

After a detailed disquisition on these customs and their place in Vietnamese history and culture, Tran remarks that he had thought this indulgent "tolerance" for the dead was peculiar to Vietnam.[18] However, coming across an American team searching for the remains of MIAs, he has begun to question this assumption. For, as he remarks with fine irony, he is struck by the great efforts the Americans are making to extend proper care to their war dead in comparison to his fellow Vietnamese, many of whom are still too impoverished to search for remains although they are much closer to home.

Two things interest me here. One is the type of "tolerance" Tran describes being extended toward the dead as a kind of attention to the needs of those perceived as having suffered, as having an unresolved grievance that demands indulgence. In the setting aside of certain places for shrines, the establishment of times for observance, and the performance of rituals and ceremonies for tending to their needs, Tran seems to trace a yielding to the dead of a special niche in the land of the living.

I believe *The Murmuring* expects and demands a similar kind of indulgence to be extended to the former "comfort women," so that they can perform their grievances and find them acknowledged in a manner hitherto denied them. And *Vive L'Amour*'s lengthy performances of loneliness beyond narrative requirements also engage the viewer in a similar kind of indulgence of the three main characters.

Another way of looking at this relation would be to think of it as witnessing testimony. In her work on the texts of Holocaust survivors, Shoshana Felman notes that in order in to perform their narratives the survivors require witnesses: "many of these Holocaust survivors in fact narrate their story *in its entirety* for the first time in their lives, awoken to their memories and to their past . . . by the presence and involvement of the interviewers, who enable them for the first time to believe that it is possible, indeed, against all the odds and against their experience, to tell the story and *be heard.*"[19]

Second, I am interested in the way in which Tran himself yields on the question of cultural specificity, allowing that a concept he thought was specifically Vietnamese may be used to describe an American activity, even though Americans themselves may not be conscious of this. I would also like to resist any cultural essentialism in my search for a concept to describe this activity. The concept I would like to adopt is *amaeru*, translated as "indulgence" in English. The Japanese psychoanalyst Takeo Doi uses *amae* to describe a passive desire for indulgence. He finds it difficult to locate a Freudian term for this desire to be indulged and tolerated, although I understand it to be taken for granted in Japanese culture. *Amaeru* is the verb denoting the activity of the person who indulges or makes a space for *amae*.[20]

Peter Dale has included Doi's *amae* in his critique of *nihonjinron*, the pseudo-academic studies that attempt to demonstrate Japanese uniqueness and work from essentialist, racist and nationalistic assumptions. Dale argues that *amae* is, in fact, a pseudo-concept no different from primary narcissism.[21] It is also easy to understand why he believes Doi's work fits such a position, not least because Doi himself describes the genesis of his ideas as occurring while he was overcome with a sense of his own cultural difference during his first visit to the United States.[22] However, two qualifications should also be noted. First, Doi acknowledges that *amae* is similar in structure to narcissism, or what Balint describes as "passive love," but also that *amae* is seen as a positive quality in Japan, whereas narcissism is seen as negative and regressive in Freudian psychoanalysis.[23] In other words, Doi argues that it is not the structure that is unique to Japan, but the positive evaluation and common social acknowledgment of it. This is indicated in his observation that although he found it in American patients, few American doctors seemed to notice it; it is also in later editions of his work, in discussions of *amae* in Western culture in a section called "*Amae* Reconsidered."[24]

In my own case, I am not adopting "indulgence" to claim there is some underlying essential "Eastern" Buddhist, Taoist and/or Confucian continuum linking *The Murmuring*, *Vive L'Amour* and *Tolerance For the Dead*. Rather, the sense of indulgence invoked by the performance of grievance, loneliness, and other negative, unresolved difficulties in these films is another spectatorial position in realist cinema. If it is to be seen as a form of desire in its own right, it is not the desire to be indulged, but the desire to be needed for the purpose of indulgence. This indulgence and performance of *amae* and *amaeru* is something people create by working together or seeming to work together. This is why I say this is where the love is in *Vive L'Amour*, or at least the love effect.

We Are With Them, They Are Still Alone

The operations of this indulgent structure are relatively straightforward in *The Murmuring*, and comparable to the testifying and witnessing Felman describes in her work with Holocaust spectators, or the acting out of unacknowledged loss that Butler speaks about in the quotation at the opening of this article. In the case of *Vive L'Amour* the effect of indulgence is more paradoxical and begs a few more questions. The characters are alone and never acknowledge the presence of a camera, so there seems to be little demand for indulgence on their part. A different kind of indulgence is required here, one that helps to sustain a paradoxical sense of simultaneous presence and absence on the part of the spectator. In this particular hyperbolic case, then, what is being simultaneously exposed and persisted in is loneliness itself. Loneliness and the condition of being alone are necessarily normally invisible to others, so it is only by performing this hyperbolic and paradoxical realism that the loneliness can be exposed and yet persisted in in such a way as to give the audience access to it.

However, if Butler is right that performance is linked to unacknowledged loss, this then begs the question of what is at stake in acting out loneliness in *Vive L'Amour*. In her discussion of drag Butler argues that it does not just expose the general foreclosure on different gender possibilities that all of us experience, but that it is more socially specific: "drag exposes or allegorizes the mundane psychic and performative practices by which heterosexualized genders form themselves through the renunciation of the *possibility* of homosexuality, a foreclosure that produces a field of heterosexual objects at the same time that it produces a domain of those whom it would be impossible to love."[25]

In terms of differentiated social roles and power, what does the performance of loneliness expose and allegorize in *Vive L'Amour*? On one level any alienated urban spectator can empathize with the general loneliness. The loneliness of all three characters is the product of modern living and the chase for a middle-class standard of living in the consumer economy. On another level the loneliness is quite specific. For, as Chang Ta-Ch'un notes in his essay on the film, what the three characters also lack is something considered especially important in Taiwan and Chinese culture: family.[26] Significantly, the Chinese term for family, home and dwelling is the same, *chia*, implying that one cannot really have a home without a family. It is this that provides a larger metaphorical significance to the three characters' professional circumstances and their loneliness. Taipei's speculative building boom has created a glut of empty luxury apartments of the type that Mei-Mei sells: homes without a family. Ah Jung's itinerant profession leaves him homeless and, by implication, without family. Hsiao Kang sells homes for the dead. His homeless/family-less condition is also signified by a game his office colleagues play. Somewhat like musical chairs, participants change position when someone calls out that a family member is going to move. Hsiao Kang, who stands silently on the sidelines watching everyone else take part, is, by implication, a man without a home or a family.[27]

Chang Ta-Ch'un reads this lack of family as a sign of social breakdown and perversion. He draws particular attention to what he sees as gender inversion in the film, signified by the fact Mei-Mei is seen out working a lot, whereas Ah Jung and, in particular, Hsiao Kang are seen washing clothes and cooking in the apartment. In contrast, I tend to read Hsiao Kang, Ah Jung, and Mei-Mei as defectors from the traditional family system, although maybe not quite as the self-conscious and deliberate defectors I have described elsewhere, half-jokingly, as "deviationists."[28] There is nothing to suggest that any of them are without family and home because of poverty. Instead, one gets the impression that it is equally likely they have been drawn to this condition and have chosen it.

Of the three, it is most difficult to speculate about the motivations of Ah Jung. Mei-Mei, on the other hand, seems to be part of the growing army of professional young Taiwan women less interested than previous generations in marriage and motherhood. Finally, we are given plenty of material enabling us to interpret Hsiao Kang as a young man gradually coming to terms with his homosexuality: the attempted suicide is followed by a growing interest in Ah Jung; a scene in which he tries on some of the women's clothes Ah Jung is selling; and finally, the morning after he has hidden under the bed on which Ah Jung and Mei-Mei were having sex, a scene in which he tentatively kisses the sleeping Ah Jung on the cheek.

However, as Chang Ta-Ch'un's reaction itself indicates, there is very little acknowledgment in Taiwan society that some people may choose to opt out of the family system. Here again Hsiao Kang's homosexuality, as the most evident character motivation in the film, stands as emblematic of this difficulty. The difficulty of coming out to family in a society where the individual's financial, social and psychological position is so dependent upon family means almost everyone keeps their homosexuality hidden.[29] Similarly, it would be difficult for a daughter explicitly to announce to her family that she has no desire to settle down and become a traditional wife and mother.

If all three characters are understood to be defectors from the traditional family system in a society that permits no space outside that same family system, other than as the space of failure and dereliction, then the performance of their isolation and loneliness, and the sense that it is being indulged, becomes an intervention. For what *Vive L'Amour* achieves is a form of performance that writes the social invisibility of those who are not part of the family system, thus making it visible and acknowledged. And by finding a form that persists in that loneliness, it rewrites realist style differently, avoiding the recuperation of these people into the family system that occurs in films like *The Wedding Banquet* (*Hsi-yen*, Ang Lee, Taiwan, 1992). As such, it also writes sexual non-conformity in Taiwan as not solely a matter of gender and object choice, but also as defined by failure or refusal to participate in existing kinship systems.[30]

8

Generational/Cultural Contradiction and Global Incorporation: Ang Lee's *Eat Drink Man Woman*

Ti Wei

Most existing literature on Ang Lee's early works treats the films in isolation from the film industry and Lee's career, focusing either on his presentation of inter-generational relationships in the Chinese family or the cultural significance of his depiction of the Chinese diaspora.[1] Ma Sheng-mei is among the relative few who discuss the impact of the internationalization of his productions on their content.[2] However, he treats this as a given rather than as a dynamic and negotiated process. This chapter aims to deepen the inquiry into the cultural issues raised by Lee's three earliest films and simultaneously link them to the dynamic trajectory of his career, as it moved from locally to globally oriented production. *Eat Drink Man Woman* is the hinge in this movement. This chapter argues that thematic transformations through his first three films, culminating in *Eat Drink Man Woman*, are closely related to the changing creative conditions under which Lee was working. Furthermore, this shift in his mode of production not only affected the content of his films but also had a significant effect on Taiwan cinema itself.

Today, Lee is perhaps the best known of the "migrant Chinese directors" who worked in Hollywood in the 1990s. Among the group, which includes John Woo, Stanley Tong and Tsui Hark, Lee is the only director from Taiwan.[3] In 1984, after graduating from New York University with a degree in film directing, he remained in New York and looked for film-making opportunities. In 1990 two of his screenplays won awards in Taiwan, and the major Taiwan film company Central Motion Picture Corporation (CMPC) financed the filming of *Pushing Hands*, which was produced entirely in New York.

Lee worked with a newly established independent production company, Good Machine, run by Ted Hope and James Schamus, to realize his debut. It was the international production of *Pushing Hands* — apart from the main characters, most of the crew was American — that helped Ang Lee develop his later career in the American film industry. *Pushing Hands* won the Best Film award at the Asia-Pacific Film Festival and two major awards at the Taipei Golden Horse Awards. A strong performance in the domestic market, which accounted for box-office revenues of NT$36 million, placed it third among Mandarin-language films released in 1991. However, *Pushing Hands* is little known in the West.

Because of its success, Ang Lee received another offer from CMPC to film what would be his second award-winning movie, *The Wedding Banquet* (1993). He continued with the independent film production model used on *Pushing Hands* and achieved even greater success. *The Wedding Banquet* was a box-office hit in its year of release — ranking 99th in the world market and first in the Mandarin-language film market in Taiwan — and won the Berlin International Film Festival's top award, the Golden Bear. Made on a budget of only US$750,000 but enjoying worldwide box-office receipts of US$32 million, *The Wedding Banquet* was the world's most profitable movie that year.[4] His third film, *Eat Drink Man Woman* (1994), was also successful overseas, although its domestic box-office performance did not match that of *The Wedding Banquet*.

Through these three films Ang Lee became the only member of the new generation of Taiwan directors to enjoy both artistic recognition and commercial success. After receiving financing from CMPC for all three, Lee was recruited by Hollywood majors to direct films with Western themes. The first of these, *Sense and Sensibility* (1995), was adapted from English novelist Jane Austen's book of the same name. *The Ice Storm* (1997) and *Ride with the Devil* (1999) both had American settings. With his Western themes, Lee had apparently also moved his career's center of gravity. It was only with the blockbuster martial-arts film *Crouching Tiger, Hidden Dragon* (2000) that he returned to Chinese themes. With the benefit of hindsight, it is clear the first three features are key to exploring his early creative thinking in reference to the changing contexts and conditions of his work.

The Father Trilogy

Ang Lee's first two films deal with encounters between Chinese and American cultures through the lives of Chinese immigrants in the US. This focus on cultural conflict intersects with another important aspect of the contradiction between old and new, and traditional and modern, which is explored through the generation gap between parents and children. As I will demonstrate, this theme runs through all three films, but is particularly salient in *Eat Drink Man Woman*.

In *Pushing Hands* Mr Chu is a Beijing tai chi master who has retired to New York to join his son's family. His son, Alex Chu, has been living in the US for more than ten years. He works as a computer engineer and has an American wife, Martha, and a son, Jeremy. Mr Chu has serious difficulties situating himself in his new environment and in Alex's "hybrid" family. He moves out to live on his own and works as a dishwasher in a Chinatown restaurant. When his boss humiliates him, Mr Chu displays his tai chi skills and police are called to arrest him. However, the incident makes Mr Chu famous, and he organizes a tai chi course at a community school.

The Wedding Banquet is also about a father-son relationship. Wai-tung is a gay Taiwanese immigrant who has become an American citizen, works in New York, and lives with his white American partner, Simon. He hides his sexuality from his parents, Mr and Mrs Gao, who constantly urge him to marry and produce a grandson for them. To avoid hurting his parents' feelings, Wai-tung and Simon decide to arrange a false marriage for Wai-tung with their friend Wei-wei, an illegal immigrant from mainland China. Mr Gao suffers a minor stroke when, unknown to anyone else, he discovers the truth. However, he eventually accepts Simon as his other "son" — or maybe as his "daughter-in-law" — without revealing he knows the secret, and returns to Taiwan with his wife at the end of the film.

In *Eat Drink Man Woman* the central tension is between father and daughter and the setting shifts to Taiwan. Mr Chu is a Chinese master chef in a Taipei five-star hotel. He lives with his three daughters in a large old house in the center of the city. Mr Chu, whose wife died sixteen years ago, falls in love with a young divorced woman, Jin-Rong, who is a friend of and only slightly older than his own eldest daughter, Jia-Jen. He plans to tell everyone about his new love at the regular Sunday family dinner, but is foiled repeatedly because of a series of unexpected announcements by his daughters. Although the sudden marriages of Jia-Jen and his youngest, Jia-Ning, see them leave the family home, Jia-Chien, who works as an airline executive, decides to stay with her father because of her sisters' decisions.

Family dinner as ritual in *Eat Drink Man Woman.*

However, all three are extremely surprised when their father finally announces his plans to sell the old house and move to a new one with Jin-Rong.

The figure of a Chinese father is a key element in all three films. In an interview, Ang Lee admits that his father's profound influence on him was probably the reason for his paternal focus in his first three films. "For me," he says, "the Chinese father is the source of pressure, responsibility, and honor, as well as the cultural incarnation of the old feudal patriarchal society."[5] The fathers in the films represent tradition, while the younger generation represents the modern. This theme is explored most fully in *Eat Drink Man Woman*, which is set in one of the most rapidly changing cities in contemporary Chinese society.

Generational Conflict

In *Eat Drink Man Woman*, the Chu family lives in an old bungalow in the center of modern Taipei City. In contrast to the speeding traffic and tall buildings outside, the space within the house is still, old-fashioned, and somewhat vulnerable. Mr Chu is trying to hold the family together by cooking sumptuous meals. His skill in preparing classic Chinese cuisine, which features prominently in the film, functions as both a representative element of tradition and a spectacle designed to attract Western audiences. This conspicuous mastery of traditional ways, however, becomes steadily less attractive to his daughters — the younger generation — who are more familiar with modern/Western culture.

At the same time, the young also experience intense internal conflicts as they struggle to adjust to the new modern world. Jia-Chien, like Alex in *Pushing Hands* and Wai-tung in *The Wedding Banquet,* embodies the contradiction between Oriental/traditional culture and Western/modern culture. Efforts to find a balance are characterized by suffering, hesitation, and struggle. Jia-Chien is the family member most eager to escape the old house. But after much thought she decides to give up her job in Amsterdam and stay with her father. She feels frustrated in the end, however, when she learns her father intends to sell the old house and marry a young woman, behavior that is hardly traditional. For her, everything is shifting and even the will to balance the new and the old fails eventually. [6]

The films do not set out to judge traditional and modern values, but they do seem to imply that the withering of tradition is unavoidable. If the older generation wants to survive and maintain its relationship with the younger generation, it has no choice but to compromise and adjust. In *Pushing Hands*, Mr Chu chooses to live on his own. Mr Gao accepts his son's true sexuality and returns home in *The Wedding Banquet.* The old family collapses in the face of change in *Eat Drink Man Woman.* Shih Shu-mei takes a different position. She argues that in all three films the resolutions reinforce traditional patriarchy, which is now seen as even more capable of containing challenge and difference, while renewing its validity through flexible negotiations and "well-intentioned" duplicity when necessary.[7] However, I think the situation is a compromise rather than a negotiation.

Diaspora and Cultural Confrontation

Generational conflict is also intimately bound up with cultural tensions, particularly in the first two films. In *Pushing Hands*, Ang Lee sets up a series of events and elements to underline the conflicts between Chinese and Western culture, represented by Mr Chu and Martha. In the opening sequence Mr Chu is shown practicing tai chi in the house in the morning, dressed in his traditional kung fu clothes. Then the camera cuts to Martha, who is using a thoroughly modern device — a computer — to write her novel. Throughout the day, they continue performing different tasks simultaneously but separately: Mr Chu watches Beijing Opera videotapes, smokes, writes calligraphy, and eats rice and fried dishes while Martha types up her work, goes jogging, and eats healthy food like wheat cookies and vegetable salad. They do not talk to each other and the wall dividing the room, shown from outside, implies a barrier between them that cannot be crossed.[8]

In *The Wedding Banquet*, Wai-tung has been living in New York for ten years and could almost pass for a typical New Yorker. Even his homosexuality seems more normal in America than it would in a Chinese society. However, he cannot bring himself to violate the most important Chinese traditional virtue, filial piety, and tries instead to find a way to make his parents happy while maintaining his chosen path. Again, the attempt to find balance fails in the end because his father, Mr Gao, who represents traditional culture, has no choice but to acknowledge the truth and accept his son's relationship with Simon.

The confrontation between Oriental and Western cultures seems devoid of an easy resolution in these two films. Nevertheless, Western culture is always shown as stronger. In *The Wedding Banquet*, after realizing his son's sexuality and relationship, an upset Mr Gao returns to Taiwan with his wife. The film's final scene, showing Mr Gao raising his arms in front of an American security officer at the airport, seems to imply a surrender to the West, the new, and the modern.

The narratives are also about the process of cultural mixing arising from diaspora. Recent writing on diaspora and cultural hybridity has tried to describe the changing cultural conditions of widely spread immigrant groups in the global era. Scholars emphasize the complexity, diversity, and fluidity of immigrant identities.[9] While this discourse celebrates the mixture of cultures, it ignores the unavoidable conflicts among ethnic groups and classes generated by this process and the socio-economic pressures that condition them. The identity formed by the migrant may be hybrid, but the discourse of hybridization cannot properly grasp the complicated process of this cultural encounter that is full of conflict, struggle, and pain arising from concrete socio-economic factors. The hybridity of the diaspora experience is not formed equally from all the cultural elements migrants ever experience. Rather, it is the outcome of struggles among unequally weighted cultural, political, and economic forces.

Ang Lee's own career also demonstrates this reality. After enduring low budgets and poor filmmaking conditions to make the three films discussed for Taiwan's CMPC, he joined the Hollywood production system. Since then he has had access to more resources and attracted much more attention because of Hollywood's tremendous industrial power and comprehensive global distribution system. This is a situation many filmmakers dream of. However, his engagement with the global Chinese community has disappeared with changes in production conditions. Indeed, changes in the main theme and the father figure in *Eat Drink Man Woman*, compared with the previous two films, parallel Ang Lee's own incorporation into the global film-industry system. Understanding the full significance of this shift, however, requires some recent background knowledge of Taiwan's film industry and its relation to the global film market.

Inside and Outside Taiwan's Film Industry

Despite prosperity throughout the 1960s and early 1970s, Taiwan's film industry entered a decline in the late 1970s from which it has never recovered. The film-production sector looked for a way out in the context of having already lost its overseas markets, the increasing domestic popularity of Hong Kong and Hollywood films, and the gradual relaxation of film censorship. Two main avenues were taken, the first of which was to offer more commercial products with plenty of sex and violence. This effort failed because it was no competition for mainstream Hong Kong and Hollywood films.

The alternative was a more artistic approach first attempted by the Kuomintang-owned CMPC, and later followed by some private companies. With the process of democratization and liberalization that had started in Taiwan in the late 1970s, the CMPC was experimenting with a new and more "open" role by placing less emphasis on overt propaganda and more on educational and cultural leadership. In 1982 it came up with the four-episode omnibus film *In Our Time* (*Guangying de Gushi*) directed by four new-generation directors. This is now seen as ushering in Taiwan New Cinema. Taiwan New Cinema films had three widely recognized main characteristics. First, most stories were about past or present Taiwan society, and not set on the Mainland or overseas. Second, the filmmakers were more consciously exploring the possibilities of film form and rejected traditional melodrama formulas. Third, the filmmakers told the story in a polysemic and ambivalent way rather than relying on simplistic and sensational devices. They thus kept a distance from the film audience, inviting them into the experience rather than pushing a message.[10]

These characteristics earned Taiwan New Cinema a reputation for high social and artistic value, but the films also had to contend with the increasingly "Hollywoodized" tastes of mainstream audiences. Viewers gradually lost patience with having to work to "interpret" the movies and, after a few early successes, most Taiwan New Cinema films failed at the box office. The situation was exacerbated by bad-quality films produced by private companies that had jumped on the Taiwan New Cinema bandwagon. Since they were interested for only as long as the films were popular, once the movement began to fail in the marketplace they withdrew as quickly as they had joined in.

The heyday of Taiwan New Cinema production is commonly considered to have ended in 1987. Although its productions (broadly defined) accounted for less than 14 percent of total local film output during the five years from 1982, it had significant consequences for Taiwan cinema.[11] It is widely agreed that the Taiwan New Cinema movement has, as Peggy Chiao puts it, fostered the development of a unique "Taiwanese film culture."[12] Nevertheless, the movement had another more significant, but usually ignored, impact on Taiwan's film industry: it forged a new link between the industry and the contemporary global film market, which I call the internationalization of art film production and consumption.

In the context of the cultural economy of globalization, the stratification of cultural capital and taste according to national societies is being restructured into a global framework. In these global cultural dynamics, along with the global Hollywoodization of the popular cinema market, the elite art-cinema market is also integrating globally. As a consequence, a global system for the production and consumption of art cinema has been shaped gradually. In this global art-cinema system, however, the markets and corporations in advanced capitalist countries — particularly the US, West European countries and Japan — still dominate. For these markets, art films from developing or under-developed societies and with exotic cultural elements are especially attractive and maintain stable market demand.

It is in this context that links have formed gradually between Taiwan New Cinema and the global film market. Indeed, at an early point in the development of the movement, some directors found that attending overseas competitions and selling products at international film festivals was an effective and helpful way to generate revenues that would sustain their creative lives. Two eminent early examples were Hou Hsiao Hsien and Edward Yang (Yang De-Chang). Their films demonstrated that revenues from overseas sales could eclipse box-office takings at home and sometimes push the films into profit. However, the more filmmakers oriented themselves to the international art film market, the farther they distanced themselves from local society and audiences. This tendency contributed much to the further downturn of Taiwan's film industry in the 1990s.[13]

The practice of "internationalizing" production has continued throughout the 1990s to today. There are two main ways for global cultural economic dynamics to incorporate the "energies" of Taiwan art cinema. The first works like a subcontract. An internationally famous director obtains investment from foreign distributors and pre-sells distribution rights (domestic or international) to investors. For example, some Japanese companies have invested regularly in Hou Hsiao Hsien's works since the 1980s and Edward Yang has attracted financing from the US, Japan, and France. Tsai Mingliang, who emerged as one of what Peggy Chiao has called the "New New Wave" directors, also attracted French capital for his latest films.[14]

Ang Lee himself represents the other pattern. Rising at the same time as Tsai Mingliang and others in the "New New Wave," he was positioned in the same way as "regular" art film directors. But his experience of making film in New York and, most importantly, his talent for telling stories in a popular and transcultural way — as shown by the great international market success of *The Wedding Banquet* and *Eat Drink Man Woman* — distinguished him from the others. The Hollywood majors preferred him to work for them directly rather than as a subcontractor. In contrast to other Taiwanese art film directors, Lee was encouraged to make popular or "Hollywood" art films for a much larger international market rather than elite art films for relatively small numbers of international art film fans. This transformation of his career influenced his creative direction, and *Eat Drink Man Woman* is key to revealing this influence.

Chinese Fathers and Global Cultural Production

Despite international co-operation on *Pushing Hands* and *The Wedding Banquet*, both are basically Taiwan-oriented productions. But the international critical and box-office success of *The Wedding Banquet* made Ang Lee a real international figure and his subsequent work, *Eat Drink Man Woman*, a real internationally oriented production. Its budget was also higher. *Eat Drink Man Woman* cost US$1.5 million to make, double *The Wedding Banquet*'s US$750,000, while *Pushing Hands* cost US$480,000. America's Samuel Goldwyn Company bought US distribution rights for US$550,000 before filming. When shooting started in October 1994, revenues from pre-selling distribution rights internationally had already equaled the budget. Lee describes the experience:

Making *Eat Drink Man Woman* was my first experience of the double pressure for artistic achievement and box-office performance. I never thought much about that when I was making *Pushing Hands* and *The Wedding Banquet*. . . . After *The Wedding Banquet* was a hit, distributors from all over the world offered high prices for my films. The international market model for my works was formed: the "mainstream popular market" in Taiwan and Asia plus the "art house cinema" in the US and Europe. . . . I began to think much more about the taste of the global art film market. . . . Therefore I found myself caught between the Chinese and the Western.[15]

The writing process demonstrates the necessary adjustment to the new market situation. Unlike the first two films, which were written by Ang Lee alone, *Eat Drink Man Woman* was the collaborative work of Lee, female Taiwanese writer Wang Hueling, and Good Machine's James Schamus. The narrative was a product of negotiations between Taiwanese/Chinese and Western cultural and market considerations. James Schamus was particularly influential in composing key plot elements and dialog because "he knows the Western audience's taste." For example, the loss and return of the father's sense of taste to imply the suppression and liberation of his desire and emotion was Schamus's suggestion.[16]

The first adjustment made in comparison with the previous two films, according to Ang Lee, was to refresh the pattern by changing the father-son relationship theme to a father-daughter relationship.[17] The change is essential and closely related to the gradually weakening father figure across the three films. The father in *Pushing Hands* is the strongest and most powerful. In contrast, the father in *The Wedding Banquet*, a retired general, displays many symptoms of aging and is sent to a hospital emergency room on one occasion. In *Eat Drink Man Woman* the father has no son and pursues his second love like a regular emotional human being, erasing the image of the authoritarian and solemn Chinese father. What Lee and Schamus aimed for was a reversal: the children disappointed their father in the first two films, but in *Eat Drink Man Woman* he disappoints them.[18]

Interestingly, the film was set entirely in Taipei, rather than in New York, as in the previous two films. The consistent theme of generational conflict remains, but the site of cultural confrontation has moved from the migrant community to local Chinese society. The diaspora experience represented in the film concerns the "Mainlanders" who went to Taiwan with the KMT from mainland China in the late 1940s rather than Chinese migrants in the US. This issue can be seen in the conversation between the hotel manager and Mr Chu when he decides to retire. He explains to the manager, who wants him to stay, the unavoidable transformation in "authentic" traditional Chinese food and by implication culture:

> *Manager:* Please reconsider it, Master Chu. The hotel needs you.
> *Mr Chu [sighing]:* There are many young chefs. You can easily find a successor.
> *Manager:* But a chef like you, who is good at Sichuan, Yangzhou, Chaozhou, and Zhejiang cuisine, is hard to find these days. . . . Your whole life has been devoted to this; it is a real waste if you retire.
> *Mr Chu [sighing again]:* People have become so vulgar. Who eats in a refined way today? Forty years after coming to Taiwan, mainland Chinese cuisine has merged with cuisine from everywhere like various rivers running into the sea. Everything tastes the same. Even slops can be passed off for "Joy Luck Dragon Phoenix."[19] What more can I say?

The change is significant. In the first two films, the Chinese immigrants are agents — albeit relatively weak ones — actively engaged in intense struggles to adjust to an alien culture and society. In contrast, when the cultural contradiction takes place between different Chinese ethnic groups, and cuisine rather than real social pressures is the bearer of the contradiction, the Chinese people in the film become more like objects laid out for our gaze. As Sheng-mei Ma puts it, "The trilogy reveals an increasing propensity toward exotic travel in search of the Other rather than nostalgic lamentation over the loss of the Self."[20]

On the one hand, these changes concerning the father figure and the main theme are Ang Lee's personal attempt to liberate the Chinese father as well as himself from traditional ethical constraints. On the other hand, they also seem to reflect the shift from primarily Taiwan-oriented to globally framed productions, as his career's center of gravity moved from his homeland in Taiwan to the US and the West. However, the substantial change in the father figure in *Eat Drink Man Woman* and in its mode of production resulted in paradoxical outcomes. The film was popular in American and European film markets. It won the Best Foreign Language Film award from the National Board of Review (US) and was nominated in the same category for Oscar, Golden Globe and BAFTA awards. Its gross revenues in the US were US$7,294,000, surpassing *The Wedding Banquet*'s US$6,933,000.[21] Yet, in comparison with *The Wedding Banquet*'s NT$120 million box-office takings in Taipei, *Eat Drink Man Woman* earned a mere NT$50 million and did not win a single Golden Horse award. As Lee recalls, it also attracted negative criticism that the film did not represent contemporary Taipei appropriately.[22]

To this day, Ang Lee finds it difficult to explain the popularity among international viewers of *Eat Drink Man Woman*, which found little favor among many Taiwanese critics. "I was confused. I did not know how the film would look," he says. "I couldn't taste it. . . . I couldn't even smell it."[23] However, he also says that financial support from overseas markets has guaranteed him more creative autonomy.[24] These contradictory statements seem to highlight his considerable difficulty in balancing the "global" and the "local." Not surprisingly, as a committed filmmaker, Lee moved toward the side that could offer more resources. The budget for his next film, *Sense and Sensibility*, financed and produced by the Hollywood major Columbia, was ten times that of *Eat Drink Man Woman*.[25] As a result, although the global film industry gained a new and popular talent, Taiwan lost a filmmaker who was seriously exploring the problems of contemporary Chinese cultures and local society.

9

On Tsai Mingliang's *The River*

Gina Marchetti

If I go back into my own family experience, I was really scared of my father as a child because he was a very hard person. . . . The very interesting thing is that when my father retired I discovered a person who had become very fragile after being so tough throughout the rest of his life. That was how I found out he had always worn a mask. . . . We found that he cried quite easily, and seeing him like that made him into someone hard to accept, almost as fragile as a woman.

—Interview with Tsai Mingliang[1]

Although Asian (and specifically Chinese) males have been coded by a racist, Hollywood-dominated, and Orientalist cinema as "queer" — outside the norms of white heterosexuality — for more than a century, and Chinese films as early as the silent era dealt implicitly with homosexuality, Ang Lee's *The Wedding Banquet* (1993) opened a transnational discourse involving issues to do with Chinese culture, nationality, ethnicity, and homosexuality at a time when the political concerns of gay, lesbian, bisexual, and trans-gendered individuals were emerging as part of an international queer cinema.[2] The issues broached in Lee's film resonated throughout "Greater China," the transnational cultural realm inhabited by the ethnic Chinese globally. Films emerged from Singapore, Canada, the United States, Europe, Hong Kong, and Taiwan, as well as mainland China, that brought to international attention the place of a Chinese queer sensibility within global cinema culture.[3] Indeed, a dialectic materialized in Chinese cinema involving queer issues and gay characters that oscillated between the use of homosexuality as a metaphor for various crises of identity involving the Chinese globally (e.g., Chen Kaige's *Farewell My Concubine*, 1993; Zhang Yuan's *East Palace West Palace*, 1997; and Wong Kar-wai's *Happy Together*, 1997) and films that dealt more directly with homophobia in the Chinese-speaking world and gay rights in Chinese communities (e.g., Shu Kei's *A Queer Story*, 1996).

Within this dialectic, Tsai Mingliang has emerged as a filmmaker whose oeuvre contains this contradiction. Tsai's feature films, *Rebels of the Neon God* (1992), *Vive L'Amour* (1994), *The River* (1996), *The Hole* (1998), and *What Time Is It There?* (2001), deal with the margins of contemporary Taiwan society and the decay (often very physical) of that world. *The River* stands out among Tsai's films for its strikingly direct treatment of homosexual angst personified by a father and son so alienated from themselves and each other that they end up having anonymous sex with each other in a bathhouse. Although the son bending over to be screwed by the father has been read metaphorically as a tacit reference to the PRC's relationship with Taiwan[4] at a time of increased political friction between the "two Chinas,"[5] the scene also resonates with issues that are a staple in international queer cinema; the pain of coming out, the invisibility and suppression of gay history, generation gaps within the gay community, and so on. This study looks at *The River* within the context of global Chinese cinema as it intersects with international queer cinema in order to explore this double articulation of issues of concern to those inside and outside the Chinese diaspora, the Chinese gay community, and the audience for international queer cinema more generally.

Tsai Mingliang was born in Malaysia in 1957. It must be kept in mind that Southeast Asia (what the Chinese call the "*Nanyang*") has a large Chinese population, with generations of ethnic Chinese making their homes there — some as sojourners, others as settlers. These "Overseas Chinese" have been wealthy merchants, colonial compradors, skilled laborers, and unskilled "coolies" (a word derived from "*kuli*" or "bitter labor" in Chinese). Many diasporic Chinese, like Tsai, come from families of "multiple" immigrants who often move for political, economic, or personal reasons from point to point within Greater China's cultural sphere. Polyglot and adaptable to a range of cross-cultural situations, many, like Tsai, bring the role of the outside observer into circumstances in which they are both "at home" as ethnic Chinese and "foreign" as members of the overseas community. Tsai, for example, experienced the process of decolonization and nation building in Southeast Asia in his youth, and he moved to Taiwan in 1977 to study drama. After working in theater and television in Taiwan, he made his first feature film there, *Rebels of the Neon God*, in 1992. He went on to direct *Vive L'Amour* in 1994 and *The River* two years later. Because all three films feature the same lead actor, Lee Kang-sheng, playing the same character, Hsiao Kang, with the same actress and actor playing his parents in *Rebels of the Neon God* and *The River*, the films have been regarded as a trilogy about the postmodern condition in Taipei, where modernity in all its forms seems to be falling apart just as leaky plumbing ruins any dreams of economic prosperity and progress. Although he seldom deals directly with the political dynamics of being gay in Asia, Tsai was among the first to address the AIDS crisis in Taiwan: in his television documentary *My New Friends* (1995) he speaks frankly with two gay, HIV-positive men.

Tsai Mingliang is associated with the "second phase" of Taiwan's New Cinema and, thus, his works are part of an international circuit of art films as well as a self-conscious push on the part of the KMT party to maintain its claim to cultural legitimacy within Greater China through its production company, Central Motion Picture Corporation.[6] Indeed, Tsai's visions of urban decay, crisis, and homosexuality are Taiwan government propaganda (at least at a certain fundamental level), and there is an irony — perhaps also a certain amount of justice — in the fact that Malaysian Tsai should become one of the most lauded and funded voices in Taiwan cinema for his queer renderings of Taipei. In fact, in many respects, *The River* falls into the same category as other mass media products of the 1990s that Tze-Lan Deborah Sang has described as "schizophrenic" in their characterization of Chinese gays and lesbians.[7] Although the media cover gay-rights parades, AIDS, and changing sexual mores to appear "liberal," "free," and topical, gay life still appears most often as "abnormal" and "pathological" under the scrutiny of the dominant media. Sang and Chang Hsiao-Hung theorize a profit motive behind the media attention to homosexuality. As in the West, the media in Taiwan attempt to draw in the queer consumer by "normalizing" homosexuality and making it more visible, while simultaneously maintaining a Confucian status quo by viewing homosexuality as a deviation from the norm.

In many respects *The River* conforms to this "schizophrenic" depiction of gay life in Taiwan. Remaining veiled in its presentation of gay life in Taipei, the film places its focus on the family. Other gay men, detailed delineation of life in the gay saunas, or any mention of the vociferous political groups agitating for gay, lesbian, bi-, and trans-gendered rights on the island remain outside the purview of the film. In fact, Taipei boasts a large gay community that has benefited enormously from the general cultural and political thaw Taiwan has experienced since the lifting of martial law in 1987.

Chang Hsiao-Hung describes what has come to be known as the *"tongzhi"* (*"t'ung chih"* in the Wade-Giles romanization system) movement as follows:

> Following the women's movement, labor movement, and aborigines' movement, the *t'ung chih* movement has gained much visibility in the shifting cultural scenes of Taiwan. The Chinese translation *t'ung chih* (comrade) of the English 'queer' has now come to designate lesbians, gays, and queers at the same time. Originally used to refer to partners who share the same revolutionary passion and ideal, *t'ung chih* is also employed to refer to members of the same political party. . . . Its straight and righteous connotations are now appropriated and queered in the process of translation. What is more, the fact that *t'ung chih* is extensively used as a title in Communist mainland China gives the term a special political edge when it is used in Taiwan.[8]

Originally used as a synonym for "gay" in Hong Kong, *tongzhi* appropriates a reviled term associated with the Communist Party and uses it to challenge the heterosexist status quo in virulently anti-Communist Taiwan.

In many ways it is not surprising that a new term associated with "otherness" (in this case, political otherness) should be transformed in the service of the gay liberation in Taiwan. Just as homosexuality was often associated with "Oriental" vices in the Western imagination, it was linked to Western decadence in many parts of Asia. In fact, when looking at the homophobic preconceptions that often frame Asian thinking about the West as well as the West's Orientalism, a striking parallel appears. Within neo-Confucian, anti-colonial rhetoric, homosexuality is often associated with Western debauchery and colonial subjugation. The "rice queen," in this scenario, uses his imperialist power to pervert the morals of Asian youth, who must submit to Western dominance manifested by the colonial pederast/Chinese houseboy dialectic.[9] Western Orientalism, on the other hand, has characterized Asia as essentially feminine — naturally subordinate and masochistic — and Asian men as "queer" by definition. The colonist is blinded by the charms of the "naturally feminine" Chinese and gives into homosexual impulses. In this "going native" scenario the Westerner would never consider a homosexual relationship with another of his race, but gives into the seductive allure of the East embodied by the young Asian gay. Homosexuality is, thus, erased from the history of each culture and displaced onto the Other; the native gay conveniently ceases to exist and he becomes a stranger in his own country. As Chris Berry points out in his essay "Sexual DisOrientations: Homosexual Rights, East Asian Films, and Postmodern Postnationalism": "Homosexuality is a convenient discursive trope — a political conjuring trick made to appear first here, then there according to the needs of the players. However it is manipulated, it is always made abject, always construed as part of the collective other and not as part of the collective self it is deployed to construct and defend."[10]

In *The River*, Hsiao Kang's father is associated with the neo-colonialism of his hang-out, McDonald's, and the colonial past associated with Japanese-style baths, while his son has all the "modern" — read "Western" — attributes of his generation, from tight jeans to motor scooters. Thus, the father-son dialectic in *The River* occupies an ideologically over-determined and contradictory position, with the father representing the PRC, KMT, the imperialist West, and Confucian tradition, and the son embodying Taiwan, the present, and an uncertain future.

The year before the lifting of martial law, *The Outcasts* (Yu Kan-Ping, 1986) broke important ground as the first commercial feature film made in Taiwan to deal openly with gay life. Like *The River*, it looks at young gay men within the context of the family. It attempts to recreate a pseudo-family for gay boys thrown out of their natal homes. However, unlike *The River*, in which an older generation of gay men remains hopelessly alienated from the younger generation of gay "sons," *The Outcasts* attempts to reconstitute the Confucian order by providing a father substitute in the form of an older gay photographer for the homeless gay youths. Although the older man dies at the film's conclusion, Timothy Liu refers to young gays burning incense to their mentor as an attempt to reconcile Confucian precepts with contemporary gay life in Taiwan. He notes: "What *The Outcasts* seems to suggest is the necessity for accepting certain Confucian forms and virtues even if such virtues also form the basis for intolerance."[11]

The River's focus is also quite Confucian, since its central concern involves the relationship of a father and his son, the most vital relationship within the Chinese patriarchy that serves as a model for all other political and social relationships in traditional Chinese society. Just as the son submits to the father, the subject submits to the emperor, the servant to the master, the wife to her husband, and so on. Any corruption of that relationship bodes ill for the entire society, and the disrupting influences of homosexual and incestuous contact in *The River* speak to a social critique outside the confines of the individual and dysfunctional household at the heart of the narrative.

Although they share a domicile, *The River*'s nuclear family communicates minimally and barely recognizes the blood ties that bind them together. As Jonathan Rosenbaum[12] and Bérénice Reynaud[13] have pointed out, the film does not reveal that the father, mother, and son are related until fairly late in the narrative. *The River*'s focus on a GenerAsian X/Generation Q[14] gay man and his gay father places queer Chinese issues within a dramatically new context and highlights many problems within the Chinese diaspora that had heretofore received scant attention. Thus, Tsai moves between allegorizing contemporary Taiwan and the Chinese diaspora and directly looking at the pains and pleasures of gay life in present-day Taipei.

Reading *The River*

In many respects *The River* has a great deal of affinity with the New Queer Cinema as a narrative feature that takes gay life as a given, without apologies or explanations for a straight audience. However, just as it is disingenuous to say that a film like *Happy Together* could have been as easily about a heterosexual couple or that the obsessive relationship in *Farewell My Concubine* could have revolved around a heterosexual love triangle, *The River* should not be dismissed too easily as "post-" queer because it does, indeed, revolve around a closeted older gay man and a younger man searching for his sexual identity within Taipei's gay subculture of cruising and bathhouses.

Before reading *The River* as a statement on gay life in Greater China, it may be useful to look at it more closely as a metaphor for the postmodern condition generally and as an allegory for Taiwan as a political entity. Although associated with sexuality, *yin*/femininity, and the sex industry in Chinese thought, water, an important destructive and unifying element in all of Tsai's films, also evokes a more specifically ethnic incarnation of the flow of the Chinese "life force" in *The River*. Thus, the title of the film itself conjures the "pure" ethnic roots of the Han Chinese in the Yellow River valley, with its transmutation into the polluted Tanshui River as a sign of the decline of civilization generally and Chinese society specifically. The water offers less of a hope for renewal through flow and movement and more of a promise of destruction through either stagnation or flooding. Although Taipei's shopping malls, department-store exteriors, hotel rooms, and other transnational commercial spaces like McDonald's restaurants offer the concretization of a modernist dream of uniform material prosperity and capitalist bliss, the "heart" of Taipei, as represented by the apartments inhabited by most of the city's population, is in ruin. Demolished buildings, construction debris, and industrial trash mar the landscape, and the family home is not only cramped and drab but also plagued by substandard plumbing. After calling in a repairman and knocking at the door of the upstairs flat assumed to be the source of the leak, Hsiao Kang's father has so little hope of eliminating the problem that he scavenges for bits of discarded roofing and PVC pipe to redirect the water he sees as an unavoidable intrusion into his bedroom. As the water threatens to wash away the home, the dysfunctional family itself serves as a metaphor for a more general social crisis involving the decline of interpersonal communication, the atomization of the individual, the isolation of the nuclear family, the malaise associated with what Herbert Marcuse has called "repressive desublimation"[15] of sexuality, and a host of other ills linked to the uncertainty of living in a contemporary metropolis like Taipei, or, more specifically, within a powerhouse economic entity like Taiwan that has next to no "official" political standing in the world polity.

Since the normalization of the relationship between the United States and the PRC, and American recognition of a "single" China under the leadership of Beijing, most countries in the world have followed suit and denied earlier Cold War claims for the recognition of Taipei as the temporary capital of "China" and even earlier promises of Taiwanese sovereignty after the expulsion of the Japanese following the Pacific War. Although Taiwan is recognized as a separate economic entity by the WTO and America has a range of military obligations and pseudo-diplomatic ties with Taiwan, the island has had enormous difficulties navigating the very tricky path between calling for independence from China and agreeing to eventual unification under a plan similar to Hong Kong's or Macau's. With the decline of the KMT's political clout since the end of martial law in 1987, the situation has become more urgent as the public sphere has opened to a greater range of political expression and the threat of invasion by the PRC if the independence movement should gain too much power. Within this maelstrom of political change, with the first direct public elections of the president in 1996 and precipitous economic downturn in 1997, *The River*'s threat to flood not only the Lee household but all of Taipei with its putrid, polluted water takes on another allegorical layer.

Although Hsiao Kang's mother finally locates the source of the apartment's irksome water and the spigot is turned off, the pressure on the island of Taiwan, represented by its "everyman" city flat, may be more difficult to locate and eliminate. Does the water come from Taiwan's Yellow River roots and hence the Mainland, or does the source of the water come from the modern plumbing associated with its global commercial, industrial, and military connections with America, Europe, and the rest of Asia? Does the water spring internally from the corruption of Taiwan's own government and domestic society or is the pressure from the outside? To put it simply, what is causing Hsiao Kang's pain in the neck, and, if Hsiao Kang represents the younger generation and the future of the island, what is causing Taiwan's malaise? Looking at *The River* as a political allegory, it comes as no surprise that no one asks about the cause of Hsiao Kang's condition, because everyone already knows and no one wants to admit it.

When looked at in this way, the allegorical significance of Hsiao Kang's relationship to his father (Miao Tien) becomes less obscure. Even though Tsai may have less of a stake in Taiwanese politics because of his Malaysian roots, working in Taiwan for a significant part of his adult life, the director has become a keen observer of the types of people who inhabit the island. Although, in some sense, Hsiao Kang's father could be any older Chinese man representing the vestiges of a hypocritical, failed Confucianism anywhere in the Greater Chinese world, he is specifically a Mandarin-speaking Taipei resident with an implicit history associated with his status as such. Thus, while it is logical to look at the father as the bigger, older Mainland lusting after the younger and smaller, but more agile, youthful, promising, and potentially prosperous Taiwan, it also makes sense to look at the father as representing the Mainland in another way. The father serves as an emblem of his generation — a member of the KMT forces that took over the island when the Mainland fell to/was liberated by Mao Zedong in 1949. As one of Chiang Kai-shek's soldiers, he is tainted not only by the corruption associated with the KMT and its lucrative but sometimes nefarious dealings with the United States and the West, but also by his absolute failure to fulfill the Confucian patriarchal dream of a stable family as the foundation for a stable nation. He is the bottom rung in a chain of command that failed from the top to re-conquer the Mainland, and he has certainly also lost control of his domicile, from the leaking walls to the cheating wife to the drifting son. He literally pissed his life away, as is manifest in a sequence that shows him taking a very long leak in the toilet. From this perspective, the father's homosexuality serves as narrative motivation for his lack of commitment to his son, his family, and, by extension, Taiwan and the island's future. As Jean-Pierre Rehm notes, Tsai Mingliang's world has "no fatherland."[16]

When confronted with his son's illness the old man tries to play the part of the dutiful father, but his sexual orientation works against him and he literally ends up screwing the object of his "good" — patriarchal and Confucian — intentions. The relationship is doomed from the start, and several bleakly comic moments highlight the pitiful absurdity of the father's attempt to fix what is ailing his son. When he sees that Hsiao Kang cannot safely ride his motor scooter without someone to support his spastic neck, the father gets on the back and supports his son's head as he drives. Although the family never eats together in their flat, the father still attempts to ensure Hsiao Kang eats properly by ordering congee from a street stall. Unfortunately, more congee is spilled on the table than enters the young man's stomach because the spasms in his neck prevent him from feeding himself efficiently. Although the two barely speak, the father takes his son to a string of doctors and, eventually, takes him out of town to a temple specializing in spiritual cures. Even after their sexual encounter the father still sleeps beside his son in their hotel room and keeps trying for the elusive cure. The struggle to connect and to endure is both absurd and poignant, and it seems to fit with the cultural climate of contemporary Taiwan struggling to connect with its own citizenry, find acceptance globally, prosper materially, and endure physically.

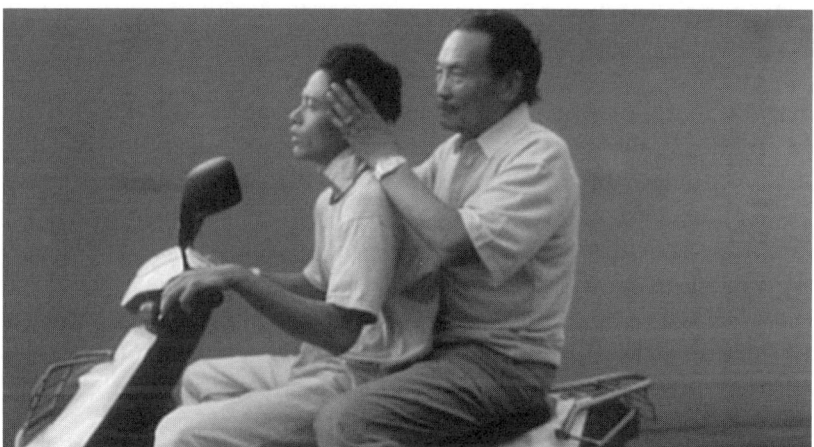

Feeling the pain: Father supports son's neck on the motor scooter in *The River*.

However, although Hsiao Kang's father is the one most literally on his back and screwing him, the young protagonist has other pressures on him that also have a metaphorical significance. Like Taiwan, Hsiao Kang drifts among various influences and often suffers as a result. The film begins with an image of an empty escalator in front of a department store. Hsiao Kang is going up and a young woman (Chen Shiang-chyi) goes down. She recognizes him, and he goes against the movement of the stairs to meet her. He says he is "just hanging around." This seems to describe his existence succinctly: he is going nowhere fast, swimming against the current, drifting, and with little sense of a fixed purpose or identity.

The girl takes Kang-sheng to a movie set where she has a job. Hong Kong filmmaker Ann Hui plays the director on the set. Hui is an appropriate choice for several reasons: she is a recognized and recognizable figure throughout Greater China, with a string of critical and commercial successes, including *Boat People* (1982), *Song of the Exile* (1990), and *Summer Snow* (1994), in which she made a cameo appearance. The appearance of Hui, who was born in Manchuria, educated in Hong Kong and London, and who has been associated with a string of international co-productions, many of which had their post-production in Taiwan to take advantage of its competitive and government-subsidized facilities, takes *The River* beyond Taiwan's borders (however porous those borders may be). Hui represents Hong Kong, but also the diaspora, and a different transnational positioning of *The River* as a metaphor for a drifting Chinese as well as a problematic Taiwanese identity. On the set, Hui has been having trouble with "authenticity," which is something that resonates more generally as an issue within the diaspora. As people move farther from China physically, they are still expected to be "Chinese" — to perform "Chinese-ness" convincingly — while also assimilating into a specific national/ local society and a competitive transnational labor market.[17] Essential identities and authentic ethnicities become problematic, while immigration restrictions, racist violence, and exilic disquiet plague those bodies marked by racial difference.

Using a dummy, Hui cannot capture a convincing image of a dead body on film, and Hsiao Kang (Taiwan), unsuspectingly munching from one of the Styrofoam box lunches found on Chinese movie sets, and already dressed in the funereal white suitable for the occasion, according to Chinese custom,[18] gives Hui both her dummy and her corpse. If his father or his dysfunctional family did not cause his pain in the neck, then the machinations of international capitalism and the desperate drive to create a convincing image of something "authentic" for global screens did. Hsiao Kang excels at being dead, and Hui gets what she needs in a single take, as does Tsai Mingliang, who is known for his long take/long shot, languorous and distant style.

The international image market has exploited Hsiao Kang, and he deteriorates afterward. Given that Tsai Mingliang "discovered" the non-actor Lee Kang-sheng hanging out on the streets of Taipei in much the way Hui "discovers" him for her movie, *The River* seems self-critically to implicate Tsai in this potentially damaging commerce. Maybe the director is the actor's pain in the neck? Here, the shift may be from political allegory to a self-reflexive metaphor for the narrative filmmaking process as explored by New Wave cinema at a postmodern remove from its original articulation. After all, Tsai, with his alienating *plans sequence*, works within the same tradition as his older Taiwan New Cinema counterparts, Edward Yang and Hou Hsiao Hsien. With Yang, in particular, Tsai shares a vision of Taipei as a city of boxes, closing in on their inhabitants, who have little possibility of escape from the untenable situation of contemporary Taiwan society.[19]

In addition, Tsai has a campy sense of taste and humor. This self-reflexive twist, derivative long take/long shot style, and sense of irony and the absurd, as well as the peculiar roles his characters embody — for example, a corpse — bring him closer to some of the key characteristics associated with New Queer Cinema. These are manifested in a camp sensibility based on theatricality, irony, humor, and mock seriousness that has its roots in the experiences of closeted gay men who must "perform" as straight men, be perfectly serious, but know it is all a sham.[20]

In the final instance, Hsiao Kang's pain in the neck is linked to his sexuality. It manifests itself after he has had sex with the female acquaintance who introduced him to the film business. Passionless and silent sex characterizes all of the erotic encounters in *The River*, and the evacuation of intimacy from intercourse and from the domestic sphere places issues of ethnicity (with patriarchy as the basis of Confucianism for traditional Chinese identity), gender (the mother's domestic duties devolve into bringing takeaway from her service job operating an elevator at a restaurant and cutting up durian on the living room floor), and sexuality (with the shift in Hsiao Kang's sexual orientation and desire) in crisis. Hsiao Kang's mother is par for the course in this respect — she cannot even seem to get sex from her pornographer boyfriend. In her vain attempts to mother her son, she gives him her dildo to use as a neck massager and stinks up the small apartment with the durian she feeds him by hand. A shot of her watching her boyfriend's dirty videos alone in bed while listening to her son using the dildo on his aching neck in the next room underscores her anomie and disassociation from the traditional roles assigned to mother and wife within the Confucian ethos. Durian or no, the Taipei domestic sphere stinks, and the public follows on the private dysfunction.

At this point, a very conservative reading of what appears to be a shockingly radical film surfaces. Rather than reading *The River* as an allegorical critique of Taiwan politics, decaying civil society, and vacuous commercial culture, the symptom can be read as the root of the malaise, and the reconstitution of the patriarchy can be seen as a potential cure. From this perspective, Hsiao Kang's homosexuality is his "disease." This reading parallels the possible meanings inherent in *The River*'s groundbreaking, gay-themed, and government-financed predecessor *The Wedding*

Banquet.[21] In that film, gay sex, misplaced maternal sentiments, and desperate Mainlanders are roped into the service of the perpetuation of the Chinese patriarchy as propagated by a Taiwan-defined Chinese diasporan existence. Both take a darkly comic approach to the maintenance of Taiwan as a distinct entity, the continuation of "Chinese-ness" as conceived of within Confucianism, and the propagation of some form of the Chinese nation. While *The Wedding Banquet* squeaks by with a "happy" ending as the patriarch waits for his grandson, the father's recognition of his son with a slap after they have been sexually intimate in *The River* does not bode well. However, *The River* ends its narrative on an indeterminate note. Even though the traditional Chinese cure promised by the trip to the temple could do no possible good, by the spiritual master's own admission, Hsiao Kang opens the hotel curtains to face a sunny day. Although it may be that he has picked a good day to jump out the window, it is difficult to say with any certainty that Hsiao Kang will, indeed, reprise the role of corpse assigned to him at the film's opening. Taking a conservative approach, looking at the ending as bleak or sunny does not really matter. The point that Taiwan's present decay is rooted in the dysfunction of the traditional family has been made.

Is There Still Something Queer Here?

When looking at *The River* as allegory, gay life becomes a metaphor for Taiwan, Greater China, and the postmodern condition generally. The father's homosexuality can be read as a sign of a decadent patriarchy and political vulnerability. Hsiao Kang can be seen as an emblem of shifting identities, loss of essence, and a questionable future. Cruising, then, becomes a metaphor for the rootlessness, anonymity, purposelessness, decadence, and lack of affect associated with postmodern Taipei, and the bathhouse serves as the dark version of the agora in which homosexuals can shop around for sex partners. However, this allegorical interpretation can potentially obfuscate reading the film as queer and concretely about the lives of gay men in the specific locale of Taipei. In "Happy Alone? Sad Young Men in East Asian Gay Cinema," Chris Berry poses the question succinctly: "Maybe it is possible to see how it [the sad gay man trope] might appeal to spectators who are not gay, lesbian or queer because of its symbolic functions as a local or even generational metaphor for alienation and a figure of the times. But how much help is it to the gay, lesbian or queer spectator to have become a sort of image of existential anomie for straight people?"[22]

Is it possible to read *The River*, as many in the local and international audience for the New Queer Cinema will desire to read it, as about gay men generally, and, more specifically, about homosexuality in contemporary Chinese culture? From this perspective, even though Tsai Mingliang has claimed his own neck pain inspired the malady portrayed in the film, Hsiao Kang's mysterious pain in the neck still bears a striking similarity to AIDS as a disease of unknown origin that devastates the young. Given Hsiao Kang's sexual encounter before the appearance of symptoms, sexual transmission seems a likely possibility. A cut between Hsiao Kang's encounter with his lover in the hotel room and his father's encounter with a lover in the bathhouse links heterosexual and homosexual intercourse early in the film as the two dark rooms with sparse key lights on semi-nude bodies pair the two spaces visually, creating a narrative parallel between the father's and the son's sexuality.

The litany of painful treatments Hsiao Kang undergoes (from traditional Chinese treatments like *tui na* [Chinese "chiropractic" medicine], acupressure, and acupuncture to Western injections and spiritual healing) mirrors the desperate attempts by many AIDS victims to seek relief for their incurable disease. Hsiao Kang is so drastically transformed by his disease that his parents fail to recognize the twitching man with a shaved head in a hospital gown as their son, and they rush by him sitting in an empty hospital corner without realizing who he is. The disease has effectively effaced Hsiao Kang's identity, just as many AIDS/HIV positive people say that the disease becomes their identity, and Hsiao Kang breaks down in hysterical tears.

Viewers must fill in the blanks that link Hsiao Kang's disease with his homosexuality. Finally unable to ride his scooter, Hsiao Kang finds himself covering the same ground on foot as an anonymous gay man (Chen Chao-Jung),[23] who has just cruised his father. Hsiao Kang walks into the entrance hall of the same Taipei bathhouse frequented by his father, and it seems inevitable the two will eventually connect in one of the dark bathhouse rooms. They both dare to open the closet door, but they are blind to what exists inside because the son never expects to find his father and vice versa. From this perspective *The River* can be seen as an indictment of the relegation of homosexual desire to the shadows. Hsiao Kang and his father, unable to communicate and representing tremendous generational differences, find themselves sequestered on the margins of heterosexual society. The bathhouse provides no public forum for the celebration of homosexual desire and queer identity; rather, the individual rooms, furtive sexual encounters, and silence speak to the isolation of Taiwan gays robbed of a voice and of a place to be "out of the closet." The father's slap can be read as a wake up call to Chinese gays that the closet cannot continue and that it is time for all homosexuals to come out of their dark cubicles and face the light of day as Hsiao Kang does in *The River*'s closing image.

Queering the Chinese Patriarchy

What is the current importance of queering the Chinese patriarchy? *The River* queers a father, a generation, and, allegorically perhaps, Taiwan and the PRC as well. This cinematic queering of the patriarch serves a number of functions, some contradictory, including a postmodern de-centering of loci of authority, origins, and absolute, phallocentric meaning; an allegory of the Chinese nation as a failed, impotent, or questionable father-figure; a liberatory icon of emancipated sexuality; a chauvinistic icon of ethnic/racial pride; a divided, conflicted, marginal figure who emerges as a corrective to homophobic rhetoric surrounding neo-Confucianism or the emergence of "Asian values"; a corrective to "rice queen" Orientalism and self-deprecation within the Asian gay community; and so on. In any event, the queer patriarch is a slippery figure who also represents the legacy of the closet and centuries of repression.

In the last instance, the queer patriarch represents the transnational/ transcultural dimensions of Greater China. Implicit in *The River* is the idea that the diaspora did not create the queer, but the queer fueled the diaspora. Flexible citizenship resembles national/cultural cruising as queer Chinese nomads wander throughout the Greater Chinese world, from the Mainland to Hong Kong, Taiwan, Canada, California, and beyond. If the assumption is made that Hsiao Kang's father came to Taiwan with the KMT, it can be extended to include the fact that he may not have been unambiguously unhappy about the prospect of being severed from his Mainland roots and the heterosexual expectations they implied. Although his wife and son testify to his ability to satisfy his Confucian obligations, his ability to drift, minimally encumbered by a few sparse possessions in a tiny flat, and freely cruising in metropolitan Taipei, where relative anonymity frees him to pursue sexual gratification in the malls and bathhouses, testifies to the fact that Taiwan exile has its advantages. In other words the history of the Chinese diaspora becomes a queer history of the sexually repressed whose exile or nomadism is over-determined by issues of sexual orientation as well as politics, economics, and other factors. The Chinese patriarch becomes the queer sojourner, and his existence can serve as a critique of nationalism, ethnocentrism, and phallocentrism, as well as homophobia throughout Greater China.

Compulsory Orientalism: Hou Hsiao Hsien's *Flowers of Shanghai*

Nick Kaldis

Our society has begun to offer us the world — now mostly a collection of products of our own making . . . that you can possess visually, and collect the images of.
— Fredric Jameson[1]

To put it another way, this is a paradigm of globalism intertwined with "fin de siecle orientalism" that permeates Western perceptions of Asia.[2]
— Xiaoping Lin

This chapter situates Hou Hsiao Hsien's *Flowers of Shanghai* (1998) within the continuing academic discussions about the "self-orientalizing" and "exoticizing" characteristics of certain Chinese films.[3] Dai Jinhua describes the process this way: "Internalizing the gaze of Western culture, Chinese national culture and national experiences [are] even more profoundly alienated, frozen in the language and representation of the Other."[4] In this vein Dai and others have argued that particular films and/ or their directors are deliberately creating and marketing exoticized representations of China for the gaze of Western viewers, the accolades of Western film critics, and international film-festival judges. These critics endeavor to show how such films reflect "third world cultural dependency on the first world . . . concocting a hybrid cultural commodity for Western consumption . . . actively and consciously seeking identification with the Western cultural hegemony."[5]

I argue that *Flowers of Shanghai* represents a new phase in this purportedly one-sided East-West cinematic exchange, a phase that problematizes the debate from this point on. To situate further my argument within the most recent contributions to these complex inter-cultural, aesthetic-theoretical exchanges, I am proposing the inclusion of *Flowers of Shanghai* as an amendment to Zhang Yingjin's discussion of particular Chinese films that have the potential to "renegotiate with transnational capital, technology, and other forces of globalization" in a cinema "that at once projects and problematizes new boundaries and desires in the era of globalization."[6]

Chu T'ien-wen wrote the screenplay for *Flowers of Shanghai*, based on Zhang Ailing's (Mandarin) translation of Han Bangqing's eponymous 1892 work, a novel that uses Wu dialect in its dialogues.[7] In the film, events are limited to the largely uneventful and subtle interactions between prostitutes, madames, maids and servants, and the rich male patrons of late nineteenth-century Shanghai's upscale whorehouses. Particular attention is given to a few of the men and their favorite prostitutes. Among them, Wang Liansheng (or Wang Laoye, played by Liang Chaowei) can be described as the story's protagonist.

Wang Laoye has been the main customer of Shen Xiaohong for five years. (He is described as Xiaohong's *xianghao* — "boon companion" — a euphemism for one's best regular client, often implying a romantic bond.) He also occasionally visits the quarters of the prostitute Zhang Huizhen, to the great displeasure of Xiaohong. There is little action in the film. The diegetic is centered on the emotional cold war between Wang and Xiaohong. A second storyline involves the prostitute Zhou Shuangzhu's successful purchase of her freedom, after negotiations with her madame (*laobao*). A final, brief addition to these events comes toward the end of the film — the unsuccessful murder-suicide attempt by the prostitute Shuang Yu of her *xianghao*, the young Wu Shaoye. Punctuating these events are four virtually identical banquet scenes.

I believe the pronounced lack of action in the film is intentional because this is definitely not a storyline that hinges on dramatic conflict, progression of narrative events, action of any kind, or plot development. Instead, I would argue, *Flowers of Shanghai* foregrounds above all else the atmosphere, adornments, and settings in which these non-events take place. Briefly stated, I argue that this film constitutes a unique contribution to the debates concerning how certain artistic works are purported to be "representing China for the Western gaze."

We are all familiar with the arguments made by critics such as Zhang Yiwu, Liao Ping-hui, Wang Yichuan, Esther Yau, Dai Jinhua, Dai Qing, Chen

Xiaoming, and others, concerning films like Chen Kaige's *Farewell My Concubine*. These critics have been particularly disparaging of Zhang Yimou and especially his film *Raise the Red Lantern*. Sheldon Hsiao-peng Lu has aptly summarized the characteristics that have facilitated the assault on Zhang's works. The "twin main aspects that underlie Zhang's film art," Lu notes, are "an indigenous cultural critique of the Chinese nation and the creation of what we may call 'transnational Chinese cinema' with the support of transnational capital. . . . His films have attracted a large international audience precisely because they are regarded as authentically 'national,' 'Chinese,' and 'Oriental.'"[8] Zhang Yingjin addresses some of these issues in his penetrating analysis of the "transnational imaginary," considering, among other issues, "whether international audiences are attracted . . . [to] the surfaces of their Orientalist details" (referring to films by Zhang Yimou and others).[9] Thus, the argument goes, "an indigenous cultural critique through the medium of national cinema becomes at the same time a cultural sellout of the Chinese nation in the international film market." Other films and directors may have been accused of similar offenses, but Zhang Yimou has drawn by far the most fire, and "has been taken as an exemplary instance of the willful surrender of Third World cinema to the Orientalist gaze, as a classic case of the subjugation of Third World culture to Western hegemony."[10]

These scholars criticize what they see as a common theme in these and other (especially Fifth Generation) films — a marketing of exoticized images of China for the Orientalizing gaze of Westerners, manipulating images of China to create an "international fantasy" and "pseudo-folklore." This process is variously termed "self-Orientalizing," "selling exotic images of China," "cultural sellout," cultural "exhibitionism," soliciting "'cultural baptism' by the West," humbly submitting cinematic "'article[s] of tribute (*Wenhua gongpin*) . . . showy and stereotypical piece[s] of curiosity (*Minsu qiwen*),'" "international fantasy," and so forth.[11] As Richard James Havis puts it in his discussion of the international marketing of Zhang Yimou films: "[the] strategy focused on objects that could be taken as representative of a Westerner's perception of 'exotic' China . . . to play upon the potential audiences' expectations of a film about China. This involves utilizing clichés of the 'mysterious, exotic East.'"[12]

The critical paradigm discussed above has dominated the academic interpretation and reception of Zhang's films and those of other Chinese directors, although dissenting voices, such as those of Xu Ben and Sheldon Lu, have argued for an alternative way of reading Chinese films in the current era of "global capitalism." Lu posits that "the entrance of Third World cinema such as Zhang's into mainstream Western film culture may indeed begin to make a 'difference.' These films offer alternative histories, stories, and images of nations and peoples that are unseen and unavailable in ordinary Hollywood films. Consequently, Zhang's film art has the potential to become an oppositional practice on the domestic front and an alternative discourse in the international arena."[13]

I would now like to take up Sheldon Lu's challenge to consider how a film like *Flowers of Shanghai* may have this "potential to become an oppositional practice on the domestic front and an alternative discourse in the international arena."

Leaving aside my differences with the majority of critics discussed above, and leaving aside the issue of directorial intention, I believe *Flowers of Shanghai* should be considered as an aesthetic — versus a theoretical — intervention into this one-way transnational commodification of nostalgic, historicized, and exoticized images of China for Western consumption.[14] Furthermore, it intervenes by means of a unique and unprecedented technique that does not arise from an essentialist assertion of China's grand cultural traditions; or from jingoistic narratives of Chinese nationalism; or through the facile attempt to celebrate China's eagerly anticipated emerging position of power in the Global Market; or, finally, from celebration of China's participation in a configuration of "transnational flows," "cosmopolitan public spheres," "postcolonial hybridity," and so on.[15] For, instead of falling into the trap of conservative cultural essentialism, reactionary nationalism, or joyous capitulation to global capitalization, *Flowers of Shanghai* actually *embraces* exotic images of China, multiplies them, reproduces them, and fixates on them, smothering the (Western) viewer in an *excess* of Orientalist fantasy.[16] This protracted over-indulgence of the senses is achieved primarily through the combination of unedited long takes, lack of dramatic action, de-emphasizing of dialogue, and redundancy in the mise-en-scène — including redundancy of scenes and settings, replication of lavish backgrounds, spectacular costumes, and attractive, sexualized (female) characters.

The entire film consists of a series of slow-paced interior shots, all of them long takes, spanning from one minute to eight minutes, the average being about three minutes long. This is very long compared with most Hollywood movies or other art films. This use of uncut, real-time long takes is not in itself a novel technique in a Hou Hsiao Hsien film, as his fans well know. However, this is, as far as I can remember, the first Hou Hsiao Hsien film in which almost nothing of narrative or dramatic significance ever actually happens in any of the long takes. Excepting one pathetic outburst by a solitary Wang Laoye, the only action to speak of takes place in the form of quotidian conversations, preparation of meals and pipes, drinking games at banquets, and subdued negotiations for a prostitute's purchase of her freedom. The non-action that characterizes each scene apparently mimics the slow-paced, leisurely world of the male Chinese elite in late-Qing Shanghai. These long takes, during which the camera laboriously pans back and forth across a room, represent the rhythm of the world for the economically privileged of the day. The upscale brothels are depicted as high-priced, restricted, semi-public spaces that exist for and adjust to the free time and social, sexual, and romantic needs of the Han elite in the nineteenth century.

Everyday life in the upscale brothel: *Flowers of Shanghai.*

However, the same lazy rhythm of the leisured class has an ugly mirror image: the interminable waiting, the stifling physical and financial servitude of the economically underprivileged women kept in these gilded prisons.[17] These women must spring to life, fully made-up and in pristine chambers at whatever hour their male clients choose to appear.[18] Hou Hsiao Hsien shows a mark of brilliance here, for he has taken the most exotic of exoticized images of historical China, the cultivated "high-class" prostitutes (also known as "art prostitutes," or *yiji*), and staged the agonizingly slow and unremarkable quality of their lives. Eschewing the devices of narrative development, conflict, or dramatic action, while favoring the exclusive employment of long takes — thirty-five in total, connected by slow fade-outs and fade-ins — *Flowers of Shanghai* force-feeds the audience several dozen helpings of these prostitutes' excruciatingly redundant lives.

This brings me to the importance of the mise-en-scène in the film, especially the settings and backgrounds. Every scene in *Flowers of Shanghai* takes place within the confines of the various private chambers and banquet rooms of a few upscale brothels in Shanghai's English concession, circa the late Qing dynasty. Much like the prostitute's redundant daily routines, the brothels' interiors are almost identical. As the film progresses, we visit and revisit the same or barely distinguishable brothels, and it becomes increasingly difficult to tell one prostitute's private chambers from another's or one banquet from another. Many of the characters are also hard to tell apart. Yoshimiro Hanno's slow, simple, redundantly droning soundtrack is perfectly matched to the pace and feeling of these lives.[19]

This lack of dramatic conflict or of any other exciting or engaging plot development, combined with the boring redundancy in scenes, causes a shift in audience attention.[20] In shot after shot, as Hou's camera pans slowly across the room, the luxuriant settings and costumes often upstage the dialogue and the characters. With little drama to engage the attention, excite, or anticipate, the audience turns to marveling at the luscious mise-en-scène. The male clients and prostitutes are elegantly dressed in multi-colored and brocaded silk garments, and adorned with bracelets, hairpins, rings, and more. In addition, the women are always immaculately made up, their hair elegantly simple or carefully combed and arranged, matched by the uniform neatness of the men's shaved foreheads and queues. As servants come and go, delivering towels, tea, food, and other items to the central characters, the camera pans leisurely from one person to the next, regardless of who is speaking to whom. That few audiences can understand the mostly Wu dialect conversations further reduces the possibility of viewers becoming interested in the minimalist plot. Žižek has analyzed a similar camera effect and its relationship to the dialogue in Godard's *Contempt* (1963):

> Godard shoots the dialogue . . . in a continuous lateral movement of the camera: instead of the standard shot/reverse-shot procedure, the camera drifts from one character to the other and back again. However, this movement does not simply follow the rhythm of their exchanges in the conversation . . . rather, it follows its own disparate rhythm . . . *its own syntax in counterpoint to the spoken word.*"[21]

But Hou Hsiao Hsien's similar camera syntax in *Flowers of Shanghai*, though somewhat defamiliarizing, does not leave the viewer in referential limbo because the mise-en-scène has been so carefully constructed, arranged, and stocked with familiar chinoiserie. Contra Zïzĕk, the lack of shot/reverse-shot does not always indicate the presence of a threatening "free-floating gaze without a determinate subject to whom it belongs" within the diegetic reality. In *Flowers of Shanghai* the sheer redundancy of this effect gradually assumes a burdensome familiarity, owing mostly to the historical (and, for most audiences, cultural) distance of the events, the lack of variety in the mise-en-scène and dramatic content in the plot, and the boring behavior of the characters.[22] Rather than pointing to or creating a disjuncture between the viewer's visual and aural perception, the slowly panning lateral camera effect leaves the audience un-sutured, emotionally disengaged with the characters' lives, and with ample time to take in every detail of these ornately decorated rooms and banquet halls. The elaborately appointed luxury quarters of the prostitutes take center stage. The spaces in front of, behind, above, and especially between the characters assume an air of importance comparable to that of the characters.

Richard Pena likens the experience of watching *Flowers of Shanghai* to reading a classic Chinese novel, in which "Objects and settings soon supersede these characters . . . [until] one begins to feel the sheer weight of the physical world."[23] For the Western viewer, these adornments are rarities, things that one can only get a hint of today in museums and antique stores.[24] A partial list of the objects found in these rooms includes: stained-glass windows, elaborate wrought ironwork on the staircases, latticework on the windows and doors, Western clocks and candelabras, antique Chinese porcelain vases, jade knick-knacks, elegant wooden tables, chairs, doors, beds, and windows. Finally, there are the ubiquitous tall-stemmed Western gas lamps and Eastern hookahs. The use of low-key lighting displays these objects in muted shades, imparting more the feeling of an opium dream than the "glossiness" of nostalgia-film objects so thoroughly dissected by Frederic Jameson. Nonetheless, the camera performs a similar function in both cases: "the ensemble of jumbled objects — bright flowers, sumptuous interiors, expensively groomed features, period fashions . . . are arranged together as a single object of consumption by the camera lens."[25]

Here and elsewhere, Jameson makes a powerful and convincing case for the interpretation of nostalgic film images as the substitutes for and displacements of an historical past of far more depth and complexity, a past in which these images would have been grounded in a context of unequal social relations, among other things. By contrast, in nostalgic cinematic representation, he argues, such images "have become enfeebled — producing something like a pseudo-past for consumption as compensation and a substitute for . . . that different kind of past[.]"[26] In the case of *Flowers of Shanghai*, however, I would argue that the exponential proliferation, the constant re-appearance/reproduction of such images constitutes an *intervention from within* the very dynamics of cinematic nostalgia and consumption exposed by Jameson. This movie frustrates the viewer's familiar modes of participating in such dynamics, but through a very novel technique. Rather than rejecting the allure of nostalgic cinematic adornment, and rather than seeking an alternative cinematic aesthetic to counter nostalgia and exoticization, this film implodes them. (Contrast this with the criticism that Zhang Yimou's films do not "attempt to resist the Orientalist discourse but rather participate in it. They lend themselves to Western appropriation . . . [through a] willful surrender to the dominant discourse of First-World culture.")[27] As the film progresses, the multiplication and overlapping of nostalgic oriental embellishments, combined with the emotional flatness of the characters, creates a kind of cinematic inertia, a ponderous ball and chain of beauty that drags the narrative down yet militates against the viewer's indulgence in pure pictorial or nostalgic pleasure.

This film, I contend, casts the viewer as a kind of non-participant observer, at first inciting the (Western) viewer's fantasy of (historical) China with visual, museum-like opulence shot mostly at a straight-on angle with the camera maintaining a detached gaze. An important factor contributing to the museum quality of the scenes is Hou's decision to film entirely on sets built in Taiwan rather than on location, as with *all* his previous films. Only within the studio setting could one create such elaborate period reproductions of (one aspect of) the elite lifestyles of a small fragment of Qing-dynasty Chinese culture, a fragment that has nevertheless come to stand for traditional Chinese culture within the (Western) imagination. (The related issue of whether this film somehow allegorically depicts Taiwan, or Taiwan-PRC issues, is a provocative one. I find no evidence in the film and am thus unable to support this interpretation). At first this selective simulacrum of an "authentic" Chinese past, to borrow Zhang Yingjin's apt phrase, "successfully satisf[ies] a demand in the global market by feeding 'self-satisfied tourist fantasies' dominant for decades and still currently prevalent in the West."[28] But as the stultifying redundancy of exotic scenes and settings accumulates and proliferates, the viewer becomes the camera's accomplice, and is implicated as part of this perversely concentrated gaze, obsessively viewing and reviewing the same suffocating, superfluous lives and assemblage of exotica.[29] The audience is repeatedly subjected to almost identical scenes, force-fed until bursting the very delights we have come to the Orient to "taste" — the precious, exotic, refined, and cultural curiosities of a historically distant, unchanging, and non-threatening "China." The result of this process is, for the viewer willing to probe his/her discomfort, the incitement toward doubt, in this case, a skepticism about "the hold over our imagination of such antiquated narrative categories," in Jameson's words.[30]

If, as many of the earlier-mentioned critics have argued, Zhang Yimou and other Chinese directors have marketed exoticized images of an antiquated and palatable pre-modern China for the sake of attracting the attention of a materialistic, acquisitive Western gaze, or to win Western film festival awards and investment dollars, then *Flowers of Shanghai* represents an internal rupture of that process. This film forces us to watch nothing but these kinds of Orientalized images for more than two agonizing hours. Rather than feasting our eyes, leisurely surveying these "timeless" images of China, time begins to drag. Soon, our overexposure to this "China" produces an opposite phenomenon — an opulence ad nauseam that alters our experience of an exotically represented China, turning a titillating historical curiosity into a question about our own culture's desire continually to postpone an authentic engagement with contemporary China in all its complex, unexotic, political and economic immediacy, not to mention its continuing social conflicts concerning matters of gender and sexuality.[31]

This infiltration and subversion of the Orientalizing cinematic mode from within leads us back to a further consideration of the camera style, as it relates to contemporary audience expectations. From start to finish, *Flowers of Shanghai* is composed of long takes separated only by fade-outs and fade-ins (formal blackouts).[32] Otherwise, there is no visible cutting, no use of shot/reverse-shot, and an absence of transition shots. Many of these devices thoroughly frustrate the viewing expectations of Western audiences long accustomed to the clear dramatic tensions, focus on plot, use of montage, and fast-paced action (with soundtrack to match) found in Hollywood-style films. Furthermore, the pace of this film in no way approximates the pace or feeling of dominant popular contemporary cinematic style(s) in either Taiwan or the People's Republic of China. For this reason, I believe the film subverts not only an East-West Orientalist aesthetic, but an intra-Asian "self-Orientalizing" aesthetic as well. In other words, the local audience is equally disoriented by the shooting style and the film's content, a contention supported by its poor box-office performance everywhere. The exotic, opulent, and elitist historical images of China represented in *Flowers of Shanghai* are not accompanied by familiar plotting devices or genres, humorous scenes or dialogue, special effects, a pop-music soundtrack, or other popular devices and themes familiar to Chinese audiences. Neither does one find the type of Hollywood packaging that would help "translate" the film to meet Western or Chinese/Taiwan audience desire and entertainment appeal. Absent are the attendant action, dramatic tension, conflict, sexual titillation, and ritualistic mystification within which similar images are often contextualized in more well-received films by Zhang Yimou, Chen Kaige, and others.[33] Nor are exotic and nostalgic images of traditional (dynastic) China juxtaposed against the violent arrival of political and economic modernity, as in films like *Farewell My Concubine. Flowers of Shanghai* does not indulge in a cinematic symbolic system of mystification and idealization, presupposing some historically unchanging Han ethnic/cultural essence around which nationalistic and/or racial sentiments can rally.

Hershatter points out that rapid, unsettling urban change and the threat of the West led to a "literature of nostalgia" one hundred years ago, one of the goals of which was "to glorify vanishing Chinese cultural practices . . . [a]nd part of that glorification was to explicate meticulously the cultivated and refined social practices of courtesans."[34] Hou Hsiao Hsien translates that "literature of nostalgia" into a cinematic grammar, excising any dramatic content, removing all reference to an exterior context, and recycling barely distinguishable scenes, settings, and characters.[35] As a result, audiences of *Flowers of Shanghai* are overindulged in their taste for images of China that would ordinarily serve to maintain our residual but persistent colonial escapist fantasies — fantasies that would keep "China" hidden away (here, in the Western quarters of Shanghai) and as a quaint, exotic holdout of the past, and a non-threatening, enclosed and isolated other.[36] But without a familiar narrative or contextualizing paradigm, without catharsis, melodrama, seduction and sex, action, conflict, or plot intrigue, we are soon stuffed to the gills with this labored presentation of Orientalist exotica from the colonial era, and then slowly forced to continue eating serving after serving of the same. For these reasons, in debates about Orientalist and self-Orientalizing representations in Chinese cinema, this film constitutes a significant artistic intervention.

11

Another Cinema:
Darkness and Light

Feii Lu

We believe that cinema can be a conscious creative activity, an art form, or even a national cultural activity that is both self-reflexive and possessed of a sense of history. However, we also realize that in most circumstances, cinema is a commercial activity. . . . But another kind of cinema (films with creative ambition, artistic direction, and cultural self-consciousness) may make an even greater contribution to society as a whole. . . . We call for a space outside the commercial cinema for "another cinema"; for this, we sign our names below.

"Taiwan Cinema Manifesto, 1987"[1]

In February 1987 about sixty Taiwan filmmakers and critics proclaimed the "Taiwan Cinema Manifesto," criticizing the government's film policy and the mainstream media's negative attitude toward the Taiwan New Cinema. The manifesto reflected the difficult situation the Taiwan New Cinema was in and urged more support for filmmakers. However, this earnest request was ignored and proved an ironic foreshadowing of the Taiwan film industry's dim future. By the end of the year film production in Taiwan had dropped sharply. As a result the manifesto has been seen as the symbolic end of the Taiwan New Cinema movement.

If, as most people in Taiwan agree, the Taiwan New Cinema ended in 1987, what came next? Has what the manifesto called for — "another cinema" — thrived or even existed?[2]

Hou Hsiao Hsien initiated his Taiwan trilogy two years after 1987 with *City of Sadness*, unquestionably the greatest achievement since the beginning of the Taiwan New Cinema. With his later works, such as *The Puppetmaster; Good Men, Good Women; Goodbye South, Goodbye; Flowers of Shanghai;* and *Millennium Mambo*, this film manifests in aesthetic form a social and historical consciousness quite different to that of films he made before 1987. Edward Yang, another leading Taiwan New Cinema director, directed *A Brighter Summer Day* in 1991, and followed it with *A Confucian Confusion, Mahjong,* and *Yi Yi.* Although he maintains his modernist film style in most of these films, his rejection of funding from government and the state-owned studio has added the flavor of independent film aesthetics to his films and distinguished them from his prior works.

Furthermore, many new directors have won critical and audience attention. Their debut films include *Pushing Hands* (Ang Lee, 1991), *Rebels of the Neon God* (Tsai Mingliang, 1992), and *Ah-chung* (Chang Tsochi, 1996).[3] Compared with the Taiwan New Cinema, the films made after 1987 deal more with contemporary Taiwan society and are more formally experimental and personal. It is fair to say Taiwan cinema's greatest achievements are not from the Taiwan New Cinema era itself (1982–87) but from the years after. In other words "another cinema" has thrived since 1987. But what do these films look like? And do they continue or differentiate themselves from those produced in the Taiwan New Cinema era itself?

I aim to answer these questions through a close analysis of Chang Tsochi's *Darkness and Light* (1999).[4] Chang is widely considered to be Hou Hsiao Hsien's and the Taiwan New Cinema's heir. Yet, along with all the hallmarks of the Taiwan New Cinema, Chang has also integrated drama into his unique manifestation of "real-life fantasy." In these ways "another cinema" both continues and differentiates itself from the Taiwan New Cinema.

In recent years the blurring of the distinction between documentary and dramatic realist conventions has marked world cinema and Taiwan New Cinema in particular, but *Darkness and Light's* unique innovations in this area mark Chang's contribution to the realization of "another cinema." To demonstrate this I first explain how filmmakers have been crossing the boundary between documentary and drama recently, and how Chang Tsochi has achieved this in his unique way. I adapt theories of suture and spectatorship to ground my analysis and develop a tool for seeing deeper into the *Darkness and Light.*

Since his debut with *Ah-chung* in 1996, Chang has inherited 1980s Taiwan New Cinema and developed an unprecedented auteurist style. He has shown a sustained concern for those on the margins of society, using highly documentary-style techniques to represent those who are otherwise neglected. Including real-life stories in his movies, he has developed a unique style that reached a new level in *Darkness and Light*. Moreover, the movie achieved a better balance between real life and script, blending the two and blurring the distinction in such a way that the audience finds it difficult to distinguish between them. In these circumstances audiences cannot ignore social inequality by simply reminding themselves that the movie is fictional.

Of course, Chang is not the first person to blur fiction and reality: this has been a growing cinematic trend since the 1980s. For example, Zhang Yimou includes increasingly more documentary elements in films, such as *The Story of Qiu Ju* and *Not One Less*, whereas documentary films such as Michelle Citron's *Daughter Rite* include more and more dramatic elements. Academic work in the New Historicism has also deconstructed the traditional definitions of reality and fiction, arguing that the fictional narratives of novels and drama are not necessarily less accurate than those of historical documentaries. Hayden White once said history is simply another kind of novel and every history is a product of processes of condensation, displacement, and symbolization.[5] In terms of representation, whether produced through words or images, all discursive representations of reality are subjective in the end; they are not objective views of the absolute truth.

But what methods are used to depict "reality" in fictional feature films that blur the boundary? Such effects are common — for example, in Hou Hsiao Hsien's *The Puppetmaster* or *The Blair Witch Project*. However, Chang's *Darkness and Light* blurs fiction and non-fiction in a uniquely sophisticated manner, further developing the cinematic inheritance of the Taiwan New Cinema.

Chang Tsochi and *Darkness and Light*

That Chang should build upon the foundation of the Taiwan New Cinema is not surprising. He was Hou Hsiao Hsien's assistant director on *City of Sadness* (1989), and is widely considered his cinematic heir.[6] Chang graduated from the film program of the Theatre Department at the Chinese Culture University and worked as an assistant director and screenwriter before making his directorial debut with *Ah-chung* in 1996. A plain and simple film close to documentary or the early Taiwan New Cinema, *Ah-chung* focused on marginal members of the working class. Since then, Chang has gone further than any other Taiwan director in working with non-professional actors, filming in the documentary style, and telling stories in a fragmented and undramatic manner that uses complex metaphor. His commitment to realistic representation of lives on the fringes of society is longstanding. Despite the trace of the heritage of the Taiwan New Cinema, *Darkness and Light* also shows his unique "real-life drama" integration of reality and drama. This may be a good example of how "another cinema" continues yet also differentiates itself from the Taiwan New Cinema.

As a relatively new director, Chang Tsochi has received less attention than Tsai Mingliang and Ang Lee. Apart from brief introductions or interviews, there is little written about him.[7] Lin Zhiming's article is a rare exception. Lin points out that under the loosely constructed plots and details there lie clear storylines.[8] Chang uses the techniques of chronicle and aphorism, extracting details from daily life and organizing them without cause-and-effect structures. As a result his films appear to be without dialectical flow. Yet each sequence proves to be a micro-*recit* or story, the pay-off for each one hidden in the next, so that ultimately they are all connected. The Taiwan New Cinema is known for a style that follows the flow of life; Chang's film inherits this but takes it to new and more accessible levels.

Narrative technique is not the only element differentiating *Darkness and Light* from the Taiwan New Cinema. In what follows I focus on the use of the point-of-view or subjective shot, borrowing ideas of suture and spectatorship. Suture theorists believe cinema needs to establish an imagined time and space to construct imagined reality and meaning. Editing creates effects of suture to produce these results.[9] The point-of-view shot combined with the reverse shot is a classic example of suture, whereby two reverse shots edited together establish an effect of seeing and being seen. Spectatorship theorists believe there are three spectators in a movie: the character, the camera, and the audience.[10]

Combining the concepts of point-of-view, suture, and spectatorship, when we see a person seeing in a movie, we are actually seeing them through the camera's "seeing." Therefore, the position of the camera may decide how we see this person and how they are seeing. The position of the camera may place us at a distance from the person or, on the contrary, lead us to empathize with them; it can produce either alienation or allo-identification.[11] In *Darkness and Light* Chang presents spectacular ways of seeing. By manipulating camera position (or how the camera sees), we the audience are placed at a distance and then placed in the position of the characters in an innovative technique that is simultaneously disguised as the conventional visual style of the Taiwan New Cinema. How is this achieved?

To understand this, first we must further examine ways of seeing in the cinema in order to understand the lexicon Chang draws upon to produce his own ways of seeing.

Ways of Seeing in the Cinema

As indicated, ways of seeing in the cinema include how the character, the camera and the audience all see. The other two only become meaningful through the mediation of the camera. There are numerous ways of putting these elements into play. A basic point-of-view shot is produced by following a regular frontal shot of a person looking with a reverse-angle shot of whatever they are looking at. The spectator is "sutured" into this structure. There are many ways of varying this pattern. If the shot order is reversed the effect is produced retrospectively. Shot distance adds further variation; the closer the shot the stronger the emphasis on the watching/being watched effect. Camera movement can also emphasize the point-of-view shot. For example, if the character watching moves her or his head or eyes, a pan can follow their gaze. Finally, a third shot or reaction shot can be added. Displaying the watcher after the act of watching, this communicates the effect of the watching.[12]

All these possible constructions of the reverse shot are based on suture, in which sequential shots are linked in such a way as to give viewers a first-person perspective. However, this can even be achieved with only one shot, an effect often neglected in elaborations of the idea of suture. This single shot can consist of a two shot (or two character shot) in which the audience follows as character A watches B or A and B watch each other in a single frame. The same effect can be emphasized with a pan as A watches B or vice versa, or it can be produced as an over-the-shoulder shot of A watching B or vice versa. (Whether or not the character's shoulder is in the frame can make a great difference to the audience's "seeing" and identification.) Finally, the effect can also be produced in a rack focus shot, where the focus is changed as a person in the foreground watches someone in the background, and the refocusing follows the gaze.

So far, these different structures have been discussed in purely technical terms, but what are their aesthetic and significatory implications? From a psychological perspective, with a horizontal camera angle — when the camera is at zero degrees and front on to the character being filmed — it is easier for the audience to enter the character's perspective. From this angle the audience can immerse themselves in that person and perceive information from the first-person perspective, identifying with the character. On the other hand, when the camera angle is more oblique, for example a profile shot close to ninety degrees to the face, the audience can see that the character is watching something but cannot easily enter the character's mind or perceive their emotions and generate similar feelings of their own.

Furthermore, if the character is in the frame of the point-of-view shot — for example, in the two-character shot, the pan, the over-the-shoulder shot, or the rack focus shot the person watching and the person being watched are both in the shot — the audience will find it harder to project themselves into the scene and empathize. Instead of taking up the position of the character, they are more likely to develop sympathy for the character.

Generally speaking, a frontal shot of the character followed by a reverse-angle shot and combined with visual movement and a reaction shot is the most effective way of encouraging identification with the point-of-view by means of suturing. On the other hand, a profile shot of two people watching each other is probably least effective in encouraging the audience to identify with the characters. In other words, blurring the three levels of spectatorship — the character's perspective, the camera perspective, and the audience perspective — can best help the audience to become involved.

When the lines of spectatorship are blurred, the audience is also likely to become very emotional. This may bring them pleasure, but they may also lose the capacity to form a distanced reflection upon the film. In the 1980s the Taiwan New Cinema and especially Hou Hsiao Hsien's films encouraged the use of realism in movies.[13] They were strongly opposed to excessive cutting and avoided shot/reverse-shot structures. At the same time, because they were materially and financially constrained, the Taiwan New Cinema directors avoided too many changes of camera angle, filming with detailed shot coverage, or using lots of sequential shots, which would have led to complicated editing structures. They also used non-professional actors in order to enhance the sense of reality and chose filming techniques that minimized interruptions of their performances. This not only led to the eschewal of reverse-shot techniques and close-ups, but also to the rise of the long shot, the profile shot, the two-character shot, and the pan shot in New Cinema. Combined, these inadvertently gave the Taiwan New Cinema a unique angle on the profilmic event, promoting a calm, distanced, and documentary-like style that eventually led to observational realism.[14]

Ways of Seeing in *Darkness and Light*

With these considerations in mind, we can now examine how Chang Tsochi's films form his own perspectival mode and identity on the basis of the Taiwan New Cinema. *Darkness and Light* is about a 17-year-old girl named Kan-yi. She goes home during the summer months to take care of her father, who is blind and works as a masseur. During this period she meets Ah-ping, her neighbor. His mother passed away when he was young, so his father went back to China to live. Ah-ping quit military school and joined a gang. He and Kan-yi become attracted to each other. However, there is a third person: Kan-yi's junior high school friend A-Lin, who considers himself her boyfriend. He disrupts Kan-yi and Ah-ping's relationship, and creates conflict. In an act of revenge Ah-ping is stabbed, ending his life at only eighteen. Kan-yi's father becomes ill, and has to enter the hospital, where he dies. The summer ends with tragedy and loss. At the end of the film Kan-yi appears once again before the window of her room and looks out at the harbor, where there are fireworks. Then the doorbell rings. She turns around to see Ah-ping coming home, and her father, who has been to Hawaii to fulfill his dream. The home is filled with warmth and happiness, and the happiness and sadness of the summer become surreal because it is impossible to distinguishable between dream and reality.

In this simple story there are eight scenes of the male or female protagonist watching or seeing. In the first scene in this structure of mutual observation, Ah-ping enters an old building. In the hallway he asks Kan-yi and her friend for directions. At this moment, the camera is placed at the end of the hallway to produce a wide-angle, long shot of their profiles. As if observing in a documentary, we see Kan-yi curiously watching the strange boy. In the second scene of watching, Kan-yi and Ah-ping meet in the hallway again. The camera position is much the same as above, using a long-profile shot and a slight positional change, moving closer in to Kan-yi (as if secretly watching them). We see a quick encounter between the two characters.

In the third scene Ah-ping and the leader of the gang are at Kan-yi's house for a massage. The camera is in the hallway, placed to one side of the entrance to the living room. From an oblique angle we see Kan-yi, Ah-ping, and others in conversation. However, we also see that Kan-yi keeps her eyes on Ah-ping. Even when Ah-ping is out of the frame, we see Kan-yi's eyes follow in his direction.

The fourth scene of mutual watching takes place in the apartment hallway again, where Ah-ping bumps into Kan-yi and her younger brother as they pass through the hallway. The camera, as if sneaking, moves in from a long to a full shot. We see Kan-yi's younger brother, who is mentally handicapped. Abruptly, he makes a gesture indicating that the two are a couple. (Later, we learn that the brother has secretly read Kan-yi's diary and found out about her secret crush on Ah-ping.)

In the fifth scene Kan-yi and Ah-ping take the trash out together. As they glance at each other the camera makes an unusual move, dollying in to turn an ordinary two-character shot, where the two characters are looking at each other, into a very dramatic and ambiguous situation.

In the sixth scene Kan-yi and Ah-ping return from a night out. On the apartment staircase Kan-yi suddenly moves to kiss Ah-ping in a medium shot of their profiles. Various over-the-shoulder reverse shots follow, linked by dissolves. As the camera cuts back and forth, we see that Ah-ping is kissing Kan-yi back.

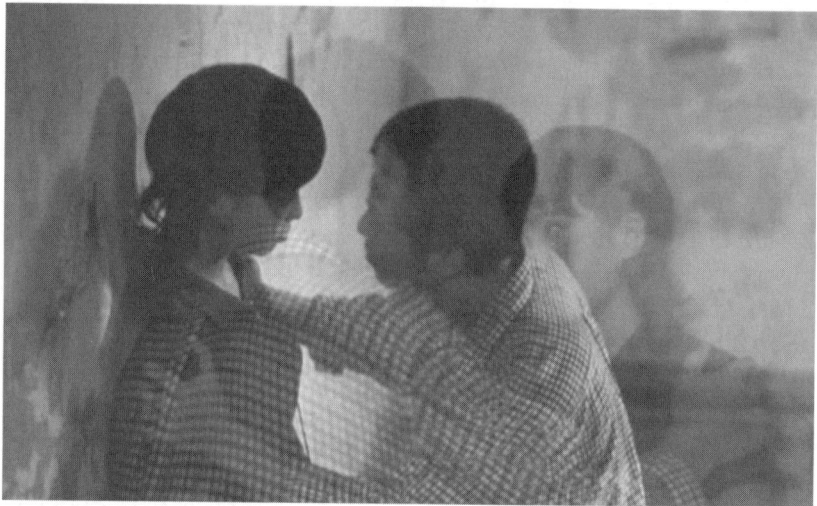

Darkness and Light: A reverse angle dissolve reverses audience identification with characters.

The seventh scene discovers Kan-yi standing by her window. This is the first shot conforming to the components of a typical suturing structure; it is a frontal close-up of Kan-yi looking down. The reverse shot completes the classic suturing structure by showing us a frontal full shot of Ah-ping across the street. In the same shot Kan-yi enters the frame and gives Ah-ping a hug. This sequence of shots follows a typical Hollywood point-of-view style.

However, it turns out that it is not aiming to connect real time and space, but rather to connect us to Kan-yi's imagination. The next cut takes us back to Kan-yi, still in her room, in a reaction shot. Her brother appears, carrying candles because there is an electrical blackout. Kan-yi quickly blows out the candles because their light is blotting out her dream.

The eighth scene takes place toward the very end of the narrative. From previous scenes we know that both Ah-ping and Kan-yi's father have died. We see Kan-yi standing in front of the window again. The shot dollies in on her. There are fireworks going off in the sky and Kan-yi looks happily at them. Again, this frontal close-up is the first component of a classic suturing shot/reverse-shot. Sure enough, the reverse shot of the fireworks outside the window follows, and then a reaction shot of Kan-yi's happy expression. In retrospect we might say that fleeting appearances of the fireworks have rekindled Kan-yi's imagination. In the same shot the doorbell rings. Kan-yi turns around. The next shot is a reverse point-of-view shot — a very subjective shot — from her perspective. It dollies toward the other side of the hallway in the apartment, a movement implying that Kan-yi is moving forward. At the end of the hallway, we see Ah-ping and the father's homecoming.

In these eight point-of-view scenes, long shots and two-character shots are most frequently used. From the first to fifth instance, the camera position and shot composition place the audience mostly in a distant, observational perspective on the story and the characters. As a result the audience is likely to feel uninvolved. However, as the story gradually builds, there is a shift in distance with the use of the closer full shot in the fourth scene, and then camera movement with the dolly in the fifth scene. These elements increase visual and emotional intensity.

As the story comes to a climax, *Darkness and Light* changes its style from quasi-documentary to drama, adopting sequential reversal shots blended together via dissolves in the sixth scene to bring the audience into the story. The repeated shots from the perspectives of the male and female protagonists draw the audience into the experience of kissing and being kissed.

Of course, *Darkness and Light's* most innovative use of point-of-view shots takes place in the seventh and eighth scenes via the use of camera position. In these two scenes, the classic suturing structure following a frontal shot with reverse and reaction shots is deployed. However, this apparent suturing of real time and space is actually used to suture the longing of the heart, which is not reality at all. This unconventional style creates two meanings. In the image we see everything is back to normal in the family. The return of Ah-ping and Kan-yi's father symbolizes the annihilation of their death. However, from previous scenes, we know that this current point-of-view shot is similar to the seventh shot, where it reflected Kan-yi's imagination rather than reality. In other words the return of Ah-ping and Kan-yi's father is merely a projection of Kan-yi's wish. A more experienced or sophisticated audience will tend to interpret the scene in this way. However, the audience may also engage in a degree of identification with the characters that leads them to believe what they literally "see" now is the story's true ending and that the previous deaths were only imagined. Thus, at this point the movie leaves two possible endings for the audience to choose from, decisively blurring the line between reality and dream. Using the same images to engender different perspectives, different identities, different stories, and different meanings is an excellent example of how traditional cinematic language can be revitalized.

Darkness and Light's basic and frequent use of long shots and two-character shots both reflects Chang Tsochi's previous experience with documentary and his inheritance of the observational realism associated with Hou Hsiao Hsien and the Taiwan New Cinema, which he takes to new heights. He regularly casts semi- or non-professional actors, adjusting his scripts on the basis of his extended acquaintance with them to bring their real lives into the films, which he also encourages them to do through improvisation. As a result, the filming often changes direction. Furthermore, to minimize distraction and capture real life elements best, the camera tends to be placed at a distance, in the manner of the Taiwan New Cinema.

However, unlike the observational style of past Taiwan New Cinema, Chan instills the sense of observation from a distance but then enters the character's feelings. In *Darkness and Light*, Chang Tsochi's real subject "is not so much doomed romance (touching though the storyline is) but rather the tensions of seeing, wishing and imagining. And so he's less interested in grungy social realism than in psychological realism."[15] *Darkness and Light* emphasizes less glamorous and socially marginal people, such as the masseur and the gang, portraying their relationships and loves. The emphasis on realism makes the progression of love seem natural, slowly revealing the story, and building a strong, moving, and almost overflowing power.

Having started with a combination of documentary and Taiwan New Cinema style in *Ah-chung* in 1996, Chang takes up a unique technique to combine fiction and reality and make a breakthrough in *Darkness and Light*. And this skill is further developed in his most recent film *The Best of Times* (2002), in which the coda of the story is repeated, first as the death of a young man and the second time as the escape of the young man from death. Both scenes are presented through the protagonist's point of view, confounding the distinction between reality and fantasy in what on the surface seems to be a work of observational realism. Although Chang Tsochi's film language derives from the Taiwan New Cinema it also divorces from its precedents, creating a new mold for Taiwan cinema, which I would call "another cinema."

12

The China Simulacrum: Genre, Feminism, and Pan-Chinese Cultural Politics in *Crouching Tiger, Hidden Dragon*

Fran Martin

The film is a kind of dream of China.

– Ang Lee

In the light of its colossal worldwide critical and popular success, Ang Lee's martial-arts romance *Crouching Tiger, Hidden Dragon* (2000) constitutes an unprecedented global cinematic and cultural event. The Mandarin-language film earned more than US$100 million at the US box-office, making it the highest-grossing foreign-language film in American film history.[1] It was nominated for ten Academy Awards in 2001 and won four: Best Foreign-Language Film, Best Art Direction, Best Cinematography and Best Original Score.[2] Ang Lee also received a personal home visit in Taiwan from President Chen Shui-bian, and Taiwan's Government Information Office proclaimed the film's success nothing short of "the greatest achievement in the history of filmmaking in the Republic of China."[3]

This chapter attempts to unpack some of the major questions that the *Crouching Tiger* phenomenon raises about contemporary cinema in a global frame. Taking a broad, cultural approach, the chapter positions *Crouching Tiger* in relation to its global audience and status as a successful crossover film, and in relation to its production of a Pan-Chinese cultural nationalism that constructs a triumphal, post-modern version of "Chineseness." I propose that the film enables particular forms of spectatorial pleasure based on the multiplicity of interpretive strategies available to the film's disparate audiences and the possibility of "allo-identification" across the lines of ethnicity and culture. In particular, I explore the use of the female warrior figure and consider the implications of the double citation performed by Zhang Ziyi's character both of the *wuxia* (knights-errant) Chinese popular film genre and of 1990s-style cinematic pop-feminism.

Ang Lee and Cinematic Chinese Transnationalism

Ang Lee is claimed enthusiastically by the government of the Republic of China as a Taiwanese director, and his films are celebrated locally as national products with the potential to educate overseas audiences about Taiwanese-Chinese identity and culture. However, the most prominent strand in the critical response to Lee's cinema in English to date has positioned it as exemplary not of a national cinema but rather precisely of the *trans*national turn in film production and consumption today, an interpretation that resonates strongly with the concerns of this chapter.

Sheng-mei Ma and Shu-mei Shih both argue that Lee's films underscore the tension between the national and the transnational in the era of intensified global cultural flows.[4] For Ma, Lee's early films appeal to nostalgia for the Chinese mainland on the part of Chinese diasporic audiences, while simultaneously constructing a tourist-friendly spectacle of exotic "Chineseness" for global non-Chinese audiences. Similarly, Shih argues that Lee's films deploy a strategy of "flexible encoding" to enable differential translations for differently positioned audiences. Wei-ming Dariotis and Eileen Fung take a comparable approach to Lee's early films, arguing that ". . . Lee's films reenvision [Chinese] 'tradition' in a . . . sympathetic light as something that is highly versatile and adaptive" to the altered conditions of global culture.[5]

Felicia Chan argues that *Crouching Tiger* in particular is exemplary of the condition of "cultural migrancy."[6] Chan reads the film as an "interstitial" site in Homi Bhabha's sense: insofar as it negotiates collective experiences of nation, community, and cultural value among regional Chinese, diasporic Chinese, and global film audiences. Chan's argument underscores the film's inscription of a "Pan-Chinese" cultural imaginary in its bringing together of stars from the four key regions of Chinese transnationalism: Hong Kong (Chow Yun Fat), mainland China (Zhang Ziyi), Taiwan (Zhang Zhen), and the Chinese diaspora in south-east Asia (the Malaysian Michelle Yeoh). The same Pan-Chinese convergence can be seen in the film's production: with a Taiwanese director, a Hong Kong action choreographer (Yuen Wo-ping) and mainland Chinese crew, *Crouching Tiger* was filmed in diverse locations across the Chinese mainland, from Xinjiang province in the north-west to the bamboo forest in China's south.

Indeed, *Crouching Tiger* has often been perceived as a film centrally concerned with the meaning and value of "Chineseness." An article on Lee in the *Taipei Review*, a Republic of China (ROC) government publication in English, frames him as a filial Chinese son: "For years, film director Lee Ang was haunted by the knowledge that his parents thought he had chosen a highly unconventional career. But then he found a way of making up for his lack of filial piety: his films kept winning awards."[7] The article then describes Lee dutifully bringing his *Crouching Tiger* Oscar home to his mother on her seventy-sixth birthday. In this narrative of Lee as the faithful son returning triumphant from his overseas successes, the director is claimed as (Taiwan) "Chinese" through the description of his filial piety — filial piety signifying as a paradigmatically "Chinese" cultural value. Comparably, but from a different perspective, an article about *Crouching Tiger* in the now-defunct *Asiaweek* magazine, titled "A Roots Trip With a Kick: After tasting success in Hollywood, Ang Lee rediscovers his Chineseness," quoted Lee saying: "It became very important for me to re-confirm and re-taste my mother tongue, to return to my cultural roots. It's a homecoming of sorts."[8] Here, the distinctively "Chinese" *wuxia* genre of *Crouching Tiger* is made to signify "Chineseness" as the rediscovered cultural identity of the film's director, the generic "homecoming" of the film paralleling the geographic homecoming of its director, post-Oscar, in the *Taipei Review* article quoted above.

The Film

Crouching Tiger is a generically hybrid film, mixing the conventions of the romantic melodrama with those of the *wuxia* film, cutting back and forth among scenes of emotionally freighted dialogue, highlighting character psychology; scenes of fantastic flight across moonlit rooftops, and fast-paced armed and hand-to-hand combat characteristic of the *wuxia* genre; and dramatic exterior shots highlighting the spectacular scenery of the mainland-Chinese locations. The story centers on five main characters: Yu Jiaolong ("delicate dragon" — "Jen" in the English subtitles — played by Zhang Ziyi), the central character, is a daughter of the Manchurian aristocracy who yearns to escape social convention for the freedoms of the fabled *jianghu* warrior underworld. When the film commences, Jen is being unwillingly prepared for an arranged marriage in Beijing. Previously, she has had an illicit affair with Luo Xiaohu ("little tiger" — "Lo" in the English subtitles — played by Zhang Zhen) in China's remote northwest Xinjiang province.

Lo, a Turkic bandit who is still in love with Jen, has followed her to Beijing to ask her to return with him to the desert wilderness. Also staying in Beijing as the film begins is Yu Shulian (Michelle Yeoh), a warrior who has brought with her the mythical sword known as the Green Destiny. The sword belongs to Li Mubai (Chow Yun Fat), who is trying to give up the bloody ways of the *jianghu* underworld to concentrate on spiritual pursuits. An unconsummated love exists between Li Mubai and Yu Shulian. The fifth character is the embittered warrior-bandit Jade Fox (Cheng Pei Pei) who has insinuated herself into the Yu family as Jen's governess. Jade Fox bears a grudge against the Wudang martial-arts school because one of its masters had sex with her but refused to teach her — an insult for which she killed him.[9]

The film's narrative is based on a series of *wuxia* popular novels by mainland Chinese author Wang Dulu. The event that catalyzes the film's central story occurs when Jen, who has secretly been studying the esoteric martial-arts techniques of the Wudang school, steals the Green Destiny. Li Mubai and Yu Shulian set about recovering the sword and, when they realize Jen is the thief, try to teach her to use her martial-arts talents for good instead of evil. But Jen sees the *jianghu* underworld as one of unfettered freedom and fails to understand the chivalric code of honor by which its warriors must treat one another. On the day of her marriage, she escapes the bridal chamber to set out in warrior-boy drag on an extended escapade in which she does battle with countless brawny fighters. Although she wins every time, she offends people left and right by failing to observe the chivalric code, instead cutting a swathe of indiscriminate destruction. Jen is then kidnapped by Jade Fox, who seeks to kill her as punishment for having concealed the true meaning of the Wudang manuals. As Yu Shulian and Li Mubai attempt to rescue Jen, Li Mubai dispatches Jade Fox to a gory death but is hit in the process by a stray poison dart. Although Jen tries to procure the antidote to revive him, she arrives too late. Finally, Jen repairs to Wudang Mountain, where she meets Lo again. Citing a Xinjiang legend he once told her, in which a person's wish may be granted if he or she is brave enough to jump off a mountain, she dives off a bridge high over a rocky abyss and disappears into the mist.

Floating Identification

There is one scene in an earlier film by Lee — *The Wedding Banquet* (1993) — that illustrates especially clearly the argument I want to make about the mode of spectatorial identification enabled by *Crouching Tiger*. The central banquet scene is interesting because it stages so directly, as part of the diegesis, the dynamics of spectacle and spectatorship that pertain to the act of watching the film itself. Formally, the scene is composed of high-angle extreme long shots and pans across the crowded banquet hall, interspersed with close-ups of people in the crowd watching the spectacle of the wedding, followed by point-of-view shots of the bride, groom, and other characters making speeches and cavorting in various games. In this way the act of watching the wedding is foregrounded: the film spectator's viewing of *The Wedding Banquet* is mirrored in the shots of wedding guests watching the wedding banquet. The key point is that in this film — which, like *Crouching Tiger*, was directed at both Chinese audiences in Taiwan, Hong Kong, and the Chinese diaspora, as well as at non-Chinese audiences in the major global film markets — the close-up shots of the spectators at the banquet show both Chinese and Anglo-American faces. At one moment the viewer is prompted to align her gaze with that of a group of gay white men as they watch in bemused distaste as bride and groom are forced to perform bawdy marital hi-jinks. The next moment the image offered for spectatorial identification is of an older Chinese man convulsed with laughter as a bridesmaid lashes out at a male wedding guest too forward in seeking her garter. The film then cuts to a white American couple giggling at the same spectacle. One might argue that what is offered here is a *choice* of identificatory points of view: images of Chinese viewers offered for local-audience identification, and images of Anglo-American spectators included to offer points of identificatory purchase for the film's non-Chinese audiences. Yet there is another possibility — one that is also suggested by the use of mobile framing in the extreme long-shots of the crowd that give the sense of the camera as a disembodied, "floating" observer. The scene allows for the possibility that viewers may "cross-identify." Indeed, given that the film as a whole enables empathy with *both* the Chinese family *and* the white boyfriend of the protagonist, Wai-tung, it is possible that this scene might prompt a non-Chinese viewer to identify with not only the mild puzzlement of the non-Chinese banquet guests but also the delight of the Chinese guests playing the goofy wedding games. It might also incite a local Chinese viewer to laugh along with the Chinese guests in recognition and to view afresh the familiar wedding rituals through the slightly bewildered eyes of the non-Chinese guests unfamiliar with the ceremony.

In its offer of a range of different points of spectatorial identification, this scene seems to hold out at least two distinct forms of spectatorial pleasure. First, it both enables and self-consciously stages the pleasure of *allo-identification*: identification with an image of an "other" or a subject significantly different in some way from the viewer's own self-identification.[10] In this case, such "othering" happens across the lines of ethnicity: the prompting of non-Chinese viewers to identify with a subject-position marked "Chinese," and vice-versa. Relatedly, the scene enables and underscores the particular pleasure of having available not just one but multiple points of identification; of moving or floating between identification with Chinese and non-Chinese positions, just as the mobile camera seems to float freely from place to place, and from point of view to point of view, about the banquet hall. Although they are not foregrounded in the later film in such an obvious way, I think these forms of spectatorial pleasure are nevertheless also central to *Crouching Tiger*, particularly in the light of the latter film's enthusiastic consumption by global audiences. As I noted above, this is a filmic text strongly and self-consciously marked "Chinese" that draws heavily on the generic conventions of a markedly Chinese form, the *wuxia* picture — and yet it has appealed on an unprecedented scale to non-Chinese audiences. As I will elaborate below, I propose that for *Crouching Tiger's* considerable and enthusiastic non-Chinese audience, as for the Western spectators pictured within *The Wedding Banquet's* diegesis, allo-identification and the pleasure of floating in and out of identification with the spectacle of "Chineseness" may constitute some of the film's key pleasures.

Parallel Citations

As is argued by both Teo and Chan, for audiences familiar with the history of the *wuxia* genre, *Crouching Tiger* reads most obviously as a commentary on and an effort to re-invent that popular Chinese film tradition.[11] Aside from the evident generic markers that include period costume, stock characters, fantastic scenes of flying and fighting, and the thematic struggle between the principles of *dao* (the proper way) and *mo* (evil), the film's citation of the *wuxia* genre is also apparent in the central place it accords the figure of the female warrior. Zhang Zhen shows that the sub-genre of the female warrior *wuxia* film dates back as far as the 1920s. She writes: "The legendary Michelle Yeoh, who . . . shone brilliantly in Ang Lee's *Crouching Tiger, Hidden Dragon*, is not a miracle woman with a 'pair of lethal legs' born in a postmodern vacuum. Rather, she is a descendant of the pantheon of female knight-errant stars . . . in a rich, if hitherto repressed, cinematic tradition."[12] Zhang identifies sixteen films made in China from 1925 to 1931, not all of whose prints have survived, that have titles indicating they belong to an extensive though under-researched "martial heroines" (*nüxia*) sub-genre.[13]

As Teo discusses, a more recent association prompted by *Crouching Tiger's* female warriors is with the 1960s and 70s films of King Hu — especially *A Touch of Zen* (1971) — whose bamboo-grove fight scene is strikingly re-interpreted in Lee's film. The association with Hu is also prompted by the casting of Cheng Pei Pei as Jade Fox: Cheng was a major *wuxia* star in 1960s Hong Kong cinema and starred in Hu's classic *Come Drink with Me* (1966). Hu is renowned for the central place his films accord female warriors, and for his creation of what Teo calls the "image of female stoicism" in the *wuxia* genre.[14] With its two female-warrior leads, perhaps as much as *A Touch of Zen*, *Crouching Tiger* recalls Hu's *The Fate of Lee Khan* (1973), whose story centers on an inn run by a group of female ex-criminal patriots and which features no fewer than six central *nüxia* characters. Certainly, something in the icy resolve and hauteur with which Zhang Ziyi plays Jen in *Crouching Tiger* recalls Hsu Feng's portrayals of lethal female-warrior villains in both *The Fate of Lee Khan* and *The Valiant Ones* (1975). The *nüxia* sub-genre also continues in different form in contemporary Kong Kong cinema — one thinks, for example, of Brigitte Lin's roles in *The Bride with White Hair* (Ronny Yu, 1993), *The Bride with White Hair 2* (David Wu, 1993) and *The East Is Red* (Ching Siu-tung, 1993). Yet, as both Teo and Chan also emphasize, *Crouching Tiger* is certainly not a

Zhang Ziyi as the rebellious Jen in *Crouching Tiger, Hidden Dragon*.

conventional martial-arts movie: its pace is far slower than that of contemporary Hong Kong action cinema and its emphasis on the love story and introduction of elements of romantic melodrama set it significantly apart from the typical *wuxia* film.

If the association with the *wuxia* genre and the figure of the *nüxia* is one obvious way to understand *Crouching Tiger* for audiences familiar with these traditions, a different set of pop-cultural associations is suggested by the film's reception in Euro-American media. For more than one reviewer the film calls up associations with the myriad feisty "ass-kickin'" heroines of 1990s globalizing Euro-American pop-feminism. *Time* magazine, for example, ran an article positioning *Crouching Tiger* as a contributor to the pop-cultural trend toward "the action heroine who is both feminist and feminine," reading it alongside the television drama series *Buffy the Vampire Slayer* and James Cameron's *Dark Angel*, the children's animation series *The Powerpuff Girls*, and the films *Josie and the Pussycats* (Harry Elfont and Deborah Kaplan, 2001) and *Lara Croft: Tomb Raider* (Simon West, 2001).[15] Elaine Showalter, too, sees Lee's film as an example of the trend toward pop-feminist film: she reads it alongside *The Contender* (Rod Lurie, 2000), *Bridget Jones' Diary* (Sharon Maguire, 2001), and *Charlie's Angels* (McG, 2000), and argues that it "speaks with luminous directness to the aspirations of contemporary women."[16] Perhaps relatedly and certainly intriguingly, Matthew Levie contends that "the real story of *Crouching Tiger* is how its main female characters reconcile (or fail to reconcile) their femininity with their professional development — a struggle any twenty-first century career woman would find familiar."[17] In commentaries like these, *Crouching Tiger* is associated not with the specifically Chinese popular form of the *nüxia* cinematic sub-genre but instead with the markedly Euro-American — though also globally extensive — pop-cultural preoccupation with the rebellious yet pretty super-heroine who, it is often argued, speaks to a generation of young Western women alienated from the "seriousness" of second-wave feminism. Jen's rebellion against the patriarchal structures of family and marriage, her yearning for personal freedom, and her gender-crossing in becoming a superior fighter and itinerant "warrior-boy" make her, in this view, less a descendant of the legion celluloid *nüxia* dating back to the Chinese cinema of the 1920s, than a far-flung sister to Buffy, Max, Lara, and Xena: creations of a decidedly 1990s Euro-American pop culture.[18]

On one hand, then, *Crouching Tiger* calls up associations with the *nüxia* sub-genre of Chinese film whose origins lie in the early twentieth century; on the other it suggests parallels with the hard-fighting third-wave feminist heroines of globalizing popular media culture who rose to prominence at century's end. As I have argued elsewhere with respect to *The Wedding Banquet*, this film also sets up a system of parallel citations or a kind of "multicoding," whereby the film's meaning becomes differentially legible to differently positioned audiences, depending on what forms of cultural background and cultural capital they bring to the film.[19] But it would be a mistake to assume that associations with the *nüxia* sub-genre would be made only by "Chinese" audiences: with the widespread cult popularity of Chinese martial-arts cinema in the West in the past fifteen years — a popularity on which Lee's film doubtless draws, in some measure, for its success in these markets — it would be wrong to think that the film's Euro-American audiences will have been universally unaware of the *nüxia* tradition. It would be equally a mistake to presume that the pop-feminist associations would be lost on Chinese audiences in Taiwan or Hong Kong: through the prevalence of both local and global forms of popular entertainment, "girl culture," "girl power" and related signifiers of pop-feminism are quite recognizable within those contexts.[20] Given the complexity of the citations the film performs and the sophistication of popular film audiences today, then, it seems reasonable to speculate that some of the pleasure *Crouching Tiger* affords its different audiences arises precisely from the multiple spectator positions offered, and viewers' ability to "float" between one and another. "Chinese" cultural capital in the form of a detailed knowledge of the *wuxia* genre may afford an American viewer the pleasure of allo-identification as she watches Cheng Pei Pei and recalls her role in *Come Drink with Me*, while the American pop-cultural knowledge possessed by a teenager in Kaohsiung might lead her to find a similar pleasure in associating Jen's steely resolution and superior fighting skills with her own appreciation of *Buffy the Vampire Slayer*, which she watches, dubbed in Mandarin, on cable TV. Equipped with the requisite crossover cultural capital, each hypothetical viewer could also enjoy the pleasure of slipping between such associative systems, seeing the film now from the point of view of "Chineseness"; now from the angle of global/American popular media culture.

The China Simulacrum and the Rebel Girl

Aside from enabling the spectatorial pleasures of floating identification, what other effects are produced by *Crouching Tiger*'s system of parallel citations? Following the success of the film at the US box office and the Academy

Awards, discussion ensued in both Taiwanese and Euro-American media about the potential of the film to transform and heterogenize Hollywood-dominated global film culture. Less has been said, though, about the reverse process: the way in which the film re-imagines and transforms what counts as "Chineseness" in world film culture today. I have already noted the film's investment in representing a particular form of "Chineseness," both through its use of the *wuxia* genre and through its construction of a Pan-Chinese cultural imaginary by bringing together stars and crew from all four areas of "greater China." While Lee Cher-jean, Deputy Director-General of the ROC's Government Information Office, has expressed the earnest hope that "American audiences will gain a deeper understanding of Chinese culture by watching *Crouching Tiger, Hidden Dragon*," Ang Lee makes a more savvy analysis when he says the film represents not any actual Chinese reality but rather his own "dream of China" — "a China that probably never existed, except in my childhood fantasies in Taiwan," fantasies constructed in large part from his reading of popular *wuxia* fiction.[21] If the "Chineseness" emphatically projected by the film reflects no social or historical reality but a self-conscious fabrication — a form of simulacral Chineseness based on generic citation — then what, precisely, are the effects of the film's wishful fantasy of "Chinese culture"? Given the film's parallel citation of not only the *wuxia* genre but also of pop-feminist media culture, I propose that a significant effect of the film's projection of a simulacral, postmodern, and transnational version of "Pan-Chineseness" is precisely to fantasize the contemporaneity of third-wave pop-feminism into the heart of a re-imagined "Chinese tradition." Presenting as it does, with its lush period costumes and quotations of *wuxia* generic formulae, such a lavish spectacle of "Chinese (film) tradition," the film pulls off the trick of revealing, at the very core of this "tradition," the anachronous pre-existence of the political values and representational strategies of 1990s pop-feminism. As popular cultural tradition is re-invented for circulation as global cinema in the twenty-first century, magically "Chineseness" turns out to be all about girl-power.[22]

These questions converge in the film's compelling final scene where Jen leaps from the bridge and soars, with an expression of enigmatic serenity, through the mist and at last out of our field of vision. As the last character we see in these ultimate, cryptic shots, Jen arguably attains a privileged symbolic status for the film as a whole. Jen is repeating the actions of the legendary hero who remained unscathed after leaping from a mountain for the sake of his sick parents, and the film refuses to imply her death — we never see her land, but only fly off magically into the mist. Given this, and the obvious fact that the *wuxia* genre is more concerned with fantasy than realism, I would resist a reading of Jen's leap into the clouds as "suicide" in any straightforward sense. Far more suggestively than this, Jen's flight signifies her desire to fulfill any number of possible wishes, according to the legend: that she and Lo be reunited in Xinjiang, as he wishes; that she had not trampled on the chivalric code of the *jianghu* underworld, leading to the death of Li Mubai; that she could live the life of freedom for which she yearns but which is denied daughters of the aristocracy. At the same time, though, Jen's flight — from her obligations in the mortal world as well as from the field of vision of the film's viewer — signifies an extension of the radical (and distinctly 1990s pop-feminist style) rebellion that has been her defining characteristic throughout the film. Instead of an expression of repentance, then, her magic flight might signify Jen's final, obdurate refusal to cleave to *any* of the social systems that structure the world of the living. Visually, her flight recalls both the supernatural aeronautics characteristic of the *wuxia* genre, and, eerily though also appropriately, that final death-defying drive off the cliff at the conclusion of the American pop-feminist classic *Thelma and Louise* (Ridley Scott, 1991) — another film that refuses visually to imply the deaths of its heroines, who seem to remain forever suspended in their ultimate trajectory. Her form soaring defiantly and eternally into the mist, Jen the "rebel girl" emerges at the conclusion of this film as the magical convergence of "China" and "the West," tradition and (post)modernity, and Chinese folk legend and global pop-feminism.

Appendix: Filmmakers and Films

This appendix includes a brief biography of the filmmakers whose works are discussed in this book, and a list of the feature films they have directed. The Chinese characters are given for their names and for the original Chinese titles of the films. Wherever possible the translations of the titles are not our own but the original English-language export titles of the films.

CHANG Tsochi (張作驥)

Chang Tsochi was born in Chiayi in Taiwan in 1961 and graduated from the film program of the Theater Department at Chinese Culture University. He entered the film field by working as a script-holder, director's assistant, and assistant director: He was a director's assistant on Yu Kanping's *People Between Two Chinas* and Yim Ho and Tsui Hark's *King of Chess*, and assistant director on Hou Hsiao Hsien's *City of Sadness*, Yu Kanping's *Two Painters*, and Huang Yushan's *Peony Bird*. During this period he also directed the television plays *What the Grass Says to the Wind* and *Teenager? Teenager!* in addition to television series. In 1989 he wrote the stage play *These People, Those People*.

In 1993 Chang Tsochi directed his debut film, *Gunshots in the Night*. However, because of a disagreement with the producer he refused to have his name appear as director. In 1996 he made *Ah-chung* independently. This film used the local "Ba Jia Jiang" folk ritual to depict the marginal lives of people living among the working class. Its plain, simple style akin to that of documentary films gave it an unexpected appeal and attracted the attention of critics. In 1999 the script for *Moving the Taxi Driver* won an Outstanding Film Script award from the Government Information Office. In the same year, his film *Darkness and Light* won the Gold award, the Tokyo Grand Prix, and the Asian Film award at the Tokyo International Film Festival, and the Grand Jury, Best Original Screenplay, Best Editing, and Audience Favorite awards at the Golden Horse Awards. *Darkness and Light* mixed realism and fantasy.

Chang is regarded as having not only inherited Taiwan New Cinema's observational realism but also created a unique cinematic language. His 2002 film *The Best of Times* was shown in the international panorama at the 59th Cannes International Film Festival, and won the three major awards at the 39th Golden Horse Awards: Best Feature Film, Best Taiwan Film, and Best Original Screenplay.

1993. *Gunshots in the Night* (暗夜槍聲)
1996. *Ah-chung* (忠仔)
1999. *Darkness and Light* (黑暗之光)
2002. *The Best of Times* (美麗時光)

HOU Hsiao Hsien (侯孝賢)

Hou Hsiao Hsien was born in 1948 in Dongmei County, Guangdong Province, and moved from mainland China to Taiwan a year later. He grew up in the Fengshan section of Kaohsiung. After completing his military service at 22 in 1969, he entered the Film Department of the National Academy of Arts. Upon graduation he worked for a year selling electronic calculators before joining the film world. He was 26. His first job was as a script-holder for the director Lee Hsing on *The Heart with a Million Knots*. The following year he was assistant to Xu Jinliang on *Clouds Without End*, and he started writing scripts when he was 28. Hou's first script made into a film was *The Peach Blossom Girl Fights Duke Zhou*, directed by Lai Yingcheng. From 1978 to 1981 he worked with Chen Kunhou on six films, all of which were box-office successes. In 1982 *The Green, Green Grass of Home*, which he wrote and directed, was nominated for Best Director at the Golden Horse Awards. In 1983 he financed *Growing Up*, a critical and box-office hit that launched the Taiwan New Cinema. *The Boys from Fengkuei* (1983), *A Summer at Grandpa's* (1984), *The Time to Live and the Time to*

Die (1985), and *Dust in the Wind* (1986) all attracted attention at international film festivals, and Hou Hsiao Hsien became known as one of the world's most original directors. In 1989 *City of Sadness* won the Golden Lion at the Venice International Film Festival and Hou's name was made.

Hou's films are grounded in observational realism and his hallmarks are the long shot, the long take, fixed camera positions, and the elision of the cause-and-effect chain in the narrative. Many critics see points of similarity between Hou's works and those of the Japanese master filmmaker Ozu Yasujiro. Hou took these aesthetic characteristics to their logical endpoint in his 1993 film *The Puppetmaster*, which used only one hundred shots with an average length of ninety seconds each. Since then Hou has gradually begun to vary his styles and subject matter. In his 1996 allegorical film *Goodbye South, Goodbye*, the focus fell on urban-rural conditions in contemporary Taiwan, and the camera position was no longer fixed. *Flowers of Shanghai* (1998) used gorgeous and luxuriant aesthetics to produce an almost abstract Qing Dynasty-costume chamber piece. *Millennium Mambo* (2001) entered the hidden world of rave music and drugs inhabited by the new urban generation.

1980. *Cute Girl* (就是溜溜的她)
1981. *Cheerful Wind* (風兒踢踏踩)
1982. *The Green, Green Grass of Home* (在那河畔青草青)
1983. *The Boys From Fengkuei* (風櫃來的人)
1984. *A Summer at Grandpa's* (冬冬的假期)
1985. *The Time to Live and the Time to Die* (童年往事)
1986. *Dust in the Wind* (戀戀風塵)
1987. *Daughter of the Nile* (尼羅河女兒)
1989. *City of Sadness* (悲情城市)
1993. *The Puppetmaster* (戲夢人生)
1995. *Good Men, Good Women* (好男好女)
1996. *Goodbye South, Goodbye* (南國再見, 南國)
1998. *Flowers of Shanghai* (海上花)
2001. *Millennium Mambo* (千禧曼波)

Ang LEE (李安)

Born in 1954 in Pingtung County, Taiwan, to parents who had recently migrated from the Mainland, Ang Lee graduated from the Motion Picture Department of National Academy of Arts in 1975. He then studied theater at the University of Illinois in the United States and film at New York University, where he worked on Spike Lee's student movie, *Joe's Bed-Sty Barbershop: We Cut Heads* (1983). After writing screenplays and looking for financial backing in the late 1980s, he won awards in Taiwan for two of his scripts and received funding from Central Motion Picture Corporation (CMPC) to film *Pushing Hands* (1991). With Ted Hope and James Schamus he established a company called Good Machine, which produced the story about the travails of an elderly Chinese migrant in the United States. A box-office success and award winner in Taiwan, it led to CMPC funding for his second film, *The Wedding Banquet* (1993).

The Wedding Banquet was Lee's breakthrough film. A poignant farce about the false marriage in New York of a gay immigrant from Taiwan, the film was a worldwide hit and prompted the Samuel Goldwyn Company to pre-purchase the US distribution rights to his next film, *Eat Drink Man Woman* (1994), another family comedy, set in Taipei. With access to international funding and audiences, Lee left Chinese themes behind for his next three movies. He directed an adaptation of the Jane Austen novel *Sense and Sensibility* (1995), scripted by and starring Emma Thompson; *The Ice Storm* (1997), a family melodrama that focuses on the sexual revolution in suburban America in the 1970s; and *Ride with the Devil* (1999), an American Civil War drama starring future Spiderman Toby Maguire.

In 2000 Lee returned to Chinese themes, reviving the swordplay film and mixing it with romance in the global megahit *Crouching Tiger, Hidden Dragon*. His most recent film was the action blockbuster, *The Hulk*, about a scientist physically transformed by exposure to radioactivity.

1992. *Pushing Hands* (推手)
1993. *The Wedding Banquet* (喜宴)
1994. *Eat Drink Man Woman* (飲食男女)
1995. *Sense and Sensibility*
1997. *The Ice Storm*
1999. *Ride With the Devil*
2000. *Crouching Tiger, Hidden Dragon* (臥虎藏龍)
2003. *The Hulk*

TSAI Mingliang (蔡明亮)

Born in Malaysia in 1957, Tsai Mingliang moved to Taiwan and enrolled in the Film and Drama Department of the Chinese Culture University when he was 20. He began working as a playwright and stage director during his student days, notching up experience with productions such as *Instant Vinegar-Soy Noodles* (1981), *A Door That Will Not Open in the Dark* (1982), and *The Closet in the Room* (1983). For several years afterwards he wrote television serials and taught classes on drama. In 1989 he wrote a series of well-received television serials and plays, such as *The Ends of the Earth*, *My English Name Is Mary*, and *The Child*. In 1993 his debut film *Rebels of the Neon God* won the Bronze Sakura Prize for Young Directors at the Tokyo International Film Festival. *Vive L'Amour* (1994) featured a stripped-down style and focus on characters, along with integrated absurdism and a passionate urban love story. It won the Golden Lion at the Venice International Film Festival, a FIPRESCI award, and the Best Director award at the Golden Horse Awards. In one fell swoop he became post-Taiwan New Cinema's most internationally acclaimed filmmaker. *The River*'s drama of father-son ethical relationships attracted spirited debate in Taiwan at the same time as it pushed the creative envelope. It won enthusiastic international praise, but after this Tsai Mingliang gradually left the arena of Taiwan film. *The Hole* (1998) and *What Time Is It There?* (2001) were made with French funding. They continued to explore the loneliness of the individual and difficulties in communication; there was also a continuation of Tsai's individual style with its water and light symbolism.

1992. *Rebels of the Neon God* (青少年哪吒)
1994. *Vive L'Amour* (愛情萬歲)
1996. *The River* (河流)
1998. *The Hole* (洞)
2001. *What Time Is It There?* (你那邊幾點)
2003. *The Skywalk Is Gone* (天橋不見了)
2003. *Goodbye, Dragon Inn* (不散)

WANG Tung (王童)

Wang Tung was born in 1942 in mainland China. While he hailed from Anhui Province's Taihe County his family — scholars and officials for generations, hence Wang's nurturing in traditional Chinese literature and calligraphy — was from Jiangsu Province. Wang moved to Taiwan to study in the Fine Arts Department of the National Academy of the Arts and won second prize in the Taiwan Fine Arts Competition. In 1966 he passed the exam to enter Central Motion Picture Corporation's studios, where he gained experience in everything related to art direction, from set painting to props to art design. He worked on the design of films by Lee Hsing, Pai Ching-jui, King Hu, Song Cunshou, Chen Yaoqi and others. In 1971 he entered the University of Hawaii to study dance and drama. On his return to Taiwan he continued to work in art design, and in 1976 he won the Golden Horse award for Art Design for his work on Pai Ching-jui's *Maple Leaf Love*. During the next fifteen years he worked on eleven films and began to direct his own. *If I Were for Real*, *Straw Man*, and *Hill of No Return* won the Golden Horse award for Best Feature Film. *Portrait of a Fanatic*, *A Flower in the Raining Night*, *Run Away*, *Banana Paradise*, and others won Outstanding Feature Film Golden Horse awards. He also won Best Director Golden Horse awards for *Straw Man* and *Hill of No Return*. In 1997 he became the head of the Central Motion Picture Corporation's studio and began to work as an administrator. In 2001 he completed work on *Away We Go*, and in February 2002 he resigned from Central Motion Picture Corporation and set up the Wang Tung Film Workshop to continue his production work. *Run Away* (1984) is considered the best example of Wang Tung's art design. With powerful visual imagery and well-researched art design, he produced a highly detailed world. He is best known to the public for his "Taiwan trilogy," composed of *Straw Man*, *Banana Paradise*, and *Hill of No Return*, as well as for his autobiographical film *Red Persimmon*.

1981. *If I Were for Real* (假如我是真的)
1981. *Don't Look at the Moon Through the Window* (窗口的月亮不准看)
1982. *One Hundred Points* (百分滿點)
1982. *Portrait of a Fanatic* (苦戀)
1983. *A Flower in the Raining Night* (看海的日子)
1984. *Run Away* (策馬入林)
1985. *Spring Daddy* (陽春老爸)
1987. *Straw Man* (稻草人)
1989. *Banana Paradise* (香蕉天堂)
1992. *Hill of No Return* (無言的山丘)
1994. *Red Persimmon* (紅柿子)
2002. *Away We Go* (自由門神)

WU Nien-jen (吳念真)

Wu Nien-jen's original name was Wu Wen-qin, and he was born on 5 August 1952 in Juifang, Taipei County. He graduated from the Accounting

Department of Fujen University's night school and started writing short stories and novels, publishing collections such as *Grabbing Hold of Spring*, *A Goose Call at the Turn of Autumn*, and *A Special Day*. He won the *United Daily News* Best Novel prize for three consecutive years.

Wu started writing scripts in 1978. In 1981, the same year *Classmates* won him a Golden Horse award for Best Original Screenplay, he joined Central Motion Picture Corporation as a script editor. The following year he worked with Xiao Ye and Tao De-zhen on the script of *The Story of Sunlight*, a groundbreaker for the Taiwan New Cinema. Since the 1980s Wu Nien-jen has been one of Taiwan's most important screenwriters. He wrote the screenplays for not only classic Taiwan New Cinema films including *The Sandwich Man*, *That Day at the Beach*, and *City of Sadness*, but also many commercial films such as *Brother with the Big Head* and *Fraternity*. As a screenwriter he has more than seventy films to his credit and has won the Golden Horse award for Best Screenplay six times. He is a rare artist who can combine the demands of art and popular culture.

In 1994 Wu Nien-jen made his film debut with *A Borrowed Life*. In 1995 he directed *Buddha Bless America* and established his own production company, making commercials. He has also used his affinity for local culture to become a television commercial actor and anchor.

1994. *A Borrowed Life* (多桑)
1995. *Buddha Bless America* (太平天國)

Edward YANG (楊德昌)

Edward Yang was born Shanghai in 1947 and moved with his family to Taiwan in 1949. He graduated from National Chiao Tung University's Control Engineering Department in 1967. In 1972 he moved to the United States to study for an MS in Computer Science; he ended up working there as an electrical engineer for seven years. In 1981 he returned to Taiwan and participated in *Winter 1905* as a screenwriter and actor. He began to attract attention when he directed the two-part *Duckweed* in the television series *Eleven Women*, produced by Sylvia Chang. In 1982 he directed *Expectation*, one film in the four-part production *In Our Time*, which was the fountainhead of the Taiwan New Cinema. His 1983 debut feature, *That Day at the Beach*, had an ingenious narrative structure and was a penetrating look at the lives of city dwellers. It established his cinematic style, which he developed in *Taipei Story* (1985) and *The Terrorizer* (1986). He and Hou

Hsiao Hsien became the leading creative forces in the Taiwan New Cinema. *A Brighter Summer Day* (1991) won him the Best Foreign Director award in the Japanese magazine *Kinema Junpo*'s annual film awards. *A Confucian Confusion* (1994) won a Golden Horse award for Best Original Screenplay. In 1996 he shot *Mahjong*, which won a Special Jury award at the Berlin International Film Festival. *Yi Yi: A One and A Two* (2000) won him international critical plaudits as well as the Best Director award at the Cannes International Film Festival, taking Yang to a new highpoint in his directing career. In 2001 Yang moved into Internet-based work and animation, establishing the miluku.com website.

1982. *Expectation* (指望) in *In Our Time* (光陰的故事)
1983. *That Day at the Beach* (海灘的一天)
1985. *Taipei Story* (青梅竹馬)
1986. *The Terrorizer* (恐怖分子)
1991. *A Brighter Summer Day* (牯嶺街少年殺人事件)
1994. *A Confucian Confusion* (獨立時代)
1996. *Mahjong* (麻將)
2000. *Yi Yi: A One and a Two* (一一)

Notes

Introduction

1. Government Information Office, Republic of China, "The ROC and the Asia-Pacific Regional Operations Center Plan," (n.d.) <http://www.taipei.org/current/aproc_1.htm> (24 May 2003).
2. On Taiwan's early history, including the disputes about the origins of its aboriginal peoples, see Simon Long, *Taiwan: China's Last Frontier* (London: Macmillan, 1991), 1–6.
3. Alan M. Wachman outlines these lines of tension in *Taiwan: National Identity and Democratization* (Armonk, NY: M.E. Sharpe, 1994), as does Christopher Hughes in *Taiwan and Chinese Nationalism: National Identity and Status in International Society* (London: Routledge, 1997).
4. See Long, 7–8, 9–11.
5. Leo T.S. Ching, *Becoming "Japanese": Colonial Taiwan and the Politics of Identity Formation* (Berkeley: University of California Press, 2001).
6. See Long, 140–2.
7. *China Times*, 26 August 1983.
8. On the early days of the Taiwan New Cinema, see Feii Lu, *Taiwan Cinema: Politics, Economics, Aesthetics* (Taipei: Yuanliu, 1998), 277–81.
9. Zhan Hongzhi, *"Minguo Qishiliunian Taiwan Dianying Xuanyan"* (Taiwan Cinema Manifesto, 1987), in *Taiwan Xin Dianying* (Taiwan New Cinema), ed. Peggy Hsiung-Ping Chiao (Taipei: Shibao, 1988), 111–118. See also Feii Lu, 303–9.
10. On the economics of the post-1987 Taiwan cinema and its globalization, see Ti Wei, "Reassessing New Taiwanese Cinema: From Local to Global," in *Taiwanese Cinema 1982–2002: From New Wave to Independent*, ed. Kim Ji-Seok and

Jongsuk Thomas Nam (Pusan: Pusan International Film Festival, 2002), 30–9. Also available on-line at <http://www.asianfilms.org>.

11. For further background, see Wi-yun Taiffalo Chiung, "Romanization and Language Planning in Taiwan," *The Linguistics Association of Korea Journal* 9, no. 1 (2001), 15–43.

Chapter 1

1. David Harvey, *The Condition of Postmodernity* (Cambridge, MA: Basil Blackwell, Inc., 1989), 191–94.

2. In 1972 Taiwan was forced to withdraw from the United Nations, and a period of diplomatic isolation in the international community followed. For more detailed discussion of the two earlier literary/cultural trends in Taiwan, see my book, *Modernism and the Nativist Resistance: Contemporary Chinese Fiction from Taiwan* (Durham: Duke University Press, 1993).

3. It cannot be a coincidence that scholars have observed the central role of this motive in cultural developments in various contemporary Chinese societies. While my book identified the quest for high culture in Taiwan, Jing Wang and Xudong Zhang both mentioned how "Modernization of the culture, the aesthetic sensibilities" underlay the PRC's "high culture fever" in the modernistic literary products of the post-Mao era. Jing Wang, "Variations of the Aesthetic Modern," in *High Culture Fever: Politics, Aesthetics, and Ideology in Deng's China* (Berkeley: University of California Press, 1996), 42–48; Xudong Zhang, *Chinese Modernism in the Era of Reforms: Cultural Fever, Avant-garde Fiction, and the New Chinese Cinema* (Durham: Duke University Press, 1997), 13.

4. See essays by Zhan Hongzhi, Xiao Ye, Li Cheuk-to, Qi Longren, and Wu Nien-jen, collected in Chapter 3 of Peggy Hsiung-Ping Chiao, *Taiwan Xin Dianying* (Taiwan New Cinema) (Taipei: Shibao, 1988), 81–124, in particular Section 5, *"Minguo qishiliu nian Taiwan dianying xuanyan"* (1987 Manifesto of Taiwan Cinema), 111–18. Two other articles on related topics, by Bai Luo and Li Cheuk-to, are included in Chapter 18 of the same book, 387–89 and 390–96.

5. Fredric Jameson, "Remapping Taipei," in Nick Browne, Paul G. Pickowicz, Vivian Sobchack, and Esther Yau, ed., *New Chinese Cinemas: Forms, Identities, Politics* (New York: Cambridge University Press, 1994), 123.

6. Peggy Hsiung-Ping Chiao, 78.

7. Peggy Hsiung-Ping Chiao, 95.

8. That Jameson contextualizes the film within the Eurocentric genealogy of literary modernism is made evident by his comparison of the multiple plot lines of the film to Western modernistic classics of the twentieth century, including Andre Gide's novel *Counterfeiters*, Jean Renoir's *Rules of the Game*, Rainer Werner Fassbinder's version of Nobokov's *Despair*, and Joseph Conrad's *The Secret Agent*.

9. See discussion and citations in Yingjin Zhang, "The Idyllic Country and the Modern City: Cinematic Configurations of Family in *Osmanthus Alley* and *The*

Terrorizer," *Tamkang Review* 15, no. 1 (1994): 82–99.

10. Fredric Jameson, 123.

11. *Shijie zhongwen baozhi fukanxue zonglun* (On studies of the *fukan* section in Chinese newspapers of the world), ed. Yaxian and Yizhi Chen (Taipei: Wenjianhui, 1997).

12. I have discussed the prominent role played by *fukan* in contemporary Taiwan's literary production in my new book *Literary Culture in Contemporary Taiwan* (tentative title; forthcoming from Columbia University Press). See also Feii Lu, *Taiwan Dianying: Zhengzhi, Jingji, Meixue, 1949–1994* (Taiwan Cinema: Politics, Economics, Aesthetics, 1949–1994) (Taipei: Yuanliu, 1998).

13. Fredric Jameson, 138.

14. Guy Debord, *The Society of the Spectacle*, trans. Donald Nicholson-Smith (New York: Zone Books, 1995).

15. In Taiwan, hard authoritarian control gradually gave way to less coercive forms, especially in the Chiang Ching-kuo era of the mid-1970s until the lifting of martial law.

16. See the essays collected in Yaxian, ed., *Zhongshen de Huayuan: Lianfu de Lishi Jiyi* (Garden of the Gods: Historical Memory of Lianfu), (Taipei: Lianjing, 1997). I have discussed this phenomenon further in the first part of Chapter 6 of *Literary Culture in Contemporary Taiwan* (Columbia University Press, forthcoming).

17. See Part II of Chapter 6, *Literary Culture in Contemporary Taiwan.*

18. Taipei: Shibao, 1988.

19. As well as Hollywood movies, examples include Asian popular culture, such as Hong Kong pop singers, Japanese popular fiction, and television drama series from Japan and Korea.

20. A number of writers and editors, notably the poet Xiang Yang, lamented around the turn of the decade in their writings and public speeches the death of "pure literature." In autumn 1994, when *Renjian fukan* sponsored a Little Theater Festival in Tianmu, Taipei, there was a shared sense among critics that the fervor for Little Theater had already subsided. See Mingder Chung's dissertation, "The Little Theatre Movement of Taiwan (1980–89): In Search of Alternative Aesthetics and Politics" (New York University, 1992). On cinema, see Mi Zou, and Liang Xinhua, ed., *Xin Dianying zhi Si: Cong* Yiqie wei mingtian *dao* Beiqing chengshi (Death of the New Cinema: from *All for Tomorrow* to *A City of Sadness*) (Taipei: Tangshan, 1991).

21. In conceptualizing transnational cinema as a "field," I am adapting Pierre Bourdieu's theory of cultural fields, originally conceived in national terms, to the international level. For Bourdieu, any social formation is structured as a hierarchically organized series of fields — the economic field, the educational field, the political field, the cultural field, and so forth — each of which is a structured space with its own internal laws and relations of force. See *The Field of Cultural Production: Essays on Art and Literature*, ed. Randal Johnson (New York: Columbia University Press, 1993), 6.

22. Each film is discussed in individual detail in essays by Haden Guest and Chris Berry in this volume.

23. David Bordwell documented Hou's influence on younger Asian directors in a paper presented at the symposium "Island of Light: A Symposium on Taiwan Cinema and Popular Culture," Center for East Asian Studies, University of Wisconsin-Madison, 7–9 March 2002.
24. I have discussed the Zhang Ailing phenomenon in 1980s Taiwan in "Yuan Qiongqiong and the Rage for Eileen Zhang among Taiwan's *Feminine* Writers," *Modern Chinese Literature* 4, no. 1&2 (1988): 201–23.
25. See Nick Kaldis's essay in this anthology for detailed discussion of Hou's film.
26. Raymond Williams, "Cultural Theory," in *Marxism and Literature* (Oxford: Oxford University Press, 1977), 108–20.

Chapter 2

1. *Dust in the Wind* is thus discussed by William Tay as a part of a group of "initiation stories" or "cinematic equivalents of the *Bildungsroman*" that run throughout Hou's early films and by Tonglin Lu as a chapter in the ongoing quest across Hou's films to "reinvent a powerful father figure." William Tay, "The Ideology of Initiation: The Films of Hou Hsiao Hsien," in *New Chinese Cinemas*, ed. Nick Browne et. al. (Berkeley: University of California Press, 1994), 151–59; and Lu Tonglin, *Confronting Modernity in the Cinemas of Taiwan and Mainland China* (Cambridge: Cambridge University Press, 2002), 18, 95–115.
2. Bérénice Reynaud, *A City of Sadness* (London: BFI, 2002); Chris Berry, "A Nation T(w/o)o: Chinese Cinema(s) and Nationhood(s)," in *Colonialism and Nationalism in Asian Cinema*, ed. Wimal Dissanayake (Bloomington: University of Indiana Press, 1994), 42–64; June Yip, "Constructing a Nation: Taiwanese History and the Films of Hou Hsiao Hsien," in *Transnational Chinese Cinemas*, ed. Sheldon Hsiao-peng Lu (Honolulu: University of Hawaii Press, 1997), 139–68.
3. Hou himself acknowledges such a division in his work in a revealing interview with *Cahiers du Cinéma* critic Emmanuel Burdeau in *Hou Hsiao Hsien*, ed. Jean-Michel Frodon (Paris: *Cahiers du Cinéma*, 1999), 72–81. Hou's early films *The Boys from Fengkuei* (1983, CMPC) and *The Time to Live and the Time to Die* (1985, CMPC) are based upon autobiographical episodes from the director's own adolescence, while *A Summer at Grandpa's* (1984, CMPC) is based upon the memoirs of Chu T'ien-wen and *Dust in the Wind* is adapted by screenwriter and director Wu Nien-jen from incidents from his own youth. These incidents are also worked through in Wu's own film, *A Borrowed Life*, considered elsewhere in this anthology.
4. This situation was compounded by the shifting demographics of Taiwan, with almost half of the population under 25, and the acceleration of video piracy on the island, flooding Taiwan with inexpensive copies of the most recent popular films and turning many away from the theaters. The problems faced by the Taiwan cinema at the end of the decade are summarized well in the series of articles on the subject collected in *Free China Review* 38, no. 2 (1988), especially

(Peggy) Hsiung-Ping Chiao, "Cinema: Struggles between Commercialism and Art": 20–25 and Eugenia Yun, "A Delicate Balance": 4–12. Also see David Bordwell's discussion of the Taiwan market as the lynchpin in the wild success of Hong Kong cinema in the late 1980s in *Planet Hong Kong: Popular Cinema and the Art of Entertainment* (Cambridge: Harvard University Press, 2000), 73–75; and the collection of articles from the 2002 Pusan International Film Festival retrospective on the Taiwan New Cinema collected at the Asian Film Connections website: (n.d.) http://www.asianfilms.org/taiwan/huigu/piffhuigu.html (14 May 2003).

5. The inaugural works of the Taiwan New Cinema, the portmanteau films *In Our Time* (1982) and *The Sandwich Man* (1983) were, in fact, produced as part of a government sponsored intervention to aid the moribund film industry, with the CMPC, Taiwan's largest film studio, reforming previously draconian censorship policies to encourage young talent to create a specifically Taiwan cinema as a viable alternative to the dominant Hong Kong model of genre production. See Bérénice Reynaud's account of the origins of the Taiwan New Cinema in her *Nouvelles Chines Nouveaux Cinémas* (Paris: Éditions Cahiers du Cinéma, 1999), 30–33. Michel Egger also offers a useful history of the Taiwan New Wave and its institutional support in his article, "Le Cinéma Chinois: Cinéma Made in Taiwan," *Positif* no. 311 (1987): 26–32.

6. Yeh Yueh-Yu discusses the controversy that followed Hou's debut, *The Boys from Fengkuei*, whose "difficult" aesthetic and narrative style immediately polarized domestic opinions about the work of Hou and his fellow directors of the Taiwan New Cinema. Yeh Yueh-Yu, "Politics and Poetics of Hou Hsiao Hsien's Films" *Post Script* 20, no. 2/3 (2001): 61–76. This critique would intensify in 1989 with the work of key figures from the Taiwan New Cinema, including Hou as producer, on *All for Tomorrow*, a promotional music video for a Taiwan military academy, a production which many claimed signaled the co-option and "death" of the new wave movement. For more on this controversy see Yeh and Chen Kuan-hsing, "Taiwanese New Cinema," in *World Cinema: Critical Approaches*, ed. John Hill and Pamela Gibson (New York: Oxford University Press, 2000), 173–77.

7. Bordwell, David. "Transcultural Spaces: Toward a Poetics of Chinese Film," *Post Script* 20, no. 2/3 (2001): 9–24. Also see Bordwell's brief discussion of *Dust in the Wind* in his *On the History of Film Style* (Cambridge: Harvard University Press, 1997), 267.

8. Yeh, 62, and (Peggy) Hsiung-Ping Chiao, in "The Distinct Taiwanese and Hong Kong Cinemas," in *Perspectives on Chinese Film*, ed. Chris Berry (London: BFI, 1991), 155–56. Chiao instead uses the term "wholesome realism."

9. Yeh, 62.

10. Ibid.

11. The film is *The Ammunition Hunters* (Ding Shan-xi, CMPC, 1971). I express my gratitude to the office of 3H Productions for this information.

Chapter 3

1. The full English version of this essay originally appeared as "Why is 'Great Reconciliation' Im/possible? De-Cold War/decolonization, or modernity and its tears," *Inter-Asia Cultural Studies*, 3, nos. 1 & 2 (2002), 77–99 and 233–51.
2. Kim Seongnae, "Mourning Korean Modernity in the Cheju April Third Incident," *Inter-Asia Cultural Studies* 1, no. 3 (2000), 461–76.
3. The standard translation of *waishengren* has been "Mainlander." Its literal meaning is "people outside the province," and "province" refers to "Taiwan province." "*Waishengren*" has no meaning except in relation to the "subject," "*benshengren*," usually translated as "Taiwanese," but literally meaning "local province people." The standard translation does not adequately capture the complexity of the local "ethnic" taxonomy, so I am sticking to the local terms.
4. Kim.
5. For lack of better English terms to render the Chinese notions of *"qingxu"* and *"ganqing,"* I am flirting with Raymond Williams's "structure of feeling." But I have to caution the reader that this translation is imprecise.
6. Wang Jingwei is portrayed in nationalist history as an exemplary traitor for collaborating with the Japanese during the Sino-Japanese War.
7. Close to half a million soldiers went to Taiwan with the KMT regime. By the 1980s they were graying, often members of the underclass, and collectively labeled as "old soldiers." In the late 1980s they were the first visible group to visit home and go to the Mainland.
8. For examples of "returning home" movies made in this period, see Wu Yong-yi *"Xiangjiao, Zhugong, Guojia: Fanxiang Dianying zhong Waishengren de Guojia Rentong"* (Banana, Pig-King, Nation: Mainlander's National Identity in Returning Home Cinema), *Chung-Wai Literary Monthly*, 22, no. 1 (1993): 32–44.
9. I am reluctant to use "representation" here for two reasons. The central concern of the paper is an emotional structure that is beyond representation. Furthermore, representation presupposes something existing beforehand to be represented and extracted, whereas these films themselves are part of the processes of social reality.
10. Because of the Sino-Japanese War, opposition to Japan has been the dominant mindset of the KMT regime. In fact, "Japan" was the imaginary Other through which the KMT version of "Chinese identity" was constructed. Until the 1980s, for instance, the import of Japanese films was highly restricted, and in propaganda films the Japanese were always represented as the enemy.

Chapter 4

1. Ernest Renan, "What Is a Nation?" Translated and annotated by Martin Thom, in *Nation and Narration*, ed. Homi K. Bhabha (London and New York: Routledge, 1990), 11.

2. The film was entered in the political film category in the Venice Film Festival in that year.

3. "A City of Sadness" website (1994, revised February 1998) <http://cinemaspace.berkeley.edu/Papers/CityOfSadness/index.html> (31 January 2003.)

4. Hou was born in China and migrated with his family to Taiwan in 1948. He grew up in Taiwan's less industrialized south with its correspondingly large measure of Taiwanese culture.

5. Qi Longren, *"Beiqing Chengshi Ererba"* (City of Sadness *Ererba*), *Dangdai* (Dangdai: A Literary Bi-Monthly) no. 43 (1989), 116.

6. See Lan Bozhou. "Huang Mache zhi Ge" (The Song of the Covered Wagon) (1988), in *Huang mache zhi ge, Lishi yu xianchang, Taiwan minzhongshi* (2) (The Song of the Covered Wagon, History and Sites, Taiwan People's History [2]) (Taipei: Shibao wenhua, 1991), 49–104.

7. Lan, 87. Jiang Biyu is Jiang Weishui's daughter and Zhong Haodong's wife.

8. There is a temporal discrepancy in the timing of the purge of the underground in Lan's reportage and the film. In the film, the leftists are purged in 1947. See Zhong Jidong, "Fulu 5: Rang Lishi buzai You Jinji, Rang Renmin buzai You Beiqing— cong 'Huang Mache zhi Ge' dao 'Beiqing Chengshi'," (Appendix 5: Let There Be No More Taboos, Let There Be No More Sadness — From "The Song of the Covered Wagon" to "City of Sadness") in *Huang mache zhi ge*, 137–65, for a discussion of the historical discrepancies in the film.

9. June Yip, "Constructing a Nation: Taiwanese History and the Films of Hou Hsiao Hsien," in *Transnational Chinese Cinemas: Identity, Nationhood, Gender*, ed. Sheldon Hsiao-peng Lu (Honolulu: University of Hawai'i Press, 1997), 143.

10. Li Tuo, "Narratives of History in the Cinematography of Hou Hsiao Hsien," *Positions: East Asia Cultures Critique*, 1, no. 3 (1993), 810.

11. Wing-tsit Chan, "Moral and Social Programs: *The Great Learning*," in *A Source Book in Chinese Philosophy* (Princeton: Princeton University Press, 1963), 86.

12. Chan, 87.

13. Yip, 151. Yip points out that the disintegration of the patriarchal family structure appears to be a leitmotif in Hou's films, 166, ftn. 36.

14. Kwok-kan Tam and Wimal Dissanayake, "Hou Hsiao Hsien: Critical Encounters with Memory and History," in *New Chinese Cinema,* Images of Asia (Oxford University Press, 1998), 52.

15. Zhong Jidong, 146.

16. Rachel Feldhay Brenner, *Writing as Resistance: Four Women Confronting the Holocaust* (Pennsylvania: The Pennsylvania State University Press, 1997), 10.

17. See Brenner for a full account of these women.

18. Tonglin Lu, *Confronting Modernity in the Cinemas of Taiwan and Mainland China* (Cambridge University Press, 2002), 103.

19. Lu, 115.

20. In avant garde feminist films, the term "cinema of correspondence" is given to films that make use of personal discourse, such as letters and diaries, in order to investigate the correspondences between emotion and objectivity and art and ideology. See Ruby B. Rich, "In the Name of Feminist Film Criticism," in *Multiple*

Voices in Feminist Film Criticism, ed. Diane Carson, Linda Dittmar, and Janice R. Welsch (Minneapolis: University of Minnesota Press, 1994), 37–38.

21. *Ererba* is referred to as the February 28 Holocaust in the Taiwan Documents Project website (2 May 2002), http://www.taiwandc.org/228-intr.htm (1 July 2001).

22. In *The Reproduction of Mothering: Psychoanalysis and the Sociology of Gender* (Berkeley and Los Angeles: University of California Press, 1987), Nancy Chodorow theorizes that a woman's "primary definition of self" is comprised of elements of empathy, connectedness, continuity and a recognition of the other (167–68).

23. Carol Gilligan, *In a Different Voice: Psychological Theory and Women's Development* (Cambridge: Harvard University Press, 1982), 22.

24. Brenner, 180.

25. Taiwan's languages include the dialects of Hokkien (Hoklo), Hakka, Cantonese and Japanese. Mandarin was introduced after 1949. In the film, Shanghaiese is the language of the black marketeers.

26. Yip, 139.

27. Chris Berry, "A Nation T(w/o)o: Chinese Cinema(s) and Nationhood(s)," in *Colonialism and Nationalism and Asian Cinema,* ed. Wimal Dissanayake (Bloomington and Indianapolis: Indiana University Press, 1994), 59.

28. Zhong's choice of this song is discussed by Lan Bozhou in "Fulu 3: Sheide 'Huang Mache zhi Ge'— zhi Tamura Shizue [Tiancun Zhijin] Xiaojie," (Appendix 3: Whose "Song of the Covered Wagon"— Reply to Ms Tamura Shizue [Tiancun Zhijin]) in *Huang mache zhi ge,* 119–129.

29. Yeh Yueh-yu and Abe Mark Normes, "Writing: Dialogism and Feminine Voice," <http://cinemaspace.berkeley.edu/Papers/CityOfSadness/swpwdia.html> (31 January 2003).

30. Peggy Hsiung-Ping Chiao, "Taiwan Dianying de Dalu Qingjie," (Mainland Plots in Taiwan Films) *Jintian,* 17 (1992), 92.

31. In "Rewriting Taiwanese National History: The February 28 Incident as Spectacle," *Public Culture* no. 3 (1993), Liao Binghui comments on a tendency to re-write Taiwanese history according to the terms of Taiwan's present-day political nationalism. Liao states that in such a re-writing the casualties of *Ererba* are the precursors of the Taiwan Independent Movement, 28.

Chapter 5

1. This article is a revised and updated version of an earlier article published in Chinese in 1993. I wish to thank Shuqing Mosley and Chris Berry for their indispensable help.

2. Mark Peranson, *"A One and a Two:* Edward Yang's Meaning of Life." *IndieWIRE:* (17 May 2000) <www.indiewire.com/movies/rev_00NYFF001004 _Yi.html> (20 April 2003).

3. Lang Tian, *"Taibei Gushi De Siwang Chengxian:* Yi Yi *De Weizhi"*

(Representation of Death in a Taipei Story: The Position of *Yi Yi*) *Dianying Xingshang* (*Film Appreciation*, Taipei) no. 108 (2001): 78–80.

4. Jonathan Rosenbaum, "Exiles In Modernity: The Films of Edward Yang," *Chicago Reader:* (11 July 1997) <www.chireader.com/movies/archives/1197/11077.html> (20 April 2003).

5. Yeh Yueh-yu, *"Yaogunyue, Ciwenhua, Taiwan Dianying:* Gulingjie Shaonian Sharen Shijian *Yu Lishi Jiyi"* (Rock and Roll, Youth Subculture, Taiwan Film: *A Brighter Summer Day* and Historical Memory) *Dianying Xingshang* (*Film Appreciation*, Taipei), no. 61 (1992): 70–78.

6. Saul Austerlitz, "Edward Yang," *Senses of Cinema*: (2002) <www.sensesofcinema.com/contents/directors/02/yang.html> (20 April 2003).

7. Tang Zhengzhao, *"Huoshuilun Yu Shidai Suming Guan"* (Femme Fatale and Historical Determinism), *Dianying Xingshang* (*Film Criticism*, Taipei) no. 108 (2001), 76.

8. Lang Tian, 79.

9. Lin Lin, *"Yangguang Canlan De Gulingjie shang, Yi Meiyou Shiqicui de Danche"* (On a Brighter Summer Day, There's No More a 17-Year-Old's Bike) *Jiangsu Wenxue* (*Jiangsu Literature*): (4 September 2002) <www.jschina.com.cn/gb.jschina/culture/lit/bbs/userobjectlai78547.html> (20 April 2003).

10. Shen Jiao Du, *"Guanyu* Gulingjie Shaonian Sharen Shijian *de Shiba Tiao Suixiang"* (18 Notes on *A Brighter Summer Day*) *Ming Ru Bao* (*Ming Ru News*): (4 January 2002) <http://mypaper1.ttimes.com.tw/user/dennischan/index.html> (20 April 2003).

11. Yang Shunqing, *"Pianchang Xingqing: Gongzuo Renyuan Paipian Shouji"* (Notes from the Film Set of *A Brighter Summer Day*) *Yingxiang Dianying Zazhi* (*Imagekeeper*, Taipei) no. 16 (1991), 124. Italics added.

12. Claude Lévi-Strauss, *The Savage Mind* (Chicago: University of Chicago Press, 1966), 20–22.

13. Yang Shunqing, 127.

14. Yang Shunqing, 125.

15. The name of the heroine, Ming, means "light" and is apparently supposed to form an ironic contrast both with the perpetual darkness of the nocturnal film and with Ming's own sexual ambivalence.

16. Yang Shunqing, 126.

17. Edward Yang (Yang Dechang) et al., Gulingjie Shaonian Sharen Shijian *Fenjing Juben* (A Brighter Summer Day: *Post-Production Script*) (Taipei: Shibao Press, 1991), 154.

18. Taipei Golden Horse International Film Festival Executive Committee, *Yang Dechang* (*Edward Yang*) (Taipei: Shibao Press, 1991), 45.

19. Taipei Golden Horse International Film Festival Executive Committee, 55.

20. Taipei Golden Horse International Film Festival Executive Committee, 57.

21. Lévi-Strauss, 21.

22. Yan Hongya, *"Gulingjie de Bianju Shiwu Yu Bianyuan Zhuangtai"* (*A Brighter Summer Day*: Script Writing and Beyond), *Yingxiang Dianying Zazhi* (*Imagekeeper,* Taipei) no. 16 (1991): 116.

23. Yan Hongya, 119.
24. Yang Shunqing, 128.
25. Yan Hongya, 117.
26. Lévi-Strauss *The Jealous Potter* (Chicago: University of Chicago Press, 1988), 195.
27. Lévi-Strauss, 1988, 197.
28. Yan Hongya, 118.
29. Yan Hongya, 119.
30. Lévi-Strauss, *The Raw and the Cooked* (New York: Harper and Row, 1969), 12.
31. Lévi-Strauss, 1969, 240.
32. Jacques Derrida, *Writing and Difference* (London: Routledge & Kegan Paul, 1978), 286.
33. Jacques Derrida, 280.
34. Zhan Hongzhi, *"Xingxiao Gulingjie"* (Marketing *A Brighter Summer Day*) *Yingxiang Dianying Zazhi* (*Imagekeeper*, Taipei) no. 16 (1991), 135.
35. Lévi-Strauss 1988, 201.
36. Lévi-Strauss 1988, 171–72.
37. Derrida, 250.
38. Lang Tian, 2001.
39. Lévi-Strauss 1988, 204.
40. Shen Jiao Du, 2002.
41. Shu Chong, *"Yang Dechang Guanyu Yi Yi de Fangtan"* (Interview with Edward Yang on *Yi Yi*), (n.d.) *Sina*: <http://suntao.myrice.com/filmcritic/yangdechanginterview.htm> (25 March 2003)

Chapter 6

1. This chapter was originally published in *Asian Cinema* 8, no. 1 (Spring, 1996), John Lent, ed.

   There are two English-language books that provide a useful orientation to Chinese puppetry: Sergei Obraztov, *The Chinese Puppet Theater* (London: Faber and Faber, 1961); Robert Helmer Stalberg, *China's Puppets* (San Francisco: China Books, 1984). Li Tien-lu participated in a documentary film titled *Art of the Hand Puppet Theater by Li Tien Lu — An Introduction to Hand Puppet Theater*. It is distributed by City Films, 95 Hang-Kou St, Section 2, Taipei, Taiwan, R.O.C. (Fax: 011-886-2-3831969). Thanks to Mei-Juin Chen and Chanjen Chen for introducing me to this documentary. Special thanks to Ying-Fen Huang and Chi Y. Lee for obtaining a videotape of *The Puppetmaster* and for extensive discussion relating to it.

Chapter 7

1. An illustrated script appears in Tsai Mingliang, *Ai-Ch'ing Wan-Sui (Vive L'Amour)*, (Taipei: Wan Hsiang Publishers, 1994), 9–142.
2. Fran Martin, "Eloquent Emptiness: Sexuality and Space in Tsai Ming-liang's *Vive L'Amour*," in *Chinese Films in Focus: 25 New Takes*, ed. Chris Berry (London: British Film Institute 2004). The works she cites are: Chuck Stephens, "Intersection: Tsai Ming-liang's yearning bike boys and heartsick heroines," *Film Comment* 32 (Sept-Oct 1996): 20–23; Tony Rayns, "Confrontations," *Sight & Sound* 7 (March 1997): 14–18; and Richard Read, "Alienation, Aesthetic Distance and Absorption in Tsai Ming-liang's *Vive L'Amour*," *New Formations* 40 (Spring 2000): 102–12. An earlier version of this essay appeared as: "Where is the Love? The Paradox of Performing Loneliness in Tsai Mingliang's *Vive L'Amour*," in *Falling For You: Essays in Cinema and Performance*, eds. Lesley Stern and George Kouvaros (Sydney: Power Publications, 1999), 147–75.
3. Key examples include Chang Hsiao-hung, "An Erotic Map of Taipei" (*Taibei Qingyu Dijing*), in *Queer Desire: Gender and Sexuality* (Yuwang Xin Ditu: Xingbie, Tongzhixue) (Taipei: Lianhe Wenxue, 1996) 78–107; and Chang Hsiao-hung, "A Queer Family Romance: *The River*'s Mise-en-scène of Desire" (*Guaitai Jiating Luomanshi: Heliu zhongde Yuwang Changjing*) in *Queer Family Romance* (Guaitai Jiating Luomanshi) (Taipei: Shibao, 2000) 111–41. For a more detailed discussion of Taiwan's queer culture in the 1990s, see Fran Martin, *Situating Sexualities: Queer Narratives in 1990s Taiwanese Fiction and Film* (Hong Kong University Press, 2003), which includes her analysis of *The River*.
4. Of course, it is not as easy as it looks, either. James Naremore discusses some of the complicated techniques required to create this effect in *Acting in the Cinema* (Berkeley: University of California Press, 1988), 40–3. On realism and the classical Hollywood style, see David Bordwell, Janet Staiger and Kristin Thompson, *The Classical Hollywood Cinema: Film Style and Mode of Production to 1960* (London: Routledge and Kegan Paul, 1985).
5. Judith Butler, *Bodies that Matter: On the Discursive Limits of "Sex"* (New York: Routledge, 1993), 234–35.
6. See, for example, Jean-Louis Baudry, "Ideological Effects of the Basic Cinematographic Apparatus," in Philip Rosen, ed., *Narrative, Apparatus, Ideology* (New York: Columbia University Press, 1986), 286–98; Raymond Bellour, "Hitchcock, the Enunciator," *Camera Obscura* 2 (Fall 1977), 69–94; and Christian Metz, *The Imaginary Signifier: Psychoanalysis and the Cinema* (Bloomington: Indiana University Press, 1982).
7. Laura Mulvey, "Visual Pleasure and Narrative Cinema," *Screen* 16, no. 3 (1975), 6–18. Gaylyn Studlar, *In the Realm of Pleasure: Von Sternberg, Dietrich, and the Masochistic Aesthetic* (Urbana: University of Illinois Press, 1988). This masochistic paradigm has been further developed in different directions by Kaja Silverman, Steven Shaviro and others. Shaviro takes a Deleuzian line presuming an active spectator that takes from the film in popular culture to counter the effect of the subject. Kaja Silverman, *Male Subjectivity at the Margins* (New

York: Routledge, 1992); Steven Shaviro, *The Cinematic Body* (Minneapolis: University of Minnesota Press, 1993).

8. Judith Butler, *Gender Trouble* (New York: Routledge, 1990). On ambivalence and reading texts, see Kobena Mercer, "Skin Head Sex Thing: Racial Difference and the Homoerotic Imaginary," in *How Do I Look? Queer Film and Video*, ed. Bad Object-Choices (Seattle: Bay Press, 1991), 169–210.

9. Chris Berry, "Tsai Mingliang: Look at All the Lonely People," *Cinemaya* 30 (1995), 18–20.

10. Huang Chien-Yeh (Edmond K. Y. Wong), *"Aich'ing Yisi—Gudu Wansui"* ("Love Is Dead—Long Live Loneliness"), in Tsai Mingliang, op. cit., 189, my translation.

11. Those familiar with Taipei recognize the park as an urban beautification project promised by the mayor and opened on deadline, even though unfinished.

12. This film has been extensively discussed in a special issue of *October*, no. 72 (1994).

13. Other examples are Zhang Kunhua's *A Half-Century's Home Sickness* (1993), about a Korean former "comfort woman" still living in China, Sekiguchi Noriko's *Senso Daughters* (Australia, 1990) about the Japanese army's treatment of women in Papua New Guinea, and Tony Aguilar's *Ianfu* (1992), on Philippine "comfort women."

14. George Hicks points out that this is equally true in Western and Asian societies in *The Comfort Women: Sex Slaves of the Japanese Imperial Forces* (Sydney: Allen and Unwin, 1995), 112–27, especially 126.

15. Freda Freiberg also discusses these issues in "Rape, Race and Religion: Ways of Speaking about Enforced Military Prostitution in World War 2," *Metro* no. 104 (1995), 20–25.

16. Hicks, 216–17.

17. When I raised this point with Byun, she told me that some Korean audiences and critics felt the film was not emotional enough, and that it was too cold and distanced for their liking.

18. The translation "tolerance" is proposed by Hanh Tran, translator of the film's script into English.

19. Shoshana Felman, "Education and Crisis, or the Vicissitudes of Teaching," in *Testimony: Crises of Witnessing in Literature, Psychoanalysis, and History*, ed. Shoshana Felman and Dori Laub, M.D. (New York: Routledge, 1992), 41. Original italics.

20. Takeo Doi, *The Anatomy of Dependence* (Tokyo: Kodansha International, 1971).

21. Peter N. Dale, "Omnia Vincet Amae," in *The Myth of Japanese Uniqueness* (London: Croom Helm, 1986), 116–146.

22. Doi, 11–20.

23. Doi, 16–27.

24. Doi, 21–22, 166–75.

25. Butler, (1993) 235.

26. Chang Ta-Ch'un, *"Ch'u-le Chu-ch'iao Hai You Shen-me? Tsai Mingliang 'Ai-Ch'ing Wan-Sui' Li De Chia,"* ("Is There More Than Just the Physical Family in Tsai Mingliang's *Vive L'Amour*?") in Tsai Mingliang, 184–186.

27. Tsai Mingliang acknowledges this metaphor. See Berry, 19.

28. "Sexual DisOrientations, or, Are Homosexual Rights a Western Issue?" in Chris Berry, *A Bit On the Side: East-West Topographies of Desire* (Sydney: EmPress, 1994), 69–104.

29. The narrative of Ang Lee's *The Wedding Banquet* (1992) dramatizes this difficulty very effectively.

30. For further discussion of the construction of the relationship between gay identity, sexual non-conformity and family in East Asian films, see Chris Berry, "Asian/Family/Values: Film, Video and Gay Identities," in *Gay and Lesbian Asia: Culture, Identity, Community*, ed. Peter Jackson and Gerard Sullivan (New York: Harrington Park Press, 2001), 211–233.

Chapter 8

1. See, for example: Peggy Hsiung-Ping Chiao, *Taiwan Dianying 90 Xin Xin Langchao* (The New New Wave of Taiwan Cinema in the 1990s), (Taipei: Cite, 2002), 8–10, 38–42, and 67–68; Wei-ming Dariotis and Eileen Fung, "Breaking the Soy Sauce Jar: Diaspora and Displacement in the Films of Ang Lee," in *Transnational Chinese Cinemas: Identity, Nationhood, Gender*, ed. Sheldon Lu (Honolulu: University of Hawaii Press, 1997), 187–220; Shu-mei Shih, "Globalization and Minoritization: Ang Lee and the Politics of Flexibility," *New Formations* no. 40 (2000): 86–101.

2. Sheng-mei Ma, "Ang Lee's Domestic Tragicomedy: Immigrant Nostalgia, Exotic/ Ethnic Tour, Global Market," *Journal of Popular Culture* 30, no. 1 (1996): 191–201.

3. Ang Lee was born on 23 October 1954 in Pingdong County, Taiwan. He lived in Taiwan until he went to the University of Illinois to study drama in 1977, and then to New York University to do his graduate studies in directing in 1980.

4. Wei Ti, *Dangqian Taiwan Dianying Gongye Zhi Zhengzhi Jingji Fenxi* (The Political Economic Analysis of Present Taiwanese Film Industry [1989–1993]), (Master's thesis, National Chengchi University [Taipei], 1994), 45.

5. Zhang Jingbei, *Shinian Yijiao Dianying Meng* (A Ten-Year Dream of Cinema), (Taipei: Shibao, 2002), 138.

6. Wei-ming Dariotis and Eileen Fung, 210–11.

7. Shih Shu-mei, 93.

8. Wei-ming Dariotis and Eileen Fung, 193–94; Sheng-mei Ma, 195–97.

9. See, for example, Stuart Hall, "Cultural Identity and Diaspora," In *Identity: Community, Culture, Difference*, ed. Jonathan Rutherford (London: Lawrence & Wishart), 222–37, and John Tomlinson, *Globalisation and Culture* (Cambridge: Polity, 1999).

10. Lu Feii, *Taiwan Dianying: Zhengzhi, Jingji, Meixue* (Taiwan Cinema: Politics, Economics, and Aesthetics) (Taipei: Yuan Liu, 1998), 274–76.

11. Lu Feii, 279.

12. Peggy Hsiung-Ping Chiao, ed., *Taiwan Xin Dianying* (Taiwan New Cinema) (Taipei: Shibao, 1988), 16.

13. In 1999, only 14 locally produced films were released. They sold less than 60,000 tickets and had box-office revenues of NT$11.6 million in Taipei. In comparison, 85 Hong Kong films were shown, with attendance of 380,000 and box-office receipts of NT$72 million. There were 239 foreign films screened, over 90 percent of which were Hollywood products. They accounted for over 70 percent of screen time, attracted over 10 million admissions in Taipei (95.9 percent of total admissions) and revenues of NT$2.4 billion (96.7 percent of total revenues). *Taiwan Cinema Database*, (n.d) <http://cinema.nccu.edu.tw/lwisdominfo.htm?MID=2#> (1 October 2002).

14. For a more detailed account, see my article, "Reassessing New Taiwanese Cinema: From Local to Global," (2002),<http://www.asianfilms.org/taiwan/> (30 April 2003). Although no separate URL is given at the site, this is located in the collection of essays under the title "Taiwanese Cinema 1982–2002" in the "Generation Introduction" section.

15. Zhang Jingbei, 130–31.
16. Zhang Jingbei, 128.
17. Zhang Jingbei, 127.
18. Zhang Jingbei, 128.
19. A deluxe Chinese dish, which contains lobster (as dragon) and abalone (as phoenix).
20. Sheng-mei Ma, 195.
21. *The Internet Movie Database* (n.d) <http://us.imdb.com/Business?0111797> and <http://us.imdb.com/Business?0107156> (30 April 2003).
22. Zhang Jingbei, 150–51.
23. Zhang Jingbei, 133–34.
24. Zhang Jingbei, 119.
25. *The Internet Movie Database* (n.d) <http://us.imdb.com/Business?0114388> (30 April 2003).

Chapter 9

1. Interview conducted by Daniele Riviere with Tsai Mingliang, "Scouting," in *Tsai Mingliang*, trans. Andrew Rothwell. Rehm, Jean-Pierre, Olivier Joyard, and Daniele Riviere (Paris: Dis voir, 1999), 99.
2. See B. Ruby Rich, "New Queer Cinema," *Sight & Sound* 2, no. 5 (1992): 30–35.
3. For a broader discussion of Asian queer cinema generally, see Andrew Grossman, "'Beautiful Publicity': An Introduction to Queer Asian Film," in *Queer Asian Cinema: Shadows in the Shade*, ed. Andrew Grossman (New York: Haworth Press, 2000), 1–29.
4. See "Love, Life and Lies: The films of Tsai Mingliang in the context of the new Taiwanese Cinema," *Toto*, (1999), <http://www.cse.unsw.edu.au/~peteg/toto/Tsai.htm> (18 April 2003).
5. The year of the first direct presidential elections in Taiwan, 1996, also saw some of the worst cross-Straits tensions with aggressive war games and missile tests

conducted by the PRC and meant to intimidate anyone calling for an independent Taiwan state. For more on Taiwan in the 1990s, see Willem Van Kemenade, *China, Hong Kong, Taiwan, Inc.,* trans. Dianne Webb (New York: Vintage, 1997).

6. For a policy statement, see "R.O.C. Film Industry Guidance Measures," (2003), <http://www.gio.gov.tw/taiwan-website/7-av/film_industry/table_3.htm> (18 April 2003).

7. Tze-Lan Deborah Sang, "Feminism's Double: Lesbian Activism in the Mediated Public Sphere of Taiwan," in *Spaces of Their Own: Women's Public Sphere in Transnational China*, ed. Mayfair Mei-Hui Yang (Minneapolis: University of Minnesota Press, 1999), 150.

8. Chang Hsiao-Hung, "Taiwan Queer Valentines," in *Trajectories: Inter-Asia Cultural Studies*, ed. Chen Kuan-Hsing (London: Routledge, 1998), 284. Italics in the original.

9. See Richard Fung, "Looking for My Penis: The Eroticized Asian in Gay Video Porn," in *How Do I Look?: Queer Film and Video*, ed. Bad Object-Choices (Seattle: Bay Press, 1991), 145–60.

10. Chris Berry, "Sexual DisOrientations: Homosexual Rights, East Asian Films, and Postmodern Postnationalism," in *Pursuit of Contemporary East Asian Culture*, Xiaobing Tang and Stephen Snyder (Boulder: Westview, 1996), 161.

11. Timothy Liu, "*The Outcasts:* A Family Romance," in Grossman, 234.

12. See Jonathan Rosenbaum, "City Without Tears: *The River,*" *The Chicago Reader* (2000), <http://www.chireader.com/movies/archives/2000/0400/000414.html> (18 April 2003).

13. See Bérénice Reynaud, *Nouvelles Chines/Nouveaux cinémas* (Paris: Cahiers du Cinéma, 1999).

14. See Robin Bernstein and Seth Clark Silberman, ed., *Generation Q* (Los Angeles: Alyson Publications, 1996).

15. See Herbert Marcuse, *Eros and Civilization* (New York: Vintage, 1962).

16. Jean-Pierre Rehm, "Bringing in the Rain," trans. James Hodges, in Rehm, Jean-Pierre, Olivier Joyard, and Daniele Riviere, 27.

17. See Ien Ang, "Can One Say No to Chineseness? Pushing the Limits of the Diasporic Paradigm," *Boundary 2* 25, no. 3 (1998): 223–42.

18. White is the traditional color for mourning and funerals in Chinese culture.

19. See Fredric Jameson, "Remapping Taipei," in *The Geopolitical Aesthetic: Cinema and Space in the World System* (Bloomington: Indiana University Press, 1995), 114–57; Chuck Stephens, "Intersection: Tsai Mingliang's Yearning Bike Boys and Heartsick Heroines," *Film Comment* 32, no. 5 (1996): 20–23; Zhang Yingjin, *Screening China: Critical Interventions, Cinematic Reconfigurations, and the Transnational Imaginary in Contemporary Chinese Cinema* (Ann Arbor: University of Michigan, 2002).

20. See Jack Babuscio, "Camp and the Gay Sensibility," *Gays and Film,* ed. Richard Dyer (London: BFI, 1977), 40–57.

21. See Gina Marchetti, "*The Wedding Banquet*: Global Chinese Cinema and the Asian American Experience," in *Countervisions: Asian American Film Criticism*, ed. Darrell Y. Hamamoto and Sandra Liu (Philadelphia: Temple University Press, 2000), 275–97.

22. Chris Berry, "Happy Alone? Sad Young Men in East Asian Gay Cinema," in Grossman, 198.
23. Chen also appeared in the other two films in the trilogy — *Rebels of the Neon God* and *Vive L'Amour.*

Chapter 10

1. Fredric Jameson, *Signatures of the Visible* (New York: Routledge, 1990), 1.
2. Xiaoping Lin, "*Red Corner:* An Orientalist Nightmare in a Globalised World," *Third Text* no. 56 (2001): 58.
3. For purposes of brevity, I have omitted parts of my discussion of the film's audience. For an interesting brief discussion of American arthouse cinema audiences and Chinese film, see Meng Yue et. al., "*Diyu, wenhua, zibenzhuyi yu houzhimin?*" (Region, Culture, Capitalism, and Postcoloniality?), *Today* 2 (1994): 6.
4. Dai Jinhua, *Cinema and Desire: Feminist Marxism and Cultural Politics in the Work of Dai Jinhua*, ed. Jing Wang and Tani E. Barlow (London: Verso, 2002), 52.
5. Xu Ben, "*Farewell My Concubine* and its Nativist Critics," *Quarterly Review of Film and Video* 16, no. 2 (1997): 157.
6. Zhang Yingjin, *Screening China: Critical Interventions, Cinematic Reconfigurations, and the Transnational Imaginary in Contemporary Chinese Cinema* (Ann Arbor: Center for Chinese Studies, 2002), 251, 253.
7. Huaye Liannong (Han Bangqing), *Haishang hua liezhuan* (Taibei: Heluo Tushu Chubanshe, 1980). The use of *Wu* dialect throughout the film is significant. For Taiwanese, Cantonese, or Mandarin speaking audiences, the frequently unintelligible or unfamiliar-sounding dialogue in the film can have a defamiliarizing effect. See Li Cheuk-to, "Flowers of Shanghai (Hai Shang Hua)," (1998) <http://www.usc.edu/isd/archives/asianfilm/taiwan/hou-flrev.html>, (21 May 2003).
8. Sheldon Hsiao-peng Lu, "National Cinema, Cultural Critique, Transnational Capital: The Films of Zhang Yimou," in *Transnational Chinese Cinemas: Identity, Nationhood, Gender*, ed. Sheldon Hsiao-peng Lu (Honolulu: University of Hawai'i Press, 1997), 105.
9. Zhang Yingjin, 75, see also 207–312, and passim.
10. Sheldon Hsiao-peng Lu, 105, 107. For Lu's succinct definition of Orientalism, see Sheldon Hsiao-peng Lu, 128. See also Lu's "The Use of China in Avant-Garde Art: Beyond Orientalism," in *China, Transnational Visuality, Global Postmodernity* (Stanford: Stanford University Press, 2001), 174; Rey Chow, "The Force of Surfaces: Defiance in Zhang Yimou's Films," in *Primitive Passions: Visuality, Sexuality, Ethnography, and Contemporary Chinese Cinema* (New York: Columbia University Press, 1995), 142–72; and Tang Xiaobing, "Orientalism and the Question of Universality: The Language of Contemporary Chinese Literary Theory," *Positions* 1, no. 2 (1993): 389–413.

11. See Sheldon Hsiao-peng Lu, 125–33; Xu Ben, 155–70; and Zhang Yingjin, 207–312.
12. Richard James Havis, "The Selling of Zhang Yimou: Marketing Chinese Images," 1995 <http://www.usc.edu/isd/archives/asianfilm/china/zhang-selling.html>, (May 12, 2003).
13. Sheldon Hsiao-peng Lu, 107.
14. For another argument that a film can constitute an "intervention" into the cross-cultural dynamics of cinematic Orientalism, see Rey Chow, "The Seductions of Homecoming: Place, Authenticity, and Chen Kaige's *Temptress Moon*," in *Cross-Cultural Readings of Chineseness: Narratives, Images, and Interpretations of the 1990s*, ed. Wen-hsin Yeh (Berkeley: Institute of East Asian Studies, 2000) 8–26.
15. For an analysis of these concepts and issues, see Shih Shu-mei, "Globalization and Minoritisation: Ang Lee and the Politics of Flexibility," *New Formations: A Journal of Culture/Theory/Politics*, 40 (2000): 86–101. See also Song Hwee Lim, "Celluloid Comrades: Male Homosexuality in Chinese Cinemas of the 1990s," *China Information* XVI, no. 1 (2002): 68–88, for a reappraisal of the "model of transnational cinema."
16. I include *Flowers of Shanghai* as a significant cinematic contribution to what Zhang Yingjin terms his project to "demythify Western [Orientalist] fantasies," *Screening China*, 112.
17. The numerous menial female servants who wait hand and foot on their (kept) mistresses remind viewers that the prostitutes are an elite among the servant class; see also Hershatter on "Shanghai's hierarchy of prostitution," in "Modernizing Sex, Sexing Modernity: Prostitution in Early Twentieth-Century Shanghai," in *Engendering China: Women, Culture, and the State*, ed. Christina K. Gilmartin, Gail Hershatter, Lisa Rofel, and Tyrene White (Cambridge: Harvard University Press, 1994), 148 and passim.
18. In the context of Zhang Yingjin's discussion of films and fiction from the 1930s and 1940s, *Flowers of Shanghai* can be likened to a contemporary (late capital era) resurrection of a pre-leftist era mode of representing women in the "traditional city," in *The City in Modern Chinese Literature & Film: Configurations of Space, Time, and Gender* (Stanford: Stanford University Press, 1996), 185. The twenty-first century desire to treat the Mao decades — and other Marxist movements — as historical aberrations is linked to nostalgia for an era of confined women and women as commodities. *Flowers of Shanghai* at first invokes such nostalgia, but at the same time, I am arguing, the form of the cinematic representation is used to counter any such nostalgic desires.
19. In many of his earlier films, Hou skillfully adds layers of historical and contextual meaning to similar long takes. See, for example, the opening scene of his 1989 *City of Sadness*, where a long take with little dialogue is given complex individual, social, and historical texture through the use of off-screen sound. This technique is assiduously avoided in *Flowers of Shanghai*.
20. See Nick Browne's essay in this volume for a lucid discussion of Hou Hsiao Hsien's use of mise-en-scène in *The Puppetmaster*, including the way it can sometimes "eclipse the action."

21. Slavoj Žižek, *The Fright of Real Tears: Krzysztof Kieślowski Between Theory and Post-Theory*, (London: British Film Institute Publishing, 2001), 96–97 (emphasis added).
22. Slavoj Žižek, 31–54 and passim.
23. Pena, Richard, "Signs in the East," *Film Comment* 34, no. 4 (1998): 9.
24. Sheldon Hsiao-peng Lu has noted similar aspects in Zhang Yimou's film art, 126.
25. Jameson, *Signatures*, 139. Zhang, *Screening China*, citing Arjun Appadurai, makes similar statements about "Chinese ethnographic cinema" and its "impressive list of exotic cultural scenarios," 249.
26. Jameson, *Signatures*, 137.
27. Summarized in Sheldon Hsiao-peng Lu, 128.
28. Zhang Yingjin, 250.
29. Rey Chow has argued that Zhang Yimou's films produce an "exhibitionist self-display that contains, in its very excessive modes, a critique of the voyeurism of orientalism itself . . . by staging and parodying orientalism's politics of visuality," "The Force of Surfaces," 171. However, *Flowers of Shanghai* does not deploy the theatrics of excess, through staging and parody; rather, it injects a surfeit of orientalist objects (and people) into a redundant, unemotional diegetic, void of parody or exhibitionism. Within the context of *Flowers of Shanghai*'s relationship to its Taiwan and People's Republic of China audiences, the film's *cinematic* critique of cinematic voyeurism also contributes to a critical re-evaluation of the "'Orientalism of Oriental societies,'" and "the reification of Chinese culture into a [tourist] commodity" Arif Dirlik, *The Postcolonial Aura: Third World Criticism in the Age of Global Capitalism* (Boulder: Westview Press, 1997), 117.
30. Fredric Jameson, *The Geopolitical Aesthetic: Cinema and Space in the World System* (Bloomington: Indiana University Press, 1992), 49.
31. In light of Hou's rather sexist, patriarchal views, as expressed in Olivier Assayas's 1997 documentary on Hou, I am not inclined to interpret *Flowers of Shanghai* as a critique or re-appraisal of traditional or contemporary patriarchally biased gender and sexual relations in China and/or Taiwan.
32. See James Udden's careful comparison of Hou's long takes to those of other directors, within Udden's larger argument against a narrow definition of Hou's "Chinese style," "Hou Hsiao Hsien and the Question of a Chinese Style," *Asian Cinema* 13, no. 2 (2002): 54–75.
33. Lu Tonglin briefly discusses the disconcerting effect of Taiwan's modernization and the influence of an imported "'Westernized' value system." She ties this to the historical process by which "the Chinese past" has come to "serve[s] mostly as an idealized aesthetic object" in the Taiwanese imagination, in *Confronting Modernity in the Cinemas of Taiwan and Mainland China* (Cambridge: Cambridge University Press, 2002), 210–11.
34. Gail Hershatter, 152.
35. The Zhang Ailing version of the novel *Haishanghua liezhuan* on which Chu T'ien-wen probably based her script has illustrations depicting scenes within each chapter, many of which could have inspired Hou's arrangement of the mise-en-scène. Notably, many illustrations in the novel portray the numerous events

which take place outside the brothels, in exterior settings, such as city streets, gardens, and piers. Hou deliberately omits these scenes, which would add visual variety and a sense of narrative development to his otherwise deliberately monotonous scene selections.

36. Anagnosts's analysis of the *fangujie* "old town" phenomenon reveals a dynamic worth comparing to cinematic "self-orientalizing." Anagnost demonstrates how the *fangujie* phenomenon reconstructs pre-capitalist, pre-modern China for the dual and contradictory purposes of commodification/profit-making (from tourist dollars) and creating a communal version of a "national past." *National Past-Times: Narrative, Representation, and Power in Modern China* (Durham: Duke University Press, 1997), 167–170.

Chapter 11

1. Zhan Hongzhi, "*Minguo Qishiliunian Taiwan Dianying Xuanyan*" (Taiwan Cinema Manifesto, 1987), in *Taiwan Xin Dianying* (Taiwan New Cinema), ed. Peggy Hsiung-Ping Chiao (Taipei: Shibao, 1988), 111–18. I would like to thank Jeng Ming-huey, Dai Ning, and Hou Chi-jan for their assistance on this chapter.

2. The manifesto drew on the concept of "alternative cinema" (*linglei dianying*). But because that term already had a fixed meaning in film history, they opted for "another cinema" (*ling yi zhong dianying*) instead.

3. Other new directors' debuts include: *Schoolgirl* (Chen Kuo-fu, 1989), *Peach Blossom Land* (Stan Lai, 1992) *A Borrowed Life* (Wu Nien-jen, 1994), *Sky Calls* (Wang Shaudi, 1995), *Tropical Fish* (Chen Yu-hsun, 1995), and *Footsteps In the Rain* (Lin Cheng-sheng, 1995).

4. *Darkness and Light* was the grand prizewinner of the Tokyo Film Festival in 2000.

5. Hayden White, "The Value of Narrativity in the Representation of Reality," in *On Narrative*, ed. W.J.T. Mitchell (Chicago: University of Chicago Press, 1980), 13.

6. In an interview, Chang Tsochi admitted that Hou's influence on him is "100%." He says, "An assistant director's function is to help ensure that the director can fully concentrate on his creation without being disrupted. To fulfill that function, I had to put myself in his shoes and be aware of everything he needed on set." Xie Renchang, "*Meiyou Guang, Qingxiang Hei'an Qingxiang Meili*" (Without Light, Tending to Darkness, Tending to Beauty), *Dianying Xinshang* (Film Appreciation), no. 112 (2002), 81.

7. See *Dianying Xinshang*, no. 112; Chen Baoxu, "*Buzhuo Shengming zhi Guang*" (Capturing the Light of Life), *Yi Zhoukan* (First Weekly), no. 69 (16 September 2002), 104–7; and "'Wo Re'ai Dianying,' Shi Zhang Zuoji Bu Bian de Xuanyan" ("I Love Film" is Chang Tsochi's Unchanging Proclamation) *Xin Guannian Yuekan* (New Idea Monthly) no. 176 (2002), 30–31.

8. Lin Zhiming, "*Hei'an zhi Guang de Guang yu An*" (Light and Dark in *Darkness and Light*), *Dianying Dang'an* (Film Archive) no. 36 (1999): 98–101.

9. Jean-Pierre Oudart, "Cinema and Suture," *Screen* 18, no. 4 (1977/78), 35–47; Daniel Dayan, "The Tutor Code of Classical Cinema," in *Movies and Methods* ed. Bill Nichols (Berkeley: University of California Press, 1985), 438–51; Barry Salt, "Film Style and Technology in the Forties," *Film Quarterly*, 31, no. 1 (1977), 46–57; and William Rothman, "Against the System of the Suture," in Bill Nichols (1985), 451–59.

10. Toby Miller, "The Historical Spectator/Audience," in *Film and Theory: An Anthology*, ed. Robert Stam and Toby Miller (Oxford: Blackwell, 2000), 337–44.

11. To identify with a character whose origin is different from the viewer him/herself. See Fran Martin's chapter in this collection for further discussion.

12. This is a main element of William Rothman's discussion. However, most point-of-view structures use two rather than three shots.

13. Before the rise of the Taiwan New Cinema, Italian Neo-realism was introduced to Taiwan and highly praised, demonstrating the longstanding high public and official valorization of realism in Chinese culture in various forms. See Feii Lu, *Taiwan Dianying: Zhengzhi, Jingji, Meixue* (Taiwan Cinema: Politics, Economics, Aesthetics), (Taipei: Yuanliu, 1998), 103–8, 271–77.

14. The term "observational" is borrowed from Bill Nichols's "observational mode" of documentary; Bill Nichols, *Representing Reality: Issues and Concepts in Documentary* (Bloomington: Indiana University Press, 1991), 38–44.

15. Tony Rayns, "*Darkness and Light*," The 18th Vancouver International Film Festival catalog (1999), 36.

Chapter 12

1. William Foreman, "*Crouching Tiger* Is an Example of Greater China's Hidden Power," *Oscars: 73rd Annual Academy Awards*, 26 March 2001, <http://awards2001.belointeractive.com/oscarnews/321908_bi_china0326.html> (8 January 2003).

2. "Oscar Glory Shines on Ang Lee," *Taiwan Headlines*, 27 March 2001, <http://portal.gio.gov.tw/can/cgi/fineprint.pl?1=http://www.taiwanheadlines.gov.tw/20010327/20010327s1.html> (7 January 2003).

3. Raye Kao, "Fame by Frame: The Lee Ang Story," *Taipei Review* 51, no. 7 (2001): 54–65; Government Information Office, "The Republic of China Celebrates Taiwan Film's Success at the Oscars," 26 March 2001, <http://www.gio.gov.tw/taiwan-website/7-av/anglee/os_4.htm> (7 January 2003).

4. Sheng-mei Ma, "Ang Lee's Domestic Tragicomedy: Immigrant Nostalgia, Exotic/Ethnic Tour, Global Market," *Journal of Popular Culture* 30, no. 1 (1996): 191–201; Shu-mei Shih, "Globalization and Minoritization: Ang Lee and the Politics of Flexibility," *New Formations* no. 40 (2000): 86–101.

5. Wei-ming Dariotis and Eileen Fung, "Breaking the Soy Sauce Jar: Diaspora and Displacement in the Films of Ang Lee," in *Transnational Chinese Cinemas: Identity, Nationhood, Gender*, ed. Sheldon Lu (Honolulu: University of Hawaii Press, 1997), 187–220, 189. See also Mark Chiang, "Coming Out into the Global

System: Postmodern Patriarchies and Transnational Sexualities in *The Wedding Banquet*," in *Q&A: Queer in Asian America*, ed. David L. Eng and Alice Y. Hom (Philadelphia: Temple University Press, 1998), 374–95; David L. Eng, "Out Here and Over There: Queerness and Diaspora in Asian American Studies," *Social Text* no. 52–53 (1997): 31–52; Cynthia W. Liu, "'To Love, Honor, and Dismay': Subverting the Feminine in Ang Lee's Trilogy of Resuscitated Patriarchs," *Hitting Critical Mass: A Journal of Asian American Cultural Criticism*, 3, no. 1 (1995), <http://socrates.berkeley.edu/~critmass/v3n1/liuprint.html> (15 February 2002); Chris Berry, "*Wedding Banquet:* A Family Affair," in *Chinese Films in Focus: 25 New Takes*, ed. Chris Berry (London: BFI, 2003); and Fran Martin, "Globally Chinese at *The Wedding Banquet*," in *Situating Sexualities: Queer Representation in Chinese Fiction, Film and Public Culture* (Hong Kong: Hong Kong University Press, 2003).

6. Felicia Chan, "*Crouching Tiger, Hidden Dragon*: Reading Ambiguity and Ambivalence," in *Chinese Films in Focus: 25 New Takes,* ed. Chris Berry.

7. Kao, "Fame by Frame," 54.

8. *Asiaweek* 26, no. 27, "A Roots Trip With a Kick: After Tasting Success in Hollywood, Ang Lee Rediscovers his Chineseness" (2000), ASWK11931214.

9. The implications of the film's vilification of the particular form of feminine fury represented by Jade Fox would be a subject worthy of a separate paper.

10. The term "allo-identification" is from Eve Kosofsky Sedgwick, who uses it in relation to gender and sexual identification in *Epistemology of the Closet,* (London: Penguin, 1990), 59–63. Chris Healy has used a related term — "allo-fascination" — in relation to culture and ethnicity in his discussion of Aboriginal–non-Aboriginal relationships in "White Feet and Black Trails: Travelling Cultures at the Lurujarri Trail," *Postcolonial Studies* 2, no. 1: 55–73.

11. Stephen Teo, "Love and Swords: The Dialectics of Martial Arts Romance," *Senses of Cinema* (November 2000), <http://www.sensesofcinema.com/contents/00/11/crouching.html> (25 September 2002).

12. Zhang Zhen, "Bodies in the Air: The Magic of Science and the Fate of the Early 'Martial Arts' Film in China," *Post Script* 20, no. 2/3 (2001): 43–60, 44.

13. Zhang, 52–55.

14. Stephen Teo, "King Hu's *The Fate of Lee Khan* and *The Valiant Ones*," *Senses of Cinema* (2002), <http://www.sensesofcinema.com/contents/02/20/cteq/king_hu.html> (10 January 2003).

15. "Go Ahead, Make Her Day: From China to California, in TV and Films, Pop Culture Is Embracing a New Image of the Action Heroine Who Is Both Feminist and Feminine," *Time* 157, no. 12 (2001): 64.

16. Elaine Showalter, "Sex Goddess," *The American Prospect* 12, no. 9 (2001): 38.

17. Matthew Levie, "*Crouching Tiger, Hidden Dragon*: The Art Film Hidden Inside the Chop-Socky Flick," *Bright Lights Film Journal* no. 33 (2001) <http://www.brightlightsfilm.com/33/crouchingtiger.html> (8 January 2003).

18. Cf. Martina Navratilova's puzzlement at *Crouching Tiger*'s popularity when, as she put it, "*Xena*'s been doing that for years!" For Navratilova, unaware of the *wuxia* tradition, the sole association of Lee's film was with the Universal Studios television series, which she assumed was the progenitor of the woman warrior

figure. *Curve* magazine, Internet edition, "Martina Navratilova: Hitting 40 Love," <http://www.curvemag.com/Detailed/142.html> (10 January 2003).

19. Martin, "Globally Chinese at *The Wedding Banquet.*"

20. For a discussion of the popularization of the figure of the rebellious girl in pop music cultures in Hong Kong, see Anthony Fung and Michael Curtin, "The Anomalies of Being Faye (Wong): Gender Politics in Chinese Popular Music," *International Journal of Cultural Studies*, 5, no. 3 (2002): 263–90.

21. Lee Cher-jean, "Address at the Celebration Party for the Film *Crouching Tiger, Hidden Dragon*," 26 March 2001, <http://www.gio.gov.tw/taiwan-website/7-av/anglee/os_2.htm> (7 January 2003); Ang Lee, "Preface," in *Crouching Tiger, Hidden Dragon: A Portrait of the Ang Lee Film*, Wang Hui Ling, James Schamus, and Tsai Kuo Jung, (New York: New Market Press, 2000), 2.

22. Although as I outline above, Chinese cinema since the 1920s reveals numerous previous examples of "rebel girls," it is the common interpretation by audiences of Jen as relating to the phenomenon of 1990s pop-feminism that implies a re-imagining by this film, in particular, of "Chinese (film) tradition" as always-already contemporary.

Index